# THE STRUGGLE
# FOR JUDICIAL SUPREMACY

# THE STRUGGLE

## F O R

# Judicial Supremacy

## A  S T U D Y
## *of a Crisis in American Power Politics*

B Y

## ROBERT H. JACKSON

NEW YORK
ALFRED · A · KNOPF
1 9 4 9

THIS IS A BORZOI BOOK,
PUBLISHED BY ALFRED A. KNOPF, INC.

*Appointed to S.Ct. 7-11-41*

Copyright 1941 by Robert H. Jackson

PUBLISHED JANUARY 20, 1941
SECOND PRINTING, APRIL 1941
THIRD PRINTING, FEBRUARY 1949

*Manufactured in the United States of America*
*Published in Canada by McClelland & Stewart Limited*

# PREFACE

President Roosevelt's proposal of February 5, 1937 to " reorganize " the federal judiciary has passed out of the field of current political issues and into history. Each side of the controversy has comforted itself with a claim of victory. The President's enemies defeated the court reform bill — the President achieved court reform.

In the debate the fundamental grievances and long-standing trends which provoked the reform proposal and the relation of the current controversy to issues as old as the Republic could be heard only as undertones in a clash of political forces. These deeper issues underlying that struggle can now be dispassionately considered.

The Court Reorganization Message of President Roosevelt was the political manifestation of a long-smouldering intellectual revolt against the philosophy of many of the Supreme Court's decisions on constitutional questions. This protest was led by outspoken and respected members of the Court itself. Among its most influential spokesmen were those in our universities distinguished for disinterested legal scholarship. It counted among its followers many thoughtful conservatives and practically all liberals and labor leadership. Among these thoughtful groups the trend of the Court was a subject of censure long before political leaders made it an " issue."

We must constantly and sharply distinguish between this intellectual revolt against the Court's philosophy and the political proposal to reorganize its personnel. The plan did not capitalize more than a fraction of the force of the revolt. It is not likely that any plan of reform could have united the protesting forces. But only as we separate the insurrection against the Court's doctrine from the court reform movement can we account for their separate fates — a failure of the reform forces and a victory of the reform.

This paradoxical outcome is accounted for by the recognition on the part of some Justices — belated but vigorous — of the validity of the complaints against their course of decision. They united with long-protesting Justices and proceeded to weaken the President's political assault by acknowledging and correcting his grievances. They confessed legal error and saved themselves from political humiliation. They subdued the rebellion against their constitutional dogma by joining it.

At the moment the Supreme Court is, in general outlook, the most liberal of any court of last resort in the land. Satisfaction with its present attitudes, however, must not obscure the fact that the struggle has produced no permanent reconciliation between the principles of representative government and the opposing principle of judicial authority. The Court has renounced no power and has been subjected to no new limitation. The effect of the attack was exemplary and disciplinary, and perhaps temporary.

For a century every contest with the Supreme Court has ended in evading the basic inconsistency between popular government and judicial supremacy. None of the really influential critics of the Court have proposed destroying it or impairing its powers, and none have been able to suggest a hopeful formula for controlling it. None of the leaders of American democracy have yet been willing to risk democracy without some judicial restraint. So now, as always before, the struggle against judicial excess has ended by leaving it to the Justices themselves to correct the errors of the Court. It is certainly easier, and perhaps wiser, to let the Justices, when they have a will to do so, work out a corrected pattern of judicial restraint than to split our society as deeply as adoption of any formula for limiting judicial power would be likely to do.

But our history shows repeated disappointment of liberal Presidents in their efforts to effect a permanent or even long-enduring change of attitude or philosophy of the Court by additions to its personnel. Why is it that the Court influences appointees more consistently than appointees influence the Court? I point out certain sustained institutional and procedural pressures towards conservatism which only the most alert Justices will sense and only the most hardy will overcome. Because of these constant pressures I would underwrite no futures even now.

Another generation may find itself fighting what is essentially the same conflict that we, under Roosevelt, and our fathers under Theodore Roosevelt and Wilson, and our grandfathers under Lincoln, and our great-grandfathers under Jackson, and our great-great-grandfathers under Jefferson, fought before them. The truce between judicial authority and popular will may, or may not, ripen into a permanent peace.

The proposal to reorganize the Supreme Court and the Court's self-reformation can only be understood as one chapter in the long and fascinating history of power politics in America. The seeds of a struggle for power were planted in the Constitution itself. That instrument set up a legislative and an executive branch, each in a large degree representative of popular will. It created on the other hand an appointive Court, whose Justices are chosen for life, and thus set up an overriding legal authority completely independent of popular will. These differently constituted institutions characteristically respond to the interests of different factions of society, as the founders foresaw they would. A struggle for power between these " equal " branches was inevitable. The Supreme Court has, from the very nature of its functions, been deep in power politics from the opening of the Court, and some of its leadership has been superb, notably so under Marshall and Hughes. It has moved with such mastery that by 1933 it had established a supremacy that could deny important powers to both state and nation on principles nowhere found in the Constitution itself, or could allocate powers as between state and nation, or between Congress and the executive departments, and could largely control the economic and social policy of the country. Exertion of such power was vigorously opposed, and the struggle for judicial supremacy aroused the most dramatic and persistent rivalry in our history.

As created, the Supreme Court seemed too anemic to endure a long contest for power. It has no function except to decide " cases " and " controversies," and its very jurisdiction to do that was left largely to the control of Congress. It has no force to execute its own commands, its judgments being handed over to the Executive for enforcement. Its Justices derive their offices from the favor of the other two branches by appointment and confirmation, and hold them subject to an undefined, unlimited, and unreviewable Congressional power of impeachment. They depend annually for the payment of their irreducible salaries and the housing and staffing of their Court upon appropriations by Congress. Certainly so dependent an institution would excite no fears.

Yet in spite of its apparently vulnerable position, this Court has repeatedly overruled and thwarted both the Congress and the Executive. It has been in angry collision with the most dynamic and popular Presidents in our history. Jefferson retaliated with impeachment; Jackson

denied its authority ; Lincoln disobeyed a writ of the Chief
Justice; Theodore Roosevelt, after his Presidency, proposed recall of judicial decisions; Wilson tried to liberalize its membership ; and Franklin D. Roosevelt proposed
to " reorganize " it. It is surprising that it should not
only survive but, with no might except the moral force of
its judgments, should attain actual supremacy as a source
of constitutional dogma.

Surprise turns to amazement when we reflect that time
has proved that its judgment was wrong on the most outstanding issues upon which it has chosen to challenge the
popular branches. Its judgment in the *Dred Scott* case
was overruled by war. Its judgment that the currency
that preserved the Union could not be made legal tender
was overruled by Grant's selection of an additional Justice. Its judgment invalidating the income tax was overruled by the Sixteenth Amendment. Its judgments re-
pressing labor and social legislation are now abandoned.
Many of the judgments against New Deal legislation are
rectified by confession of error. In no major conflict with
the representative branches on any question of social or
economic policy has time vindicated the Court.

Yet, by 1933, by the efficacy of its words, the Court
had not only established its ascendency over the entire government as a source of constitutional doctrine, but it had
also taken control of a large and rapidly expanding sphere
of policy. It sat almost as a continuous constitutional con-

vention which, without submitting its proposals to any ratification or rejection, could amend the basic law. And it had used that supremacy to cripple other departments of government and to disable the nation from adopting social or economic policies which were deemed inconsistent with the Justices' philosophy of property rights.

This political role of the Court has been obscure to laymen — even to most lawyers. Its members since the Jeffersonian threat of impeachment, which was as wholesome as it was unsuccessful, have generally abstained from party politics. It speaks only through the technical forms of the lawsuit, which are not identified with politics in its popularly accepted sense.

Yet these lawsuits are the chief instrument of power in our system. Struggles over power that in Europe call out regiments of troops, in America call out battalions of lawyers. When the Court decides where power will be recognized, it often thereby settles whether that power can ever effectively be exercised. A given power held to reside in the states becomes at once a power subdivided into forty-eight sections, each circumscribed by a state's boundaries — a power which can easily be defeated, evaded, or cancelled by playing one state against another. The same power held to reside in the nation is quite another matter in its effectiveness. So, too, serious practical consequences wait upon the distribution of power between the President and the Congress. When the Court

held that N.I.R.A. code-making could not be delegated
to the President and the executive agencies, it destroyed
any possibility of the code technique of self-government
in industry, for everybody recognized the impossibility of
Congressional action on hundreds of codes.

Nearly every significant decision of the Supreme Court
has to do with power — power of government, power of
officials — and hence it is always concerned with the social and economic interests involved in the allocation, denial, or recognition of power.

Two kinds of power seem always in competition in our
democracy: there is political power, which is the power of
the voters, and there is the economic power of property,
which is the power of its owners. Conflicts between the two
bring much grist to the judicial mill. The basic grievance
of the New Deal was that the Court has seemed unduly to
favor private economic power and always to find ways of
circumventing the efforts of popular government to control or regulate it.

Thus, as we shall see, the Court conducted a dual campaign against the powers which the Congress thought had
been granted it by the Constitution. On the one hand, it
*narrowed* the scope of the great clauses of the Constitution granting powers to Congress. It seriously contracted
the interstate commerce power and it read startling ex-
emptions into the taxing power. Simultaneously, it *expanded* the scope of clauses which limited the power of

the Congress, such as the " due process clause " and the
clauses withholding power from the federation. At the
same time it used the " due process " concept to cut down
the effective power of the states. Division of opinion on
constitutional interpretation ceased to be along the classic
lines of a liberal as against a strict construction. The same
Justices used both in the interests of private economic
power: they were strict and niggardly in construing *powers* of government and liberal to the point of extravagance
in construing *limitations* — even inventing such limitations as " freedom of contract " where none existed in the
Constitution.

It was this manifestation of judicial supremacy which
threatened legislative and Executive paralysis and provoked the revolt against the Court's prevailing doctrine.
The story of the cases that led to the revolt makes that fact
plain. Our struggle has been one to restore effective government — the only means through which the will and
opinion of the people can have any expression.

The fight of 1937 was not a fight to destroy the Court
or to impose legal limitations on its powers. The Roosevelt administration never refused obedience to any mandate of the Court. It made no attack on the tenure or integrity of any individual Justice. Its attack was on what
it regarded as an abuse of power, not on the institution
itself. It recognized the Supreme Court as a necessary institution in our federation and acknowledged its evolution-

ary accretions of customary authority to be quite as valid as its less specific written authority.

But liberal-minded lawyers also recognized that constitutional law is not a fixed body of immutable doctrine. We knew its rules had their beginnings and endings, their extensions and their recessions many times in the checkered history of the Court. We saw that those changes were identified with the predominant interests or currents of opinion of past epochs, though they were often made in the name of the Constitution itself. The peculiar character of judicial tenure had enabled a past that was dead and repudiated in the intellectual and political world to keep firm grip on the judicial world. What we demanded for our generation was the right consciously to influence the evolutionary process of constitutional law, as other generations had done. And my generation has won its fight to make its own impression on the Court's constitutional doctrine. It has done it by marshalling the force of public opinion against the old Court through the court fight, by trying to influence the choice of forward-looking personnel, and, most of all, by persuasion of the Court itself. It must not be forgotten that many of the most important changes in legal theory were announced before there was any change in Justices.

The struggle which this book recites makes plain the direction of the turn the Court has taken. The unifying principle running through all of our constitutional litigations has been the recognition that the Constitution contemplated a really effective government. It has been in the nature of a Constitutional Renaissance — a rediscovery of the Constitution itself. Constitutional law had become, not the law of the Constitution, but the law *about* the Constitution. We are back to the original sweep and vigor of those clauses which confer power on the Federal Government, and those which limit it are reduced, if not to their original meaning, at least to tolerable approximations. And the National Government has won a long fight to free itself from an unwholesome dominance of the vested private interest over the public welfare.

The preservation of democracy on this continent may well depend on an effective government through which it may function. If we are now able to organize our economy effectively to support national defense against totalitarianism, it will be because it no longer can be slowed up by the obstacles to effective government which were interposed in the path of our national defense against depression.

No doubt another day will find one of its tasks to be correction of mistakes that time will reveal in this structure in which we now take pride. Our innovations will then have become the established order, and only fanatics underestimate the power of an established order. As one who knows well the workmen and the work of this generation, I bespeak the right of the future to undo our work when it no longer serves acceptably. The precedents of this period should receive only the respect due to the deeds of men who with earnest heart and troubled mind have sought gropingly but honestly for what was best for their day.

Because I am sure no finality can attach to our own contributions to constitutional law, because I know that there will be strong pressures on the Court to resist departures from today's decision which the future may need to make, because, in short, the court fight may at some distant period — a generation or two hence, perhaps — have to be repeated, I think it may be useful to assemble and record, however imperfectly, what has been done, or attempted, in this historic struggle of some of the Justices to maintain judicial supremacy over the legislative process and on the part of other Justices and of the Administration to confine judicial power to its traditional and proper sphere.

My purpose is to set the Roosevelt Court proposal and the Court's own steps to reform in their historical and constitutional perspective. I am not writing a legal text book or a history of the Supreme Court, even for the period under consideration. I hope Charles Warren will extend his excellent historical studies to cover this significant period. I am not writing a defense of the court plan. I did that as well as my powers permitted when it was timely.[1]

[1] Hearings, Senate Judiciary Committee, S. 1392, 75th Cong., 1st sess., March 11, 1937, Part I, p. 37.

Nor am I concerned at all with the personal and political factors in the court fight. These have been related by others.[2] Neither do I purpose to persuade as to the wisdom of any policies of the Administration. The social or economic background of legislation, the pressures upon government to take some action, the evils aimed at, and the effects of adverse decision are set forth only to show the field in which the Court was substituting its judgment for that of the Congress and the manner in which judicial review governed our society or economy, as well as its mere effect on legal doctrine.

It has been my duty and good fortune, chiefly as Solicitor General of the United States, but also as Attorney General, and in earlier posts, to present to the Supreme Court many Administration cases which called for a reconsideration of what we regarded as offending precedents. It is inevitable that I will reflect an Administration point of view on the constitutional struggle. I do not profess the neutrality required for the ultimate appraisal of our work. It will be a generation before the effects of what we have done will fully unfold, and at least as long before it can be disinterestedly assessed.

I consider it no part of my duty to worship the Supreme Court or its Justices. One of them has written of another: " Like all human institutions, the Supreme Court, he be-

---

2 Alsop and Catledge: *168 Days*. New York: Doubleday; 1938.

lieved, must earn reverence through the test of truth." [3]
So I have no hesitation in pointing out what seem to me
its mistakes or shortcomings. On the other hand, I could
not, if it were asked of me, write with malice or ill will for,
in addition to the ordinary obligation of a lawyer to the
Court, I have a personal one because of its patient and
courteous consideration of my advocacy, even when the
tensions between the Court and the Administration, which
I represented, were greatest.

Nor should criticism of the trend of decisions be construed as denying either the ability or disinterestedness of
the Justices. There may have been times in its history,
particularly in the late 1800's, when the intellectual level
of the Court was low. That is the view of one of its ablest
members, Mr. Justice Miller.[4] William Howard Taft,
when President Harrison's Solicitor General, referred to
the Justices as " a lot of mummies " and expressed great
irritation and contempt for their attitude.[5] Certainly no
small part of our present troubles dates from precedents
created during that period when the Court was saturated

[3] Frankfurter, Felix: *Mr. Justice Holmes and the Supreme Court.*
Cambridge: Harv. Univ. Press; 1938, p. 94. The author quotes an address
by Mr. Justice Brewer from which I take the following: " It is a mistake
to suppose that the Supreme Court is either honored or helped by being
spoken of as beyond criticism. . . . True, many criticisms may be, like
their authors, devoid of good taste, but better all sorts of criticism than
no criticism at all."

[4] Fairman, Charles: *Mr. Justice Miller and the Supreme Court.* 1862–
1890. Cambridge: Harv. Univ. Press; 1939.

[5] Pringle, H. F.: *The Life and Times of William Howard Taft.* New
York: Farrar & Rinehart; 1939. Vol. I, p. 115.

with the doctrines of *laissez faire*. But at no time during my government service, even at times of which I am most critical, have the Justices rated as a " lot of mummies." It has been a sharply divided Court, but it has not been an inferior or contemptible Court. Charles Evans Hughes has been a Chief Justice in the great tradition. Each side of questions on which the Court has disagreed has been represented by Justices of ability and earnestness and deep conviction.

And a word of caution to the reader is in order. In tracing a rising tide of dissatisfaction with the Court, culminating in the struggle of 1937 and the Court's retreat from some of its former basic assumptions, we tend to magnify the proportion of questionable judgments rendered. We must not forget that the blunders and deficiencies upon which I have concentrated in this book were vastly diluted in a stream of judicial duties acceptably, if not always brilliantly, performed. We are selecting for discussion only the debits, but there are many credits which, though not relevant to our present purpose, must enter into any balanced judgment of the work of the Court.

This manuscript was originally written in odd intervals between arguments in Court as Solicitor General. It has been revised as opportunity was found. Such intermittent attention leaves much to be desired. Without assuming responsibility for the views expressed herein, others have given me valuable help. I am heavily indebted to

Paul Freund for many helpful criticisms of my text, and for the index. Heading the staff of the Solicitor General's office from 1933 to 1939, the government briefs during this critical period bore the impress of his scholarship and judgment. I turn to his counsel from habit. I am also indebted to Professor Louis Jaffe of the University of Buffalo Law School for contributions and suggestions. And to Miss Ruth Sternberg for the preparation of the manuscript, reading of proofs, and all the really burdensome duties of authorship. This leaves the book's errors and defects as contributions of my own.

ROBERT H. JACKSON

September 23, 1940
Washington, D. C.

*Appointed to SCt*
*9-11-41*

# CONTENTS

I     Foundations of Judicial Supremacy
                    (1787–1865)     3

II    Evolution of Judicial Supremacy
                    (1865–1932)    39

III   The Court Hesitates between Two Worlds
                    (1933–34)    75

IV    The Court Nullifies the New Deal
                    (1935)     86

V     Law and Politics       (1936)     124

VI    The Challenge                     176

VII   The Court Retreats to the Constitution
                    (1937)    197

VIII Consolidating the New Position
                    (1938–40)    236

IX    Government by Lawsuit        286

X     The Political Nature of Judicial Supremacy     311

APPENDIX

     Court Reorganization Message of President
        Roosevelt     328

     President Roosevelt's Speech of March 9, 1937    340

     Wheeler-Bone Resolution to Submit Judiciary
        Amendment     352

     O'Mahoney Resolution to Submit Judiciary
        Amendment     353

TABLE OF CASES CITED     354

INDEX                 *follows page*   361

# THE STRUGGLE
# FOR JUDICIAL SUPREMACY

# Chapter I

# FOUNDATIONS OF

# JUDICIAL SUPREMACY

# 1787–1865

" We are under a Constitution, *but the Constitution is what the judges say it is*, and the judiciary is the safeguard of our liberty and of our property under the Constitution." (Italics supplied.) So spoke Charles Evans Hughes, later to become the tenth Chief Justice of the United States.[1]

The Constitution nowhere provides that it shall be what the judges say it is. How, then, did it come about that the statement not only could be made but could become current as the most understandable and comprehensive summary of American constitutional law?

What the Constitution does say is:

---

[1] *Addresses and Papers of Charles Evans Hughes.* New York and London: G. P. Putnam's Sons; 1st Ed. 1908, pp. 139–140; 2d Ed. 1916, pp. 185–186. Note: Chief Justice Hughes is the eleventh Chief Justice if we count John Rutledge, who received a recess appointment, sat for a short time, and was refused confirmation.

"The judicial Power shall extend to all Cases . . . arising under this Constitution . . ." [2] and that

"This Constitution, and the Laws of the United States which shall be made in Pursuance thereof . . . shall be the supreme Law of the Land. . . ." [3]

It is probable that many, and it is certain that some, members of the Constitutional Convention appreciated that these provisions would spell out a power in the Supreme Court to pass on the constitutionality of federal legislation. But it was the least debated of any of the important implications of the instrument. Nor was this significant probability stressed, though it was mentioned, in the debates before the people and before ratifying state conventions. Most lawyers have believed that the implication is clear; others, that it is at the very best ambiguous. But certain it is that any explicit grant of this power was omitted and that it was left to lurk in an inference. Thus, in an instrument setting up a government of carefully limited powers, the most final and uncontrolled of powers, vested in a body of least responsibility to the people or their representatives, has no written word to grant, define, or check it. Perhaps no formula could have been agreed upon. Perhaps it was the part of wisdom to leave so controversial a subject to settlement by events.[4]

---

[2] Article III, Sec. 2.
[3] Article VI.
[4] Dean William Draper Lewis in *Interpreting the Constitution* (Charlottesville: The Michie Company; 1937), says at p. 12:

In any case political evolution has supplied the omission, and the course of history has established that power in the Supreme Court.

Since the power was not disclosed by the instrument, it follows that it was not limited or regulated by it. When the power should come into play, by what caution and safeguards it would be hedged, to what extent judicial opinion should bind the political action of the other departments were left unsettled. In this indefiniteness were the makings of a controversy that has been with us from the beginning and that is certain to vex us to the end of the Republic.

In view of the use in our own time of the judicial power to regulate more or less the fundamental economic and social orders of the country, it is interesting to review the reasons for creating a federal judiciary, the early assertions of the judicial power, and the gradual evolution of what we know as " Judicial Supremacy."

The Constitutional Convention was comprised of men of remarkable learning in the history and theory of gov-

---

" There is one explanation of this failure by the Convention to act that I submit with diffidence. It is that there existed among the leaders the fear that, should the matter be seriously argued in the Convention with an insistence on a definitive decision, the Constitution's adoption by the Convention or its adoption by the people of the several States would be jeopardized because it would create a long wrangle over who should be the final interpreter, the Congress, the Supreme Court, or some body especially created for that purpose. Perhaps also there was the belief that if nothing were said the Supreme Court or the Congress would become the ultimate arbitrator, either of these solutions being satisfactory to the more federal-minded members."

ernment, but it would be a grave mistake to think of them
as theoreticians detached from the conflicting interests of
an emerging industrial and financial economy. Their
short lives had experienced several forms of government,
including monarchy, a parliamentary cabinet system, colonial governments under a variety of charter powers
and limitations, and a confederation of the independent
states.

Although the industrial revolution was only beginning,
the American people had begun to think in terms of economic interest when the Constitutional Convention was
held. Adam Smith's *Wealth of Nations* was published in
the year that witnessed the Declaration of Independence.
Its theme was the relation between economic and political
power, between well-being and government. The Constitutional Convention was born of the economic distress of
the time, and the power grants of the Constitution were
framed with a view to end by political action one of the
worst of American depressions. Financial distress was
widespread, much property and many sources of the
slender colonial revenues had been destroyed, imports had
drained the land of specie, and a paper money craze
among the states had provided an era of inflation during
which George Washington said he would like to hang all
speculators. When inflation collapsed, farmers threw
away milk, used corn for fuel, let their apples rot on the
ground while food grew scarce in cities. Shipping and

trade were at a standstill. Shays' insurrection challenged the state's ability to maintain government and order. The states began to make commercial war on one another, and the old confederation was powerless to bring order out of the chaos.[5]

The founders of our government had no misunderstanding of the fact that they were creating not only a political government but an instrument of economic control as well. One of Madison's papers in the *Federalist* clearly set forth this awareness. He said:[6]

". . . the most common and durable source of factions has been the various and unequal distribution of property. Those who hold, and those who are without property, have ever formed distinct interests in society. Those who are creditors, and those who are debtors, fall under a like discrimination. A landed interest, a manufacturing interest, a mercantile interest, a moneyed interest, with many lesser interests, grow up of necessity in civilized nations, and divide them into different classes, actuated by different sentiments and views. The regulation of these various and interfering interests forms the principal task of modern Legislation, and involves the spirit of party and faction in the necessary and ordinary operations of the Government."

---

[5] Fiske, John: *The Critical Period of American History*. Boston and New York: Houghton, Mifflin and Company; 1899, pp. 134–185.

[6] *Federalist* — No. 10.

The men who framed the Constitution were, in the main, men of property, having a conservative background and interest, and believing generally in " government by the wise, the good and the rich." The doctrines of equality set forth in the Declaration of Independence had been hard-tested by the trying times that had followed and the Constitution represented something of a counter-revolution. While the Declaration was directed against an excess of authority, the Constitution was directed against anarchy.

Among the founders of our government, none knew more clearly what he wanted than Hamilton. A life-tenure judiciary during good behavior he regarded as one of the " modern improvements in the practice of Government " because it was an " excellent barrier to the encroachments and oppressions of the representative body." He saw it as a " safeguard against the effects of occasional ill humors in the society " and as " mitigating the severity, and confining the operation " of " unjust and partial laws." [7] Hamilton's use of the polite language of the creditor class of his day hardly concealed his fear of the debtor class and its influence in lawmaking. More than any other of his time he wanted a check on Congress, and better than any other he estimated the effect of the federal judiciary as such.

Hamilton's desire was aided also by necessity. The pur-

-----

[7] *Federalist* — No. 78.

pose of the Convention was to create a federation of states, and the central problem was how to distribute governmental authority within the federation and between it and the component states, and how to keep it within the bounds of the grant. Some arbiter is almost indispensable when power is distributed among many states and the nation and is also balanced between different branches, as the legislative and executive, and when written and fundamental limitations on all governmental agencies, such as the Bill of Rights, are set up for protection of the citizen. Each unit cannot be left to judge the limits of its own power.

In some federations conflict of power between the several parts of government is treated as a political question to be settled by vote of the national legislature. Our own Constitution adopted this technique as to imposts or duties on imports and exports necessary for executing state inspection laws, which are made specifically subject to the " Revision and Controul of the Congress." [8] But other questions, regarded in many nations as political, are made legal questions, to be settled by adjudication by the judicial power, rather than by political processes. No doubt it was the hope of obtaining greater consistency and neutrality of decision that led our forefathers to entrust the keeping of the equilibrium of the Federal Union to a court rather than to the Congress. The result, however, has been

---

[8] U. S. Const. Article I, Sec. 10, cl. 2.

to give us the most legalistic system of government in the world with the judicial power penetrating and legal philosophy governing our whole national life.

However vague the general contours of the judicial power over federal legislation, the Constitution set up in the Supreme Court, as the judicial head of such federal court system as the Congress might establish, jurisdiction out of which there was certain to accrue a vast power over political and economic policy. It prescribed that this judicial power shall extend " to all Cases, in Law and Equity, arising under this Constitution, the Laws of the United States, and Treaties made, or which shall be made, under their Authority; — to all Cases affecting Ambassadors, other public Ministers and Consuls; — to all Cases of admiralty and maritime Jurisdiction; — to Controversies to which the United States shall be a Party; — to Controversies between two or more States; — between a State and Citizens of another State; — between citizens of different States, — between citizens of the same State claiming Lands under Grants of different States, and between a State, or the Citizens thereof, and foreign States, Citizens or Subjects." [9]

Thus was cast upon the Supreme Court the duty of being, within its proper jurisdiction, the voice of the Constitution speaking the final word in composing conflicts within our complicated political system. No greater task

---

[9] U. S. Const. Article III, Sec. 2.

has challenged the vision and statesmanship of any little group of men calling themselves a court. This is made clear if we examine the several sources of conflicts that have vexed the Court in the past and will do so in the future.

## CITIZEN V. CITIZEN

It will be seen that the federal judicial power included controversies between individual parties, provided they were citizens of different states. Such controversies were not confined to those involving questions under federal law. The purpose was to open to the non-citizen of a state a forum to sue a citizen thereof, a forum more likely to be neutral than those of the state. This purpose had its roots in colonial creditor experience where the local courts were not always hospitable to non-resident claimants. Congress at once exercised its power and set up a nation-wide system of federal courts with jurisdiction to decide any cases where the parties were of diverse citizenship. The result of this was that — after waiting about three years for business — the Supreme Court began to deal very largely with common law questions — quite foreign to any peculiarly federal function. For the greater part of a century the Court was largely occupied with the conventional function of courts: the adjustment of grievances between man and man.

The Supreme Court for years has been of declining importance as a conventional common law court to put at rest ordinary controversies between private litigants. What was left of its function as a common law court was virtually abdicated in the recent remarkable doctrinal somersault in *Erie Railroad* v. *Tompkins*,[10] which held that federal courts can no longer exercise an independent judgment as to the common law but will accept as conclusive the rule of law declared by the highest court of the state whose law applies. This substantially ends the influence of the Supreme Court as a source of a uniform or federal common law. It becomes, for better or for worse, more exclusively a source of public law, a real third branch of the national government.

### STATE V. STATE

The Constitution extends the federal judicial power to all " Controversies between two or more States " ; and the Supreme Court is given original jurisdiction of cases in which a state shall be a party. Thus it made many intergovernmental conflicts judicial, rather than political, problems to be settled by litigation rather than by diplomacy or military strength or by legislation.

Suits between states fortunately have been infrequent and have involved mainly disputed boundaries or the diversion of waters to the alleged injury of others. Lately

---

[10] 304 U. S. 64. See discussion Ch. VIII.

states have sued each other in disputes of an economic character. The Court recently entertained and decided a controversy between several states, in each of which a rich decedent had made some show of residence, to determine which was entitled to resort to his assets for payment of death tax claims.[11] This is not to be taken, however, as indicating a general policy of adjudicating conflicting tax claims of states.[12] This jurisdiction to settle controversies between states, while important, has not been very controversial and does not promise to become so.

## CITIZEN V. STATE

The Constitution in unmistakable terms included in federal judicial power the settlement of cases or controversies " between a State and Citizens of another State." But when the Court began to exercise its jurisdiction to bring a state to its bar on the complaint of a citizen of another state, great resistance was encountered. This is a strange chapter in our constitutional jurisprudence. Two citizens of South Carolina, as executors of a British creditor, filed suit against the State of Georgia. Chief Justice Jay wrote the most extended of his few judicial opinions to hold that the Supreme Court had jurisdiction.[13] Georgia resented

---

11 *Texas* v. *Florida,* 306 U. S. 398.

12 *Massachusetts* v. *Missouri,* 308 U. S. 1; see, also: Warren, Charles: " The Supreme Court and Disputes between States," Bulletin of The College of William and Mary, Vol. 34, No. 5 (June 1940).

13 *Chisholm* v. *Georgia,* 2 Dall. 419.

being haled before a national court and passed a statute making it a felony for any person to execute the process of the court under a penalty of " death, without benefit of clergy, by being hanged." The judgment which the Court rendered against Georgia was never executed.[14] The decision caused considerable excitement, the more, no doubt, because the beneficiaries of this decision chanced to be British creditors. Virginia joined the protest, and soon the Eleventh Amendment was adopted to protect the states against such suits. It provided that the judicial power should not extend to any suit against a state " by Citizens of another State." Thus the Court was reversed by amendment, and the states felt secure from suit.

Ninety years later a clever lawyer brought in the Supreme Court a suit against Louisiana on behalf of some of its own citizens, pointing out that the Eleventh Amendment was so drawn as to prevent only suits brought by citizens of a state other than of the one sued. The Supreme Court then decided that the Constitution had never authorized a suit by a private citizen against a state, unless it had consented and waived its sovereign immunity.[15] It thus appeared that by its later doctrines no amendment was ever needed, and, if it had been, the one adopted was probably defective. However, the policy which the Eleventh Amendment sought to establish is the law, and pri-

---

[14] Bates, Ernest Sutherland: *The Story of the Supreme Court.* New York: The Bobbs-Merrill Co.; 1936, p. 56.
[15] *Hans* v. *Louisiana,* 134 U. S. 1.

vate citizens may not use the Supreme Court process to bring suit against non-assenting states.

But, irrespective of immunity of the state itself from suit, the Supreme Court has exercised in other cases the power of determining whether state legislation conflicted with provisions of the federal Constitution as the supreme law of the land. Such a power rests on quite different foundations than does the power to strike down *federal* legislation as unconstitutional.

It is important to observe that the power of the Supreme Court to declare acts of the *states* void under the federal Constitution presents an entirely separate issue in our history. This controversy has really revolved around the issue of *federal* supremacy in the fields allotted to the Federal Government rather than around the issue of judicial supremacy as such. It is accepted that whenever state action is reviewable on constitutional grounds, the review with exceptions not here important should be by the Supreme Court. Other experiments in federation which did not place such emphasis on judicial authority have felt obliged to vest a power in the general legislature to overrule state or provincial legislative acts deemed an interference with federal powers. It is generally agreed that no union can stand without some central veto over local encroachments. All of the parts are represented in the central legislature, and it is under a political and practical restraint from injuring its own constituency. The local government, however, does not represent the whole and has no political restraint. It has frequent temptations to further a local power or interest at the expense of the broader or national welfare.

The difference in the necessity for these two veto powers was never better expressed than by Mr. Justice Holmes who said: [16]

" I do not think that the United States would come to an end if we lost our power to declare an Act of Congress void. I do think the Union would be imperiled if we could not make that declaration as to the laws of the several States."

Notwithstanding the obvious necessity for such power and a general agreement that it did and should reside in the Supreme Court and its prompt and emphatic assertion by the Court, it was repeatedly, and at times successfully, challenged.[17] Before 1809 the Pennsylvania Legislature had adopted resolutions denying such jurisdiction and directing the Governor to " protect the just rights of the State " and had resisted federal court decrees.[18] Virginia and Georgia both refused to recognize the Supreme Court

---

[16] Holmes, Oliver Wendell: *Collected Legal Papers.* New York: Harcourt, Brace and Company; 1920, pp. 295–6. Address, Feb. 15, 1913, Harvard Law School Assn. of New York.

[17] Warren, Charles: *The Supreme Court in United States History.* Boston: Little, Brown and Company; 1935. Vol. I, pp. 63–69.

[18] Id. pp. 369–88.

decisions.[19] On one occasion state authorities executed a prisoner, ignoring the pendency of proceedings in the Supreme Court to review the conviction under state statutes, the constitutionality of which was in question.[20] Again the authority of the Court was denied; this time under the Fugitive Slave Law. The Wisconsin Supreme Court refused to file the mandate of the United States Supreme Court in a case under that Act, and the State Legislature resolved that the state was the ultimate judge of federal power.[21] Such resistance practically ended with the Civil War. It is now an accepted part of our constitutional doctrine that conflicts between state legislation and the federal Constitution are to be resolved by the Supreme Court and, had it not been, it is difficult to see how the Union could have survived.

## STRIKING A BALANCE BETWEEN NATIONAL AND STATE AUTHORITY

The exercise of a reviewing authority over state legislation, especially when supplemented by similar review of

---

19 Virginia in *Fairfax* v. *Hunter,* 7 Cranch 602 (1813) discussed in Warren, supra, Vol. I, pp. 446–8; Georgia in *Worcester* v. *Georgia,* 6 Pet. 515 (1832) discussed in the same work at Vol. I, pp. 768–9.

20 Beveridge, Albert J.: *Life of Marshall.* Boston and New York: Houghton Mifflin Company; 1916–19. Vol. IV, pp. 542–52; Warren, Charles: *The Supreme Court in United States History.* Boston: Little, Brown and Company; 1937. Vol. I, pp. 733–4.

21 See Lewis, William Draper: *Interpreting the Constitution.* Charlottesville: The Michie Company; 1937, p. 36; *Booth* cases 18 How. 476

Congressional enactments, made the Court the arbitrator of those most persistent and difficult of our inter-governmental conflicts — those between state and nation. This has come about although there is no express grant of jurisdiction over controversies between state and nation as there is over those between two states.

At the Supreme Court bar federal regulations of interstate commerce, exertion of the power to tax and appropriate for the general welfare, the extension of the bankruptcy forums to municipal corporations, and many other federal legislative efforts are challenged as invading the power reserved to the states.

On the other hand, state legislation is assailed upon the ground that it trespasses on federal power in that it burdens or interferes with interstate commerce by regulating it or taxing it, or because it creates unlawful trade barriers or restrictions. The Court has had great difficulty in preventing the state and federal authority from coming into collision because of overlapping. It has also had great difficulty and less success in keeping the two from being pulled apart so as to leave a " no man's land " or a " twilight zone " between state and national authority in which powerful interests could escape being effectively governed by either.

The whole subject is one of great delicacy and recurring

(1855), 21 How. 506 (1858), 11 Wis. 498 (1859) Joint Resolution No. 4 Wis. General Laws 1859.

vexation. To draw the line truly is, as Mr. Justice Frankfurter well says, " subtle business, calling for great wariness " and he adds: [22]

" Especially is wariness enjoined when the problem of construction implicates one of the recurring phases of our
federalism and involves striking a balance between national and state authority in one of the most sensitive
areas of government."

The history of the country shows that our national
legislators, except during the reconstruction days, have
shown a pretty consistent solicitude for the integrity of
the states. Any wise national system would create states
if they did not already exist. Indeed, from our western territory we have often done so. The need for state governments for local purposes has been so evident that the original states have repeatedly diluted their voting power in
the national legislature, especially in the Senate, to set up
new states on an equality with themselves. In neither the
acts nor the philosophy of men who comprehend the practical limitations on national government is there a place
for hostility to the states or rivalry with them.

It is often assumed, however, that powers which the
Court denies to the Federal Government fall in consequence to the state governments and that its frequent denial of federal power, therefore, makes the Supreme Court

---

22 *Palmer* v. *Massachusetts,* 308 U. S. 79, 83.

a protector of the states. This is questionable. Few decisions of the Supreme Court can be cited in which any state of the Union has been able to obtain protection from the Court of its own constitutional rights, *upon its own demand.*

The State of Massachusetts in 1922 sued Secretary of the Treasury Mellon to enjoin the administration of grants-in-aid under the Maternity Act. The Court's opinion describes the plea of the state:

" The State of Massachusetts in its own behalf, in effect, complains that the act in question invades the local concerns of the State, and is a usurpation of power, viz.: the power of local self-government reserved to the States."

The Court dismissed that plea for want of jurisdiction and without considering the merits by holding:

". . . the State of Massachusetts presents no justiciable controversy either in its own behalf or as the representative of its citizens." [23]

A little later, in 1926, the State of Florida asked the Court to enjoin enforcement of a taxing law the provisions of which, Florida said, according to the Court's opinion: [24]

". . . constitute an invasion of the sovereign rights of the state and a direct effort on the part of Congress to coerce the state . . ."

[23] *Massachusetts* v. *Mellon,* 262 U. S. 447, 480.
[24] *Florida* v. *Mellon,* 273 U. S. 12, 16.

The Court, however, refused to allow Florida even to bring its suit because it said the threatened acts would not constitute " a direct injury " to the state, and that the state could not sue to prevent injury to it through its citizens.

But, though the state will not be heard, questions of states' rights may be raised by the private litigant for his own benefit and the Court will decide them for him. In the *Carter Coal* case the Court struck down the Bituminous Coal Act of Congress on the plea by the owners of the Carter Coal Company that the Congress had invaded states' rights.

Seven states appeared and joined with the Federal Government in support of the Act — no state appeared against it. Nevertheless, the Court spoke of the danger of the states' being " despoiled of their powers " and being reduced to " little more than geographical subdivisions of the national domain." [25] When the state seeks protection, it is told that its rights raise *political* questions which the Court cannot decide. When private interests make the plea, it is transmuted into a justiciable question which the Court will answer.[26] Thus " states' rights " have tended to

---

[25] *Carter* v. *Carter Coal Co.,* 298 U. S. 238, 295, 296.

[26] In *United States* v. *Butler,* 297 U. S. 1, no state complained that aid to its farmers invaded its rights. The processors were the sole objectors as well as the beneficiaries of the states' rights plea. However, the Court has lately allowed state authority to stop enforcement of a federal law deemed to invade states' rights. This may prove an opening of the door to the states themselves. (*Hopkins Savings Assn.* v. *Cleary,* 296 U. S. 315.)

become a vested private interest in federal impotency rather than a positive privilege of the states themselves.

CIVIL RIGHTS V. SOVEREIGN POWER

The Supreme Court is also the voice of the Constitution in vindicating the rights of the individual under the federal Constitution against both the national and state governments. These liberties which the Federal Government must not transgress are chiefly found in the first ten amendments, which we know as our Bill of Rights.

These prohibit Congress from enacting any law respecting an establishment of religion or prohibiting the free exercise thereof; or abridging freedom of speech, or of the press; or the right of the people peaceably to assemble, and to petition the government for a redress of grievances. They prohibit violation of the right of the people to be secure in their persons, houses, papers, and effects against unreasonable searches and seizure. They preserve the right to be held to answer for infamous crime only on indictment by a grand jury, prohibit double jeopardy for the same offense, and compulsory self-incrimination. They prevent deprivation of life, liberty, or property without due process of law, and taking of private property for public use without just compensation. They give an accused the right to a speedy trial by an impartial jury in the district where the offense was committed, the right to be informed of the charge, to be confronted with the witnesses against him, to have compulsory process for witnesses in his favor, and to have the assistance of counsel for his defense. Trial by jury is preserved in civil cases, and excessive bail or fine, or cruel and unusual punishments, are prohibited.

After the Civil War, Amendments Fourteen and Fifteen established federal protection for the citizen against his state government as well. States were forbidden to " abridge the privileges or immunities of citizens of the United States; nor shall any State deprive any person of life, liberty, or property, without due process of law; nor deny to any person within its jurisdiction the equal protection of the laws." All persons born or naturalized in the United States and subject to the jurisdiction thereof were declared citizens of the United States — a citizenship theretofore denied by one school of thought to exist.

There is room for controversy as to whether the Supreme Court has always adequately and consistently enforced all of these rights in the cases coming before it. And there can be little question that it has expanded the " due process clauses " into greater limitations than they originally were meant to embody.[27] But there can be no doubt that whatever of value these legal rights do have is

27 See Edgerton, Henry W.: " The Incidence of Judicial Control Over Congress," 22 Cornell L. Quar., 299, a comprehensive study of the practical effects and tendencies of judicial supremacy, which concludes that enthusiasm for judicial control over Congress is only logical in one identified with the " well-to-do minority " of the population

because of the existence of a Court with power to enforce them. There can also be no doubt of an increasing judicial vigilance in this field.


JUDICIAL POWER TO NULLIFY ACTS OF CONGRESS

The assertion of a power to disregard acts of the Congress as unconstitutional is the cause of the Court's long controversy with the Executive. Such supremacy over its " coordinate branches " of the same government is not, as Mr. Justice Holmes pointed out, authenticated by necessity. Its history is one of singular caution by the Court in the beginning and singular recklessness in the end. The first step in establishing supremacy of the judicial over both other departments in constitutional matters was taken by the Supreme Court in 1803 in *Marbury* v. *Madison*.[28] Over half a century was to pass before in 1857 it took a second step in the *Dred Scott* case which played its part in precipitating the Civil War.[29] The first step was as shrewd and successful as the second was reckless and disastrous. The Marshall strategy laid a foundation so deep that no later excesses have undermined it. *Marbury* v. *Madison* deserves examination.

In the fall of 1800, Jefferson and his followers won a sweeping victory over the Federalists but the new Presi-

[28] I Cranch 137 (1803).
[29] *Dred Scott* v. *Sandford*, 19 How. 393 (1856).

dent and the new Congress could not take office until March 4, 1801. The defeated Federalists used this waiting period to entrench themselves in the judiciary, where tenure was for life or good behavior and salary could not be reduced. These constitutional provisions were as good as old age pensions to the discredited Federalist politicians, for if they could once get into judicial office they could be dislodged only by death or impeachment.

This expiring Federalist Congress passed an act on February 13, 1801, reorganizing the federal judiciary, creating sixteen new circuit judgeships and also providing that on the death of the next Supreme Court Justice the number of such Justices should be reduced to five. This was to prevent Mr. Jefferson from naming a successor to the aged and ailing Cushing. On February 27, this Congress passed another act authorizing the appointment of an unlimited number of Justices of the Peace in the District of Columbia. President Adams, up to midnight of March 3, was busy filling these new judicial offices with faithful Federalists. His chief aid in the work was John Marshall, who held both the office of Secretary of State in Adams' Cabinet and of Chief Justice of the United States. He, too, had just been sworn in to the Chief Justiceship in February, 1801.

But Marshall's two jobs seem to have overtaxed his time, and James Madison, his successor as Secretary of State, on March 4 found a batch of judicial commissions on the desk Marshall had relinquished. He had failed to deliver them to the appointees. Among them was one appointing Marbury a Justice of the Peace. Madison, on instruction from Jefferson, refused to deliver it. Marbury obtained the aid of Charles Lee, Adams' Attorney General, and applied to the Supreme Court for a writ of mandamus to compel Madison to deliver the commission. The case involved some pretty legal questions. Today it would also involve an ethical standard which would forbid Marshall to sit in a case founded on acts and omissions to which he had been a party. He not only sat, but he wrote the opinion.

Marshall first held that Marbury was entitled to receive his commission, that Madison in withholding it was violating the law, and that the Congress had given the Court power to redress the wrong by issuing its writ. The Jeffersonian legal staff in court must at that point have felt that the Court was about to test its strength by ordering the Jefferson administration to deliver the commission. Not so. The shrewd Marshall was to give the Jeffersonians a victory almost as annoying as a defeat. Marshall proceeded to announce that the act of Congress giving his Court this power to command Madison to deliver the commission was unconstitutional, because it gave to his Court an original jurisdiction greater than that given by the Constitution. Marshall then asserted the power of the Court in a case before it to refuse to enforce or apply a federal law believed by the Court to be unconstitutional. In this he adopted Hamilton's argument in the 78th number of the *Federalist.* Hence he declared that despite the law the Court was without jurisdiction.

The strategy of giving the Jeffersonians a victory by invoking a doctrine of which they were the bitter opponents was masterly. Marshall knew his politics as well as his law. The Jeffersonians could not well arouse the people against the doctrine by which they had won their case. Marshall had fixed in the law the doctrine of judicial supremacy, and he had fixed it in a most sheltered position. Had he declared the doctrine in a case where the decision went against Mr. Jefferson, there is little doubt that the President would have defied the Court and at that time the people would probably have sustained him. But Jefferson could not defy a decision in his favor; he could make no issue over a legal theory. Judicial supremacy in constitutional interpretation was so snugly anchored in a Jeffersonian victory that it could not well be attacked. Meanwhile, the profession took it to be the law, and it became a part of the tradition of the Court and of our constitutional habit of thought.

It was well for the doctrine that its incubation period was thus sheltered, for there was no end of strife between the courts and the Jeffersonians. The doctrine came near being abandoned by Marshall himself during the battle over the Chase impeachment. He was ready to bargain it

away for security in the judicial office. Samuel Chase was
a Justice whose partisanship overpowered his judgment
and who in open court often assailed the Jeffersonian
party. He had been savage in his enforcement of the Alien
and Sedition Laws. No judge ever deserved censure more.
But the proceedings to impeach him took so wide a sweep
that the whole Federalist judiciary felt itself likely to be
removed if Chase were convicted. They may have been
right.

Marshall plainly was frightened and wrote to Chase an
amazing letter proposing to scrap the whole pretension to
judicial supremacy.[30] He said:

" I think the modern doctrine of impeachment should yield
to an appellate jurisdiction in the legislature. A reversal
of those legal opinions deemed unsound by the legislature
would certainly better comport with the mildness of our
character than (would) a removal of the Judge who has
rendered them unknowing of his fault."

This indicated no strong confidence that judicial judgment was to be final. However, the impeachment failed by
a narrow margin, and the Marshall doctrine, uncompro-
mised, remained in " the law."

Andrew Jackson was no friend of the Court and denied
its claim to supremacy. After it sustained the constitu-

---

[30] Beveridge, Albert J.: *Life of Marshall.* Boston and New York:
Houghton Mifflin Company; 1916–19. Vol. III, p. 177.

tionality of the Bank of the United States,[31] Jackson re-
asserted its unconstitutionality; Marshall to the contrary
notwithstanding. Thus he paid his respects to the Court
in his message vetoing the act rechartering the Bank:[32]
" The opinion of the judges has no more authority over
Congress than the opinion of Congress has over the judges,
and on that point the President is independent of both.
The authority of the Supreme Court must not, therefore,
be permitted to control the Congress or the Executive when
acting in their legislative capacities, but to have only such
influence as the force of their reasoning may deserve."

The view of Jackson, as it probably was of Jefferson
before him and Lincoln after him, was that though the
Court might pass upon questions of constitutionality in a
case before it, the Executive and the Legislature in performing their duties might, indeed must, form their own
views of constitutionality and act accordingly.

This veto message was written for Jackson by Roger
Taney, then serving as his Secretary of the Treasury. On
December 28, 1835, Taney was appointed Chief Justice
to succeed Marshall. After a fierce contest he was confirmed. Taney was beyond question one of the ablest men
ever appointed to the Court, and his early years of service
were characterized by opinions which recognized the newer
economic and social forces with which political power was

---

[31] *McCulloch* v. *Maryland,* 4 Wheat. 316 (1819).
[32] Richardson, James D.: *Messages & Papers of the Presidents.*
Washington: Government Printing Office; 1896. Vol. II, p. 582.

coming to grips. The earlier Taney Court resisted the urge to take unto itself political problems. It refused to throw the judicial power into a political quarrel in Rhode Island arising out of Dorr's Rebellion where the rebels demanded removal of property qualifications from voting; the Court held that the Constitutional guarantee of republican government presents political questions for Congress to decide, rather than legal questions for the Court.[33] But the next great fight between the Court and the elected branches of the government found Taney, now an exponent of slaveholding interests, championing to the point of disaster the power of the Court to declare laws unconstitutional.

In the famous *Dred Scott* case the question at issue was the status of a Negro who had been carried by his master from a slave state into a territory made " free " by the act of Congress known as the Missouri Compromise and was then taken back into a slave state. Dred Scott claimed that once on free soil he was forever emancipated. But Taney held that Congress was without power to legislate upon the issue of slavery even in a territory governed by it and that therefore Dred Scott had never become free. Congress, he held, was powerless to check or limit the spread of slavery.

After Taney read the *Dred Scott* decision (1857), Abraham Lincoln challenged him in language that must

---

[33] *Luther* v. *Borden,* 7 How. 1.

have reminded the aging Taney of the words he had written for Andrew Jackson: [34]

". . . all that I am doing is refusing to obey it [that decision] as a political rule. If I were in Congress, and a vote should come up on a question whether slavery should be prohibited in a new Territory, in spite of the Dred Scott decision, I would vote that it should."

and later he expressed his opposition to

". . . that decision as a political rule which shall be binding . . . on the members of Congress or the President to favor no measure that does not actually concur with the principles of that decision. . . . We propose so resisting it as to have it reversed if we can, and a new judicial rule established upon this subject."

On March 4, 1861, Taney administered the Presidential oath to this critic of his Court and heard the newly made President declare in his inaugural:

". . . the candid citizen must confess that if the policy of the Government upon vital questions affecting the whole people is to be irrevocably fixed by decisions of the Supreme Court, the instant they are made in ordinary litigation between parties in personal actions the people will have ceased to be their own rulers, having to that extent practically resigned their Government into the hands of

---

[34] See *Political Debates between Lincoln and Douglas* (Sparks Edition. Cleveland; 1895) pp. 29, 299.

that eminent tribunal. Nor is there in this view any assault upon the court or the judges. It is a duty from
which they may not shrink to decide cases properly
brought before them. . . ." [35]

Soon Lincoln and Taney were in open collision. As a
war measure Lincoln took stern measures to suppress dis-
loyalty and suspended the right to habeas corpus, the writ
which serves to test a denial of liberty. Taney held that
only Congress could suspend the writ of habeas corpus.
His condemnation of military interference with the civil
liberties of the citizen was severe. Lincoln disregarded
Taney's opinion, and his writs were disobeyed. The Supreme Court passed into eclipse during the war. Taney,
however, prepared opinions holding both the Legal Tender Act and the Conscription Law to be unconstitutional,
but they were never used. [36] Taney died as the war closed.

Lincoln knew that some of his war-time acts were on
dangerous ground in a strict view of the Constitution.
He confided that he chose Salmon Chase as Chief Justice
to succeed Taney chiefly because: ". . . we wish for a
Chief Justice who will sustain what has been done in regard
to emancipation and the legal tenders." [37] Chase had been

---

[35] Richardson, James D.: *Messages & Papers of the Presidents.*
Washington: Government Printing Office; 1897. Vol. VI, pp. 9–10.

[36] Swisher, Carl B.: *Roger B. Taney.* New York: The Macmillan Co.;
1936, pp. 540–572.

[37] Bates, Ernest Sutherland: *The Story of the Supreme Court.* Indianapolis, New York: The Bobbs-Merrill Co.; 1936, p. 172. Also, Warren, Charles: *The Supreme Court in United States History.* Boston:
Little, Brown, & Co.; 1937. Vol. II, pp. 400–401.

Lincoln's Secretary of the Treasury — as Taney had been Jackson's — and had supported the Legal Tender Acts of 1862–3 which changed the country's fiscal system to a paper basis as a war measure. Thus Lincoln sought to guard his vital measures against the judiciary, whose power he distrusted but recognized.

### JUDICIAL REVIEW MIDWAY IN THE LIFE OF THE NATION

As we reached midway in the life of the nation we saw the foundations firmly laid for a measure of judicial control of government that probably exceeded the hopes even of Hamilton. The Supreme Court had taken its position at the switchboard where power was turned off or on in many agencies. Power could be confirmed or denied to state or to nation or to one or another branch of the government. Moreover, power could be shut off from all government and turned on for private interests.

Up to midway in our national life, however, the movement of the time was an establishment of this judicial power, rather than its exercise. The doctrine of judicial review, during the first half of our history, only twice struck down acts of Congress. The first decision, *Marbury* v. *Madison,* had the effect of limiting the Court's own power more closely than the Congress had done. It decided that the Court could not be required by Congress to exercise more jurisdiction than was conferred by the Constitution. Such a decision would not appear to present any serious obstacle to popular government. Jackson's later difference with the Court passed off without incident. The Court had *upheld* the constitutionality of the Bank Act. He refused to sign a new act rechartering it because he believed it unconstitutional; he might have refused for any other reason. His veto measure was directed more to those in Congress who relied on the Court's decision than to the Court. The real issues in the Bank fight were of policy; on these the Court did not purport to bind him; there was no conflict of power or of jurisdiction between President and Court, for the Court conceded more power to Congress and the President than Jackson would admit. So there was no judicial threat here to the lawmaker.

In the early days, assertions by courts of the power to set aside an act of the legislature were generally tempered by the qualification that the power would never be exercised save in a clear case, a case in which the incompatibility of the statute with the provisions of the Constitution was beyond honest dispute.[38] If the matter was in fairness

---

[38] See the scholarly and wise discussion by J. B. Thayer, *The Origin and Scope of The American Doctrine of Constitutional Law,* 7 Harv. L. Rev. 129, 156 (1893). Thayer, the colleague of Holmes and teacher of Brandeis, wrote:
". . . the safe and permanent road towards reform is that of impressing upon our people a far stronger sense than they have of the great range of possible harm and evil that our system leaves open, and must leave open, to the legislatures, and of the clear limits of judicial power; so that responsibility may be brought sharply home where it belongs. The

arguable, the legislative act must stand, and redress be sought through the processes of representative government. The courts had some difficulty in even imagining the sort of statute that it would be proper to declare invalid; one judge thought of an imaginary statute which transferred the executive power to a committee of the House of Representatives.[39] The validity of a law, as another judge put it, should not be questioned unless so obviously repugnant to the Constitution that on being pointed out the repugnancy would be perceived by " all men of sense and reflection in the community." [40] Judge Cooley, the eminent authority on constitutional law, epitomized the principle by observing that a member of the legislature who voted against a measure as being in his judgment unconstitutional might later, on becoming a judge, find it his duty, though he had in no degree changed his opinion, to declare the measure constitutional.[41]

These professions of judicial self-restraint have never been avowedly repudiated. But the history of judicial review is the story of the wavering adherence to, and the

---

checking and cutting down of legislative power, by numerous detailed prohibitions in the constitution, cannot be accomplished without making the Government petty and incompetent. This process has already been carried much too far in some of our States. Under no system can the power of courts go far to save a people from ruin; our chief protection lies elsewhere. If this be true, it is of the greatest public importance to put the matter in its true light."

[39] Id. p. 141.
[40] Id. p. 142.
[41] Cooley, Thomas McIntyre: *Constitutional Limitations*. Boston: Little, Brown & Company. 6th Ed., p. 68.

growing departure from, this self-denying ordinance in practice.

The *Dred Scott* decision was a significant departure and an ominous portent. It is true that in a formal sense it had no immediate effect. The Missouri Compromise, which it declared to have been invalid, had already been repealed. But the decision was a deliberate attempt to destroy or neutralize Congressional power to deal with the single most important issue of the moment. This was a challenge, indeed, to popular and, probably more, to federal government. It took a Civil War to answer the challenge.

But, for another reason, to those who might be preternaturally far-seeing, Dred Scott was a portentous name. It first suggested the " due process " clause as a basis for reviewing federal legislation and so foreshadowed the enormous scope of the judicial power which was later to be exercised. The Constitution included, nearly from the beginning, the Fifth Amendment prohibiting *Congress* from taking " property . . . without due process of law." Yet it had never served as the basis for judicial review of the content of legislation, though similar provisions in state constitutions had been so used by an occasional court. But in this same ominous *Dred Scott* case Taney had suggested that the abolition of slavery might run contrary to it; the suggestion was not much noticed and was forgotten by most. In part, it is true, this may have been the result not merely of judicial abstinence but of the fact that there was little Congressional legislation at least that would offend conservative minds. *Laissez faire*, to some degree, was the philosophy of the legislature, as it was of the Court. It is partly this fact which obscured the potentialities of *Marbury* v. *Madison* and, even more, of *Dred Scott*.

Another reason why the storm signal was little heeded was that the prestige of the Court suffered greatly during and by reason of the Civil War. Taney was antipathetic to Lincoln and his purposes. His judicial mandate was ignored.

But the tree of judicial power so precariously planted by Marshall had struck deep roots. It showed wonderful vitality and hardiness. The renewal of this power, after the blight which it suffered in the Civil War, to such strength that it could strike down for the next seventy years many acts of social and economic reform, could sterilize other acts which embodied popular measures, could render ineffective much of the effort to aid the cause of labor and, at last, could mutilate in two years the whole reform and recovery program of the New Deal, is one of the most amazing chapters in the history of popular government. While in the first seventy years of its existence it set aside two acts of Congress, in the second seventy years it set aside fifty-eight. In ten years between 1920 and 1930, it set aside nineteen. It took over into its control the whole range of the national economy. It tried to

stem the increasing recession from *laissez faire* and to make
the teachings of *laissez faire* a part of our constitutional
law. It told the Congress what it could and could not tax.
It extended the due process clause to cover a review by the
Court of legislative wisdom. It conjured up such doctrines
as " freedom of contract " to defeat legislation, though
the Court later found that the Constitution did not men-
tion it.[42] At length the persistent effort of the Court to
judge the legislation of the New Deal by the measure of
*laissez faire* brought on the court fight of 1937.

---

[42] *West Coast Hotel Co.* v. *Parrish* (Washington Minimum Wage
Case), 300 U. S. 379 (1937).

# Chapter II

# EVOLUTION OF

# JUDICIAL SUPREMACY

# 1865–1932

To win the Civil War the Northern industrialists and financiers joined forces with the small farmer and free labor. Together they destroyed the slave power. The struggle then set in, or recommenced — and it has never since abated — among these former allies. The central problem of democratic government became one of working out a tolerable balance among these forces, of moderating the always threatening power of those whom society permits to own or control its economic resources.

Our history demonstrates that our legislatures saw the answer roughly in this way: *first*, there must be a tax policy, based on ability to pay, sufficient to support social services for those upon whom systematic inequalities bore most harshly — in short, an income tax; *secondly*, there must be regulation of the power of wealth where the premise of competition failed; *thirdly,* those without wealth must be protected in their efforts to organize. The instrument of these policies was, of course, legislation. The final refuge of property from unwelcome legislative restrictions or burdens was the courts. Its advocates beat incessantly upon the big bass drum of the Constitution and, when that did not work, argued for an " interpretation " of statutes which would eviscerate them.

The outstanding constitutional development of the era following the Civil War was the growing frequency with which the Supreme Court refused on constitutional grounds to enforce acts of Congress of far-reaching economic importance. As each instance became a precedent for more, the power was in a constant process of extension. Enumerated by decades, the number of laws of Congress declared invalid by the Supreme Court is as follows: [1]

| | | | |
|---|---|---|---|
| 1790 — 1800 | 0 | 1860 — 1870 | 4 |
| 1800 — 1810 | 1 | 1870 — 1880 | 9 |
| 1810 — 1820 | 0 | 1880 — 1890 | 5 |
| 1820 — 1830 | 0 | 1890 — 1900 | 5 |
| 1830 — 1840 | 0 | 1900 — 1910 | 9 |
| 1840 — 1850 | 0 | 1910 — 1920 | 7 |
| 1850 — 1860 | 1 | 1920 — 1930 | 19 |

[1] Bates, Ernest Sutherland: *The Story of the Supreme Court.* Indianapolis, New York: The Bobbs-Merrill Co.; 1936, p. 263.

But in just three years, beginning with the October 1933 term, the Court refused to recognize the power of Congress in twelve cases. Five of these twelve decisions occurred during a single year: that is, the October 1935 term; four of the five, by a sharply divided court.

In spite of the Court's condemnation of the theory that " parties have an appeal from the legislature to the courts," [2] powerful interests from the time of the Civil War were encouraged by the trend of decisions to carry to the Supreme Court all causes lost in Congress, and the power of judicial review came more and more to resemble a political veto. But there was opposition within the Court itself to being cast in the role of censor. Led by the brilliant and forceful Miller,[3] it resisted for a few years the ceaseless pressure of creditors, bondholders, railroads, and coupon-clippers. The first ominous rumble of what lay in the future was heard in the famous *Legal Tender Cases.*

The Lincoln administration to finance the war turned to printing paper money, which Congress made legal tender. As the greenbacks depreciated, creditors resisted accepting them in payment. In the test case which came before the Court [4] the depreciated paper money was offered in payment of a contract made before the Act. There were at the time only eight Justices. One of them, Grier, was

---

[2] *Chicago etc. Railway Co.* v. *Wellman,* 143 U. S. 339.

[3] Miller's story is well told in Fairman: *Mr. Justice Miller and the Supreme Court.* Cambridge: Harvard University Press; 1939. See, also, *Gelpcke* v. *Dubuque,* 1 Wall. 175.

[4] *Hepburn* v. *Griswold,* 8 Wall. 603.

senile. In conference he first voted for constitutionality.
That made the score 4 to 4. Since the case was on appeal
from a judgment in favor of the law, this meant an affirm-
ance. Poor Grier was then induced to change his vote, and
the score was 5 to 3 against the law. Miller objected furi-
ously to a decision being made under such circumstances.
He demanded that the judges wait until the Court be restored to its full strength. But the opponents of the law
thought in the terms of a political campaign and insisted
on pressing their fortuitous advantage. Before the decision was announced, Grier resigned, and the score was announced 4 to 3 against the constitutionality of the provision making the greenbacks legal tender. The opinion was
written by Chief Justice Chase who as Lincoln's Secretary
of the Treasury had supported the Acts, if reluctantly,
and had issued the money as valid legal tender. As this
remarkable decision was being read, President Grant
sent to the Senate the names of two new Justices: one
to fill Grier's place; the other, a new place just created
by Congress which in 1866 had reduced the size of the
Court to prevent Johnson from making an appointment
lest he name a man who might strike down the Reconstruction Acts which he had vetoed as unconstitutional. Grant
carefully chose men who he had reason to believe would
uphold the Legal Tender Acts.[5] Four days after the con-

---

[5] Ratner, Sidney: "Was the Supreme Court packed by President
Grant?" Political Science Quarterly, Vol. 50, p. 343 (September 1935).

firmation of the new Justices the Attorney General created
a sensation in the Courtroom by moving for argument of
two other legal tender cases. A bitter fight broke out on
the Bench. The Chief Justice maintained that there had
been an understanding that all of the pending legal tender
cases were to be governed by the disposition of *Hepburn* v.
*Griswold*. Miller and his following denied this and seem
to have been right. In *Knox* v. *Lee* [6] the Court by a five
to four vote reversed itself and held the Legal Tender Acts
valid, both as to contracts made before and after their
enactment. Yet it was an ominous portent that the power
of a democratic people to regulate its currency — whether
for good or ill is immaterial — should rest on the uncertain
tenure or the questionable sanity of one or two mortals.

Charles Evans Hughes in 1927 said of this incident: [7]

" The action of the Court, taken soon after their confirmation, in ordering a reargument of the constitutional question and then deciding that the legal tender act was constitutional, the two new judges joining with the three
judges, who had dissented in the *Hepburn* case, to make a
majority, caused widespread criticism. From the stand-
point of the effect on public opinion, there can be no doubt
that the reopening of the case was a serious mistake and

---

[6] 12 Wall. 457.
[7] Hughes, Charles E.: *The Supreme Court of the United States.*
New York: Columbia Univ. Press; 1928, pp. 52–3.

the overruling in such a short time, and by one vote, of the previous decision shook popular respect for the Court. . . . Stability in judicial opinions is of no little importance in maintaining respect for the Court's work."

Ten years play havoc with one's philosophy, and a decade after writing this Mr. Hughes was destined as Chief Justice to lead the Court not only to one but to several reversals. Some were reversed with a shorter lapse of time, and some, with no new judges at all. He evidently came in a decade to the belief that to be right is a better way of maintaining respect than to be stable in the wrong. I quite agree with the Chief Justice and disagree with Mr. Hughes.

Passing beyond this spectacular episode in the history of judicial supremacy, let us recall the story as it relates to the central efforts of the legislatures, that I have already enumerated, to maintain a democratic society — the taxing of wealth according to ability to pay, the regulation of business enterprise, and the protection of labor.

### THE COURT AND TAXATION ACCORDING TO ABILITY TO PAY

After the *Legal Tender Cases* the attack upon legislative power raged on, and for a time it was touch and go. Finally in the *Income Tax Case*,[8] the opponents of majority rule won a brilliant and smashing victory. The Civil

---

8 *Pollock* v. *Farmers' Loan & Trust Co.,* 157 U. S. 429; 158 U. S. 601.

War had been in part financed by income taxes, and in 1894 an income tax of two per cent on all incomes over $4,000 was enacted by Congress.

Joseph Choate argued that the law was unconstitutional. The Constitution (Article I, Sec. 9, cl. 4) provides that: " No Capitation, or other direct, tax shall be laid, unless in Proportion to the Census or Enumeration herein before directed to be taken." Mr. Choate argued that a tax on income derived from real or personal property was a " direct " tax on that property and so must be apportioned among the states: for example, a state with two per cent of the population, whatever its income, must contribute no more — and no less — than two per cent of the whole amount collected nationally. The requirements of apportionment would obviously defeat the very object of the income tax. Against Mr. Choate's position were historical purpose, judicial precedent, and economic logic. He was aware of this and resorted to other devices more adequate to his purposes. His argument struck as low a note as any great lawyer ever sounded before the court. Its tone may be judged from a few quotations. He recited from a personal conversation with the dead President Hayes a prediction that he would live to see a tax on estates that would take all of the larger estates, and continued: [9]

---

[9] Hicks, Frederick G.: *Arguments and Addresses of Joseph H. Choate.* St. Paul: West Publ. Co.; 1926, pp. 422, 423.

". . . It is far more communistic in its purposes and tendencies than anything President Hayes apprehended. It is defended here upon principles as communistic, socialistic — what shall I call them — populistic as ever have been addressed to any political assembly in the world."

" Now, if you approve this law, with this iniquitous exemption of $4,000, and this communistic march goes on and five years hence a statute comes to you with an exemption of $20,000 and a tax of 20 per cent. upon all having incomes in excess of that amount, how can you meet it in view of the decision which my opponents ask you now to render? There is protection now or never."

Choate knew his Court. It held that a tax on income from real or personal property was a direct tax on that property and so must be apportioned. This tax being unapportioned, was invalid. An income tax on earnings such as wages and salaries was not a direct tax and need not be apportioned. It decided (rightly, of course) that Congress would not have levied a tax on salaries alone. So the whole Act fell. A mysterious shift in the vote of one Judge emphasized again the element of caprice upon which the fate of such great issues may hang.

Though the Court's opinion purported to rest on the loftiest logic, Mr. Justice Field in his concurring opinion revealed that some, at least, had responded to the Choate demagoguery of wealth. " The present assault upon capi-

tal is but the beginning," he said.[10] The dissent was vigorous. Justice White referred to the decision as " judicial
amendment of the Constitution." [11] Justice Harlan said
the decision was being made " principally, for reasons of
an economic nature " and that its practical effect is " to
give to certain kinds of property a position of favoritism
and advantage inconsistent with the fundamental principles of our social organization. . . ." [12] Justice Jackson
said it disregarded the principle of taxation according to
ability to pay and " This decision, in effect, works out a
directly opposite result, in relieving the citizens having the
greater *ability*, while the burdens of taxation are made to
fall most heavily and oppressively upon those having the
least ability." [13] Justice Brown bluntly said: ". . . the
decision involves nothing less than a surrender of the taxing power to the moneyed class." [14]

The people agreed with the minority and in February
1913 ratified the Sixteenth Amendment which gave Congress power to tax incomes " from whatever source derived." During the eighteen years before the amendment
the men who were piling up tremendous fortunes as a result
of the national growth and their favored position to exploit resources or manpower were saved vast sums in taxes.
And the country soon learned that even after this amendment the Court would not allow Congress to tax stock

[10] 157 U. S. 429, 607.
[11] 157 U. S. 429, 639.
[12] 158 U. S. 601, 684, 685.
[13] 158 U. S. 601, 705.
[14] 158 U. S. 601, 695.

dividends,[15] judicial salaries,[16] nor profits of oil operators who leased state lands.[17]

## THE COURT AND THE REGULATION OF RATES, PRICES, AND WAGES

During the post-Civil War period, also, came the great era of expansion of the " due process " clause from its origins designed to provide a fair trial to a device for judicial control of the whole range of the national economy. The prohibition directed to Congress against depriving any person of life, liberty, or property without due process of law existed in the Constitution, in the Fifth Amendment, for almost a century without constituting a serious limitation of the substance of federal legislation.[18] It was only when the making of the Constitution ceased to be something within the memory of man that the clause began to take on a new and expansive meaning. After a similar clause was inserted in the Fourteenth Amendment, it became the rallying point for those who resisted the efforts of the states to control the excesses and relieve the oppressions of a rising industrial economy. This is only to paraphrase what the Supreme Court itself took occasion to say

[15] *Eisner* v. *Macomber*, 252 U. S. 189.

[16] *Evans* v. *Gore*, 253 U. S. 245. *Miles v. Graham*, 268 U. S. 501.

[17] *Burnet* v. *Coronado Oil & Gas Co.*, 285 U. S. 393.

[18] The cases before the Civil War in which " due process " clauses in state constitutions were urged against state legislative regulation are canvassed by Professor Corwin in " The Doctrine of Due Process of Law Before the Civil War," 24 Harv. L. Rev. (1911) 366, 460.

in 1877, just nine years after the Fourteenth Amendment was adopted. Speaking through Justice Miller, the Court observed, with reference to the due process clause: [19]

" It is not a little remarkable, that while this provision has been in the Constitution of the United States, as a restraint upon the authority of the Federal government, for nearly a century, and while, during all that time, the manner in which the powers of that government have been exercised has been watched with jealousy, and subjected to the most rigid criticism in all its branches, this special limitation upon its powers has rarely been invoked in the judicial forum or the more enlarged theatre of public discussion. But while it has been a part of the Constitution, as a restraint upon the power of the States, only a very few years, the docket of this court is crowded with cases in which we are asked to hold that State courts and State legislatures have deprived their own citizens of life, liberty, or property without due process of law. There is here abundant evidence that there exists some strange misconception of the scope of this provision as found in the fourteenth amendment. In fact, it would seem, from the character of many of the cases before us, and the arguments made in them, that the clause under consideration is looked upon as a means of bringing to the test of the decision of this court the abstract opinions of every unsuccessful liti-

---

[19] *Davidson* v. *New Orleans,* 96 U. S. 97, 103.

gant in a State court of the justice of the decision against
him, and of the merits of the legislation on which such a
decision may be founded."

While the Court was under the influence of Justice
Miller and of Chief Justice Waite this attitude prevailed,
though by the barest majorities. It was during this period
that the Court upheld the power of the states to regulate
the rates and services of public utilities.[20] If the legislature should abuse its power, said the Chief Justice, " the
people must resort to the polls, not to the courts."

But the lawyers persisted, despite the admonition of the
Court, and their efforts were finally rewarded. Beginning
about 1890, it was a fortunate and relatively innocuous
piece of reform legislation that was able to run the gantlet
of the due process clause. Two hundred and twenty-eight
times thereafter the Supreme Court set aside state legislative action under the Fourteenth Amendment.[21] The figures do not tell the whole story, because a single decision
may have caused the death of similar legislation in many
states and prevented its birth in others.

I have taken 1890 as the beginning of the era of nega-
tion under the due process clause. The late Judge Hough,
of the Second Circuit Court of Appeals, was more specific.
He dated it from the decision of *Chicago, Milwaukee &*

[20] *Munn* v. *Illinois,* 94 U. S. 113.
[21] The cases are listed in Frankfurter, F.: *Mr. Justice Holmes and
the Supreme Court.* Cambridge: Harvard University Press; 1938. Appendix I, through the 1937 term.

*St. Paul Ry. Co.* v. *Minnesota,*[22] rendered on March 24
of that year. In that case the Court decided that in establishing rates for railroads the question of their reasonableness cannot be left by the legislature to a state commission,
but must be subject to judicial review. Three members of
the Court, Justices Bradley, Gray, and Lamar, delivered
a dissenting opinion, in which they charged that the decision " practically overruled " *Munn* v. *Illinois* and the
other granger cases. " It is complained," they said, " that
the decisions of the board are final and without appeal. So
are the decisions of the courts in matters within their jurisdiction. There must be a final tribunal somewhere for deciding every question in the world. Injustice may take
place in all tribunals. All human institutions are imper-
fect — courts as well as commissions and legislatures." A
majority of the Court disagreed. " It is from that decision," said Judge Hough, " that I date the flood." [23]

Judicial review of all of the facts entering into rates set
by utility commissions has become an effective process for
slowing down and obstructing effective regulation of public utilities. The Supreme Court holds that the utility
must be permitted to earn a " fair " rate on the " fair
value " of the capital invested.[24] The " value " of the
investment, however, is not determined solely by the actual

22 134 U. S. 418.
23 Hough, Charles M.: " Due Process of Law — Today." 32 Harv. L.
Rev., 218, 228.
24 *Smyth* v. *Ames,* 169 U. S. 466.

investment. Together with this figure the Court says the Constitution requires that there must be taken into account the amount which it would cost to reproduce the plant at the time when the rate is fixed.[25] Contemplate for a moment the job of valuing, let us say, the New York Telephone Company. What incredible, lengthy, and hopeless hypotheses must be entertained. And this process is to be repeated every time a rate is set! It becomes·impossible to establish a solid, adequately supervised, permanent valuation on the basis of sound accounting. Since due process required that the utility be allowed a fair return on a so-called present value which, at a time when price levels had been rising, was greater than the investment, it might be supposed that when price levels started downward the rate base could be reduced by use of a comprehensive index figure to chart the extent of the price decline. But the commissions learned that this was forbidden by the same clause of the Constitution.[26] After a time-taking, costly investigation into each item is completed, the Court then permits — may indeed compel — the matter to be examined anew in a trial before a judge. It may take from five to fifteen years to set a rate which when finally determined is already out of date;[27] many commissions have given up regulation and bargain for rates with the utilities; and the legis-

---

[25] *St. Louis & O'Fallon R. Co.* v. *United States,* 279 U. S. 461.
[26] *West* v. *Chesapeake & Potomac Tel. Co.,* 295 U. S. 662.
[27] See Brandeis, J., on time consumed in valuation proceedings in *St. Joseph Stock Yards Co.* v. *United States,* 298 U. S. 38, 73.

latures, harassed and defeated in their efforts at regulation, turn to public ownership and the " yardstick." " Due process " seems to have come to mean " undue process."

The Supreme Court has drawn out of the big top hat of due process some rabbits even more astounding. Public utility rates, it decides, must be " reasonable " but, until very recently, it has held that prices of other commodities and of labor cannot be regulated at all. There is nothing in the Constitution which provides that there shall be no power to regulate prices or wages. Still less is there anything in the Constitution which provides that while it is a lawful function of government to regulate the hours of labor of women,[28] it is not a lawful function to regulate their rate of pay.[29] Though the distinction is not to be found in the Constitution, it was deduced from the prohibition against deprivation of property without " due process of law " — the same provision that had already supported a distinction between an eight-hour day for miners, held to be permitted by the Constitution,[30] and a ten-hour day for bakers, held to be prohibited by the Constitution.[31]

What constitutional principle explains these results? ". . . freedom of contract is . . . the general rule and restraint the exception," said the Court in the *Adkins* case.

---

[28] *Muller* v. *Oregon*, 208 U. S. 412.
[29] *Adkins* v. *Children's Hospital*, 261 U. S. 525.
[30] *Holden* v. *Hardy*, 169 U. S. 366.
[31] *Lochner* v. *New York*, 198 U. S. 45.

But the Constitution says nothing of freedom of contract, much less about a general rule and exception to it. When the people adopted the Fifth Amendment did they mean to·outlaw legislation which fixed wages or prices? Did the states which ratified the due process clause of the Fourteenth Amendment understand that they were renouncing the power?

Mr. Justice Holmes did not think so. In his now-vindicated dissent in the *Adkins* case he said: [32]

". . . the only objection that can be urged [against a minimum wage law for women in the District of Columbia] is found within the vague contours of the Fifth Amendment, prohibiting the depriving any person of liberty or property without due process of law. To that I turn.

" The earlier decisions upon the same words in the Fourteenth Amendment began within our memory and went no farther than an unpretentious assertion of the liberty to follow the ordinary callings. Later that innocuous generality was expanded into the dogma, Liberty of Contract. Contract is not specially mentioned in the text that we have to construe. It is merely an example of doing what you want to do, embodied in the word liberty. But pretty much all law consists in forbidding men to do some things that they want to do, and contract is no more exempt from law than other acts."

---

[32] 261 U. S. 525, 568.

Before the *Adkins* case, in the case of the ten-hour law
for bakers, he had stated the whole matter of judicial review under the Fourteenth Amendment with what must
now seem unanswerable eloquence, though to his brethren
it did not. He said: [33]

" This case is decided upon an economic theory which a
large part of the country does not entertain. If it were a
question whether I agreed with that theory, I should desire
to study it further and long before making up my mind.
But I do not conceive that to be my duty, because I
strongly believe that my agreement or disagreement has
nothing to do with the right of a majority to embody their
opinions in law. It is settled by various decisions of this
court that state constitutions and state laws may regulate
life in many ways which we as legislators might think as
injudicious or if you like as tyrannical as this, and which
equally with this interfere with the liberty to contract.
Sunday laws and usury laws are ancient examples. A more
modern one is the prohibition of lotteries. The liberty of
the citizen to do as he likes so long as he does not interfere
with the liberty of others to do the same, which has been
a shibboleth for some well-known writers, is interfered with
by school laws, by the Post Office, by every state or municipal institution which takes his money for purposes
thought desirable, whether he likes it or not. The Four-

---

[33] *Lochner* v. *New York*, 198 U. S. 45, 75.

teenth Amendment does not enact Mr. Herbert Spencer's Social Statics. . . . Some of these laws embody convictions or prejudices which judges are likely to share. Some may not. But a constitution is not intended to embody a particular economic theory, whether of paternalism and the organic relation of the citizen to the State or of *laissez faire*. It is made for people of fundamentally differing views, and the accident of our finding certain opinions natural and familiar or novel and even shocking ought not to conclude our judgment upon the question whether statutes embodying them conflict with the Constitution of the United States."

As far as the Supreme Court was concerned, it was unconstitutional to protect purchasers from excessive gasoline prices,[34] ticket brokerage charges; [35] or to protect the unemployed from exorbitant employment agency fees.[36] The Court set itself up as the arbiter of what businesses were " affected with a public interest." Unless the business fell within that narrow class the public was without power to set limits to the rates which a business might charge. " Due process," meant uncontrolled prices except where the Court saw fit to hold otherwise.

Aside from public ownership and the " yardstick," legislatures know two methods of curbing the excesses of our

---

[34] *Williams* v. *Standard Oil Co.*, 278 U. S. 235.
[35] *Tyson & Bro.* v. *Banton*, 273 U. S. 418.
[36] *Ribnik* v. *McBride*, 277 U. S. 350.

economic system: regulation of acquired power, and prevention of its growth. The Court pulled the teeth of regulation. What success has Congress had with prevention?

## THE COURT AND THE STRUGGLE AGAINST MONOPOLY

In 1890 a public aroused by the growth of giant combinations controlling transportation, industry, and commerce at strategic bottlenecks, demanded, and Congress passed, the Sherman Anti-Trust Law. It aimed to stop the alarming concentration of wealth and economic power, and mastery by a few of American economic life. It condemned every contract, combination, or conspiracy in restraint of trade, and declared every attempt to monopolize any part of the trade or commerce among the several states to be illegal.

The first case under it reached the Supreme Court in 1895.[37] This combination controlled ninety-eight per cent, of the sugar refining business of the whole United States, but the Court held that its activities were manufacturing and " bore no direct relation to commerce between the States or with foreign nations," and hence either were not " intended " by Congress to be within the Statute or could not constitutionally be reached by Congress.

---

[37] *United States* v. *E. C. Knight Co.*, 156 U. S. 1, 17.

So conservative an observer as William H. Taft has said: [38]

" The effect of the decision in the Knight case upon the popular mind, and indeed upon Congress as well, was to discourage hope that the statute could be used to accomplish its manifest purpose and curb the great industrial trusts. . . . So strong was the impression made by the Knight case that both Mr. Olney and Mr. Cleveland concluded that the evil must be controlled through State legislation, and not through a national statute, and they said so in their communications to Congress."

The effect of the decision was to nullify the Sherman Act during the period when most of the great trusts were being formed, and to shelter them during their period of growth.

The Court ten years later receded from its position in the sugar trust case,[39] but it then amended the law in another respect after Congress refused to do so. In the *Trans-Missouri* case the Court held that the Act meant just what it said — all combinations in restraint of trade were illegal.[40] Then in the words of Justice Harlan: [41]

" But those who were in combinations that were illegal did not despair. They at once set up the baseless claim that the decision of 1896 disturbed the ' business interests of

[38] Taft, William Howard: *The Anti-Trust Act and the Supreme Court.* New York: Harper & Bros., 1914; p. 60.
[39] *Swift and Co.* v. *United States,* 196 U. S. 375.
[40] *United States* v. *Freight Association,* 166 U. S. 290.
[41] *Standard Oil Co.* v. *United States,* 221 U. S. 1, 91.

the country,' and let it be known that they would never be content until the rule was established that would permit interstate commerce to be subjected to *reasonable* restraints."

But the Court stuck to its guns, so the interests went to Congress, but Congress refused to amend the law in order to let them restrain trade if they could prove that they were " reasonable " about it.[42]

Two years later this precise amendment was accomplished by the Court, which, in the *Standard Oil* and *Tobacco* cases, held it would allow the defense of reasonableness that Congress had rejected. Judge Harlan protested vigorously and said: " In short, the court now, by judicial legislation, in effect amends an act of Congress relating to a subject over which that department of the Government has exclusive cognizance." [43] He went further and said ". . . To overreach the action of Congress merely by judicial construction, that is, by indirection, is a blow at the integrity of our governmental system, and in the end will prove most dangerous to all." [44]

There was judicial supremacy at work subduing the self-preservation impulses of democracy. Regulation or destruction of monopoly was an issue going to the very foundation of our economic system. Popular government

[42] Sen. Rept. 848, 60th Cong., 2d Sess., Jan. 26, 1909, p. 11.
[43] *United States* v. *American Tobacco Co.*, 221 U. S. 106, 192.
[44] *Standard Oil Co.* v. *United States*, 221 U. S. 1, 105.

demanded a curb on the growing financial and industrial giants. The courts put a curb on the popular will
instead.

After many years of disappointing efforts to enforce
the antitrust laws through the Court, Congress, under the
leadership of President Wilson, enacted the Clayton and
the Federal Trade Commission Acts. These statutes out-
lawed " unfair methods of competition " and certain specific practices which, as experience demonstrated, were the
weapons for suppressing competition. The theory of the
legislation was to prevent the growth of monopoly rather
than to break it up after it had been achieved. The Federal Trade Commission was established so that a specialized, expert body might function with ceaseless vigilance
to ferret out incipient symptoms of the death of competition and revive the patient before the fact of monopoly
became irreversible. It was thought that if the courts
found the vigorous enforcement of the antitrust laws un-
congenial they at least would not presume to block the
efforts of an autonomous body. This hope was in the main
disappointed.

The Commission was expected, after investigation, to
determine what practices were unfair methods of competition. The Court promptly decided: " It is for the courts,
not the commission, ultimately to determine as a matter of
law what they include." [45] The statute said that the Com-

---

[45] *Federal Trade Comm.* v. *Gratz,* 253 U. S. 421, 427.

mission's " findings of fact " should be final. But time and again the Court was indisposed to accept the fact finding of the Commission, and it would say that as a " matter of law " that is not " the fact." [46] The climax was reached in *Swift and Co.* v. *Federal Trade Commission.*[47] The Clayton Act forbids a corporation to acquire the stock of a competitor, the acquisition of which would tend to eliminate competition. Swift and Company acquired the stock of a competitor in defiance of this provision. It then used the stock to acquire the assets of the competitor. The Commission ordered Swift and Company to divest itself of the stock and of the assets. A majority of the Supreme Court held that though the Commission might order Swift and Company to sell the illegally acquired stock, it was without power to dislodge Swift's control of the assets secured as a result of the acquisition of the stock. If Swift were swift enough and secretive enough it could make fools of the Commission, of Congress, and of the public. In a later case under the same section, the Commission had decided that the International Shoe Company had bought the shares of a competitor in order to lessen competition. But the majority of the Supreme Court felt that the Commission had thereby done the Shoe Company a great injustice: [48]

---

46 For example, see *Federal Trade Comm.* v. *Curtis Co.,* 260 U. S. 568.
47 *Swift & Co.* v. *Federal Trade Comm.,* 272 U. S. 554.
48 *International Shoe Co.* v. *Federal Trade Comm.,* 280 U. S. 291, 299, 302.

". . . the officers . . . testified categorically that there was in fact no substantial competition between the companies . . . , but that at most competition was incidental and so imperceptible that it could not be located. The existence of competition is a fact disclosed by observation rather than by the processes of logic; and when these officers, skilled in the business which they have carried on, assert that there was no real competition . . . their testimony is to be weighed like that in respect of other matters of fact."

". . . the officers, stockholders and creditors, thoroughly familiar with the factors of a critical situation and more able than commission or court to foresee future contingencies, after much consideration, felt compelled to choose [this course of action]. There is no reason to doubt that in so doing they exercised a judgment which was both honest and well informed; and if aid be needed to fortify their conclusion, it may be found in the familiar presumption of rightfulness which attaches to human conduct in general."

The incredible implication of these words that the self-serving professions of those on trial work like a spell to paralyze the Commission tells more than whole volumes of the attitude of that Court — at least its majority — toward the effort of the public to mitigate the encroachments of monopoly.

## LABOR AT THE BAR OF JUSTICE

A failure to enforce the antitrust laws against the real offenders would have been bad enough, but they were turned to strengthen the forces bearing down upon labor as it tried to find through self-organization and with legislative aid the voice with which to bargain on equal terms with the masters of industry. In 1908, the Supreme Court averred that labor unions were illegal combinations in restraint of trade if they attempted to boycott the goods of any firm that sold its product in interstate commerce.[49] Those who enjoy comparative studies of the judicial process will find it suggestive to note that restraint placed by labor upon interstate commerce, without weighing its reasonableness in the circumstances, was held to be an illegal restraint. Yet restraints by industrialists were illegal only when " unreasonable." The United States Steel Corporation which had assiduously bought up over fifty per cent of the steel business was " reasonable ";[50] yet a refusal by the members of a stone cutters' union to work upon stone quarried by men hostile to their unions was " unreasonable."[51] Said Mr. Justice Brandeis dissenting:

" The Sherman Law was held in *United States* v. *United States Steel Corporation*, 251 U. S. 417, to permit capi-

[49] *Loewe* v. *Lawlor,* 208 U. S. 274.
[50] *United States* v. *United States Steel Corp.,* 251 U. S. 417.
[51] *Bedford Co.* v. *Stone Cutters Assn.,* 274 U. S. 37, 65.

talists to combine in a single corporation 50 per cent. of the steel industry of the United States dominating the trade through its vast resources. . . . It would, indeed, be strange if Congress had by the same Act willed to deny to members of a small craft of workingmen the right to co-operate in simply refraining from work, when that course was the only means of self-protection against a combination of militant and powerful employers. I cannot believe that Congress did so."

The federal judiciary thus erected barriers against self-help by labor. Even more significant was its position that, should a state liberalize its law, labor might still be caught up by the great dragnet woven by the Supreme Court out of that dubious yarn, the unreasonable restraint of interstate commerce.[52] This story has been many times told; just for that reason there is a danger that we may forget its moral.

Long ago there began that course of legislative action designed to overcome the effects of business and judicial hostility to labor activity. Each effort was duly presented to the Court for decapitation. Sometimes the axe was labeled " the Constitution," and at others " interpretation." But, however it was called, its hard steel was basically the notion that the Rule of the Constitution between master and servant was the judicial conception of *laissez faire.*

[52] *United States* v. *Brims,* 272 U. S. 549.

The Court held that neither state nor federal statute could prevent any employer from discharging workers for joining a union.[53] It struck down a law which forbade an employer from making it a condition of employment that the worker should not join a union, the so-called " yellow-dog " contract.[54] What is more, it enforced these " yellow-dog " contracts by injunction. It enjoined anyone from even urging an employee under such a contract to join a union.[55] In this way the employer, by foisting a contract upon an employee only too eager for work, was able to build up around his employment relationship a little kingdom into which no one dared enter. The courts acted as his policeman, and the Supreme Court told the legislature it was powerless to interfere with this monopoly of the very law itself.

It seemed that even the employer's right to an injunction, which rested on no more than a pure judicial invention not much earlier than 1885, was now protected constitutionally by the Fourteenth Amendment which much antedated it. In 1921, the Supreme Court decided, against the protest of some of its most respected members, that no state could stop its own judges from granting injunctions in labor disputes. Mr. Justice Holmes protested: [56]

---

53 *Adair v. United States,* 208 U. S. 161.
54 *Coppage* v. *Kansas,* 236 U. S. 1.
55 *Hitchman Coal & Coke Co. v. Mitchell,* 245 U. S. 229.
56 *Truax* v. *Corrigan,* 257 U. S. 312, 344.

" There is nothing that I more deprecate than the use of the Fourteenth Amendment beyond the absolute compulsion of its words to prevent the making of social experiments that an important part of the community desires, in the insulated chambers afforded by the several States, even though the experiments may seem futile or even noxious to me and to those whose judgment I most respect."

A similar fate awaited legislation which attempted directly to improve the conditions of labor. We have already mentioned the Court's treatment of laws fixing minimum wages for women; of laws setting maximums to the fees which employment agencies could charge. These were struck down as interfering with " liberty of contract " and so as denying " due process of law." Maximum hour legislation illustrates the crazy zig-zag line between validity and invalidity which can be drawn by a Court which has taken to " finding " its social judgments in the Constitution. An eight-hour maximum for miners was held good; [57] a ten-hour maximum for bakers, bad; [58] and a ten-hour maximum for laundries restricted to women, good.[59] Finally a majority of the Court capitulated and held valid a ten-hour law applied to men and women.[60]

In 1918 the Supreme Court, against the protest of Jus-

---

[57] *Holden* v. *Hardy*, 169 U. S. 366.
[58] *Lochner* v. *New York*, 198 U. S. 45.
[59] *Muller* v. *Oregon*, 208 U. S. 412.
[60] *Bunting* v. *Oregon*, 243 U. S. 426.

tice Holmes and an able minority, held that Congress was powerless to stop traffic among the states in goods made by the labor of children.[61] By this decision the free labor of every section of the country was forced to compete with children, too young to make valid contracts themselves, and hence bound into service by others. That decision forced labor, and employers as well, to bargain under threat of being undersold by those who were willing to sell along with their goods the health and the opportunity of their children. This was held to be required by the Constitution. The Court argued that the motive or intention of Congress was to regulate child labor. Because this was the purpose, therefore it was said not to be a regulation of interstate commerce! This reasoning had been rejected in the lottery and oleomargarine cases. There the Court decided that the motives or purposes for which Congress regulated interstate commerce were not the Court's business.[62] But in the *Child Labor Case* the Court warned Congress that though it could regulate as much as it wished lotteries, oleomargarine, and narcotics, it must not use its power to interfere with any phase of the employment relationship. Such a relationship was entirely a matter for state regulation. A state, however, which wished to abolish child labor would find its ability to compete with other states impaired. It could not protect even its home market,

---

[61] *Hammer* v. *Dagenhart,* 247 U. S. 251.

[62] *Champion* v. *Ames,* 188 U. S. 321; *McCray* v. *United States,* 195 U. S. 27.

for it could not prohibit the importation of goods made elsewhere by child labor. That would interfere with interstate commerce.

Justice Holmes summed up the situation: [63]

" I have not yet adequately expressed the more than anxiety that I feel at the ever increasing scope given to the Fourteenth Amendment in cutting down what I believe to be the constitutional rights of the States. As the decisions now stand, I see hardly any limit but the sky to the invalidating of those rights if they happen to strike a majority of this Court as for any reason undesirable. I cannot believe that the Amendment was intended to give us *carte blanche* to embody our economic or moral beliefs in its prohibitions."

The sky had been the limit to the striking down of important economic and social experiments undertaken by the states. The nation had as yet shown little disposition to experiment. We might not be fumbling with the labor problem in 1940 if we had let the states try out industrial courts, collective bargaining guarantees, anti-injunction laws, and minimum-wage and maximum-hour laws when they wanted to. We would have learned from their experiments what was practical and wholesome and what was unworkable or vicious.

[63] *Baldwin* v. *Missouri*, 281 U. S. 586, 595.

## THE DILEMMA OF FEDERALISM

Thus by the Constitution each state gave up its power to protect itself from the harmful economic conduct of other states but received no compensating protection from the national authority. The effect of this " dual federalism " which the Court superimposed upon the Constitution was to remove child labor and kindred subjects from any effective regulation at all, and so to leave the nation to the mercies of private power. In the words of Professor Corwin, " ' Dual Federalism ' thus becomes *triple* federalism — inserted between the realm of the National Government and that of the states is one of no-government — a governmental vacuum, a political ' no man's land.' " [64] This, indeed, became the critical dilemma of federalism in the depression that began in 1929. The crisis of our economy was a national crisis. The collapse of markets and of commerce was a national collapse. Yet there was no national authority to deal with it. Congress was explicitly given constitutional power to regulate commerce among the several states. But the Court had held that the power to regulate interstate commerce may not be exercised where in the opinion of the Court its effect or purpose is to regulate a subject exclusively within state control, even though nothing in the Constitution indicates that any particular sub-

[64] Corwin, Edward S.: " Congress's Power to Prohibit Commerce," 18 Cornell L. Quar. 477, 498.

ject is within the exclusive control of the states. The dilemma of federalism, which reached its most acute state in 1935, was not inherent in the federalism of the Constitution but in the federalism of the Supreme Court.

### JUDICIAL SUPREMACY IN THE SADDLE

Thus, at the threshold of the New Deal the Court had established itself as a Supreme Censor of legislation. It expanded the concept of " due process," and tore it loose from its ancient connotations; it restricted the concept of the power to regulate interstate commerce, and cut down the significance which John Marshall had attributed to it. With these instruments it approved or disapproved each law, grudgingly giving consent to any departure from *laissez faire*, or to any serious interference with the power of property and employers. I do not mean to say that it never did give consent. The Federal Government was confirmed in important powers over railroads, grain and cattle dealings, and many kindred subjects. Workmen's compensation, factory standards, and maximum hours of labor finally became established, though in some cases only after years of judicial obstruction. But this only emphasizes the fact that the Court, and not the legislature, became the final judge of what might be law, for in certain crucial cases — child labor, minimum wage, " yellow-dog " contract, and a whole range of similar subjects — the judicial veto stood firm.

Again, the picture would not be complete if we did not acknowledge that the Supreme Court has rendered civil liberties decisions of substantial value. The record has been a variable one, but, of course, perfect resistance to forces of hysteria which sometimes permeate the whole social fabric is not to be expected from any institution. It cannot completely escape the climate in which it lives though it may come nearer doing so than can Congress.

The Court has protected pretty consistently the writ of habeas corpus,[65] fair trial,[66] the franchise,[67] freedom of the press,[68] and free speech.[69] Thus, toward the older liberalism of the eighteenth century, which was embodied in the Bill of Rights, the Court has generally been sympathetic, but it has been cold to social reform and to economic control when attempted by twentieth-century liberalism.

Chief Justice Hughes in speaking of decisions setting aside acts of Congress once intimated that " few of these cases have been of great importance in shaping the course of the Nation," and has said: [70]

---

65 *Ex parte Milligan*, 4 Wall. 2.
66 *Powell* v. *Alabama*, 287 U. S. 45; *Moore* v. *Dempsey*, 261 U. S. 86.
67 *Nixon* v. *Herndon*, 273 U. S. 536.
68 *Near* v. *Minnesota*, 283 U. S. 697.
69 *Fiske* v. *Kansas*, 274 U. S. 380.
70 Hughes, Charles E.: *The Supreme Court of the United States*. New York: Columbia Univ. Press; 1928, pp. 95–6.

" It must be conceded, however, that up to this time, [1927] far more important to the development of the country, than the decisions holding acts of Congress to be invalid, have been those in which the authority of Congress has been sustained and adequate national power to meet the necessities of a growing country has been found to exist within constitutional limitations."

I agree with the latter statement, but think he gravely underestimates the consequences of the decisions holding laws unconstitutional. Certainly if they can be dismissed as unimportant it is only because they were overthrown. We could not think it unimportant if the *Dred Scott* case were still the law, or if federal currency could not be made legal tender, or if we could not tax income from property, or were denied the right to enact social legislation. These decisions have cost dearly in time, in the diversion of energies, and in the discord involved in their belated correction.

By 1933 the Court was no longer regarded as one of three equal departments among which the powers of government were distributed. Instead, Simeon Baldwin spoke of it as " being invested with acknowledged and *supreme* authority," and the whole conservative and property philosophy became oriented around " judicial supremacy."

This doctrine of judicial supremacy came to include three elements, though rarely stated in combination:

*First.* It was defined by Professor Charles G. Haines in

his book *The American Doctrine of Judicial Supremacy,*[71] as:

" The principles of law and political practice which place the guardianship of the expressed and implied terms of written constitutions primarily in courts of justice, and the dominance of judge-made law in accordance with common-law standards and principles, constitute the bases of what may appropriately be termed *the American doctrine of judicial supremacy.*"

*Second.* The supremacy was in practice extended by use of the " due process " clause to review the wisdom and policy of legislation. One of the few frank avowals that this was its scope was by Mr. Justice McReynolds in this language: [72]

" But plainly, I think, this Court must have regard to the wisdom of the enactment. At least, we must inquire concerning its purpose and decide whether the means proposed have reasonable relation to something within legislative power — whether the end is legitimate, and the means appropriate."

*And lastly,* as Judge Van Orsdel, in setting aside the Minimum Wage Act, naïvely said: [73]

---

[71] Haines, Charles Grove: *The American Doctrine of Judicial Supremacy.* California: University of California Press; 1932. 2nd Ed., p. 27.
[72] *Nebbia* v. *New York,* 291 U. S. 502, 556.
[73] *Children's Hospital* v. *Adkins,* 284 Fed. 613.

" It should be remembered that of the three fundamental
principles which underlie government, and for which
government exists, the protection of life, liberty, and
property, the *chief of these is property.* . . ." [*Italics
supplied.*]

Franklin D. Roosevelt came to power in 1933 with his
party in a majority in both Houses of Congress. But they
would have to reckon with this concept of judicial supremacy which had an uncertain number of devotees among the
Justices of the Supreme Court.

# Chapter III

# THE COURT HESITATES

# BETWEEN TWO WORLDS

## 1933–34

On March 4, 1933, Chief Justice Hughes administered the presidential oath to Franklin Delano Roosevelt. It is not likely that either participant in this ceremony could foresee that he was destined to lead opposing forces in the most significant struggle over judicial supremacy since the days of " reconstruction." Certainly neither of them willed such a contest. The President on his part was to be surprised when his program encountered a destructive and relentless opposition from a majority of the Court. The Chief Justice on his part would again and again try to temper that opposition with the restraints of reason and of judicial tradition and at last would protect his place in history with open protests.

A clash between the precedents of the old order and the

necessities of any new one was inevitable. We have already traced the century of precedent-making during which the majority of the Court, always against the objections of an able minority, had impregnated constitutional doctrine with a philosophy of federal inaction and impotence in dealing with the economy of the nation and the designs of private power. The business and financial world had found *laissez faire* to be in line with its interests, and its servants in the legal profession and among publicists had fostered its inculcation in the law and politics of that long and lush period. This old order had yielded place to a new one in the presidency, but the Justices had, by reason of their life tenure, stayed on.

The people had awaited with unconcealed impatience the transfer of executive power to a new administration. Symptoms of deep social unrest, following economic collapse, were insistent and could be ignored only at great risk. By necessity, no less than by conviction and temperament, the Roosevelt administration was committed to reform and to active use of legislative power to arrest and reverse the economic trends. This very purpose, no matter in what particular program it might be expressed, was itself a challenge to the old philosophy, so well entrenched in juristic thought.

When it came to translation of this purpose into a concrete program, there was little guidance to be had from American experience. If there was to be any marked departure from *laissez faire*, it must be frankly experimental. Enthusiastic groups pressed proposals for reform in many fields, and in most, reform was long overdue. Separate groups brought forth plans on such subjects as banking, monetary policy, industrial practices and labor relations, agricultural distress, security frauds and stock exchange manipulation, utility holding companies, tax evasion and reform, relief, public works, loans to restore the capital structure of banks and insurance and industrial companies, unemployment insurance, and old-age benefits. The President was the only unifying force in an otherwise scattered endeavor. He sought to get the separate and sometimes overlapping or conflicting proposals welded into a unified New Deal. The " 100 days " following his inauguration marked the most active period in American legislative history.

The measures of the Administration were framed with a conscious and conscientious effort to keep within the Constitution. But they were framed by men of liberal background, who accepted generally the liberal interpretation given that instrument by such Justices as Holmes and Brandeis, and they thought of federal power in the broad terms of Marshall and Hughes. The Supreme Court at the moment was playing no significant part in events, but most of the Administration's advisers were well aware of its " brooding omnipresence." They knew that the constitutional doctrine on which they were relying had thereto-

fore won adherence from only a minority of the Court.
But they acted on it from conviction as well as necessity.

The year 1933 passed without significant decisions by
the Court, although controversies were brewing which ad-
monished that the New Deal was headed for a rendezvous
with the Justices. Friend and foe of the Administration
were watching the Court for some sign. It was not until
1934 that cases involving government power to deal with
depression problems caused the Court to speak. These decisions, to the lay public, were rather reassuring in their
results, because they sustained state economic legislation
framed under the newer philosophy of state responsibility
and power. But those who went behind the face of the prevailing opinions were not reassured. They noted a division
among the Justices which might spell peril for the New
Deal. The margin of safety by which this state legislation
had survived was but a single vote.

In January 1934, the Court decided that the Minnesota
State Mortgage Moratorium Law was valid.[1] The law involved was, of course, no part of the New Deal federal program, but the case called forth statements of attitudes
that would have great weight in deciding New Deal cases.
The majority opinion by the Chief Justice declared that,
while an emergency does not create power, an emergency
may furnish the occasion for the exercise of power. He
repudiated the doctrine that the Constitution is " to be

---

[1] *Home Bldg. & Loan Assn.* v. *Blaisdell,* 290 U. S. 398.

read with literal exactness like a mathematical formula."
" The economic interests of the State," he said, " may
justify the exercise of its continuing and dominant protective power notwithstanding interference with contracts." He refuted the contention that the great clauses
of the Constitution " must be confined to the interpretation which the framers, with the conditions and outlook of
their time, would have placed upon them." He thus spoke
a language that was much on the lips of men of the Administration.

Many of them failed to take note, however, that the
Chief Justice spoke for only half of his associates. Mr.
Justice Sutherland, Mr. Justice Van Devanter, Mr. Justice McReynolds, and Mr. Justice Butler joined in a dissent. They denied that any state had any power to give
any relief to the debtors, and their reasons were the economic arguments which always had been invoked by the
creditor against a distressed debtor class. They declared: [2]

" The present exigency is nothing new. From the beginning of our existence as a nation, periods of depression, of
industrial failure, of financial distress, of unpaid and un-
payable indebtedness, have alternated with years of plenty.
The vital lesson that expenditure beyond income begets
poverty, that public or private extravagance, financed by
promises to pay, either must end in complete or partial

---

[2] *Home Bldg. & Loan Assn.* v. *Blaisdell,* 290 U. S. 398, 471.

repudiation or the promises be fulfilled by self-denial and painful effort, though constantly taught by bitter experience, seems never to be learned; and the attempt by legislative devices to shift the misfortune of the debtor to the shoulders of the creditor without coming into conflict with the contract impairment clause has been persistent and oft-repeated."

In other words, Justices of the Supreme Court lacking only one of a majority warned that it was their philosophy that a debtor who had overborrowed could have no relief from the state, and that the Constitution required that the law must be kept wholly at the service of the creditor who had overloaned.

Again the Court spoke. It sustained the State of New York's price-fixing legislation known as the Milk Control Law.[3] The prevailing opinion was by Mr. Justice Roberts, and it took liberal ground, which encouraged all who sought legislative measures to aid in the battle against depression. It said:

". . . there can be no doubt that upon proper occasion and by appropriate measures the state may regulate a business in any of its aspects, including the prices to be charged for the products or commodities it sells.

" So far as the requirement of due process is concerned, and in the absence of other constitutional restriction, a

---

[3] *Nebbia* v. *New York*, 291 U. S. 502.

state is free to adopt whatever economic policy may reasonably be deemed to promote public welfare, and to enforce that policy by legislation adapted to its purpose. The courts are without authority either to declare such policy, or, when it is declared by the legislature, to override it."

But, again, there was an ominous dissent on behalf of the same four Justices. It was written by Mr. Justice McReynolds. The most significant feature of the dissent was the bold declaration that

". . . this Court must have regard to the wisdom of the enactment. At least, we must inquire concerning its purpose and decide whether the means proposed have reasonable relation to something within legislative power. . . ."

Not only was the legislation, in the view of the dissenters, unconstitutional, but they characterized it as a " fanciful scheme," in spite of the fundamental tenet of judicial review that not the wisdom or policy of legislation, but only the power of the legislature, is a fit subject for consideration by the courts. Their idea of its wisdom was a flat contradiction, also, of the conclusions of the New York legislature based on long experience and careful study.

As yet, however, Mr. Justice McReynolds spoke only for a minority. The opinions which had the support of

the majority carried the prestige of being the opinions of
" the Court," and thus the surface indications confirmed
the optimists in their belief that the Court would sustain
reform and experimental legislation. Realists within and
without the Administration noted the dangerously narrow
margin of success in these cases which had come up from
the states. They were acutely aware, as Professor T. R.
Powell put it, that five-to-four decisions are won by having
half a judge more than half of the judges. They were not
so sure that the same half-a-judge margin could be depended upon to support the federal legislation. Federal
legislation is more effective and less easily avoided than
pronouncements of separate legislatures and always
arouses greater fears and opposition.

Clearly, however, the lines were forming for a battle for
power with consequences far beyond any single piece of
legislation under consideration. Four of the Justices, Van
Devanter, Sutherland, McReynolds, and Butler, within
one of a majority, were asserting a power and duty in the
judiciary to stop any governmental body — state or federal — from interfering with an economy of *laissez faire.*
The Constitution, in their view, permitted no restriction of
established privileges of property and authorized no new
burden of regulation, and they asserted the power of the
judiciary as the final arbiter of these limitations in the
American Federation. Three of the Justices, Brandeis,
Stone, and Cardozo, were felt to favor a construction of the

Constitution that would concede to government fairly broad powers to deal with the emergency and would leave the choice of policy to the legislative branch. They asserted for the judiciary only a very limited power to interfere with the policy and detail of legislation adopted by the popularly elected branches of the government. If these justices found any measure of the new administration unconstitutional, as in some cases some or all of them did, then it stood no chance at all.

This left two — Chief Justice Hughes and Mr. Justice Roberts — about whom speculation turned. To be sustained, Administration legislation would apparently need the support of both of them. Both were men of keen intelligence and incorruptible character. Both had held law school lecture posts and had also enjoyed large courtroom law practices, and combined learning with practical experience. Both had had conservative professional relationships, and both, by the standards of professional rewards, had prospered. Moreover, both were Republicans and had been on intimate terms with and owed their positions to Republican presidents, against whose viewpoint and philosophy of government the New Deal was a revolt. The Chief Justice, however, as an investigator of insurance scandals just after the turn of the century and, as Governor of New York and as an Associate Justice of the Court, had a liberal record. Here was a career that puzzled forecasters.

The life of Justice Roberts had been much preoccupied
with professional work of a highly creditable quality but
which revealed little of his philosophy of government. His
public service had been largely legal, rather than policy-
making in character. His opinion in the New York milk
case indicated a comprehension of the problems of the depression and no irreconcilable opposition to efforts by
government to help solve them. It was plain, however, that
if the New Deal program crossed the convictions of either
Chief Justice Hughes or Justice Roberts at any point, it
would be lost. Human nature being what it is, that was a
good deal of a risk, as the event proved.

The judicial hazards to which legislation had become
subjected seemed rather personal ones, considering the
tradition that ours is a " government of laws not of men."
Viewed in retrospect it is clear that this division among the
Justices represented, and probably stimulated, a like division among forces that were gathering for conflict. They
would soon precipitate an epic struggle in American power
politics — the stake being judicial power to revise and
control the legislative policy of the Republic.

The year 1934 came to a close with little awareness of
the impending struggle. New Deal experiments were under way and economic improvement noticeable. The election returned an overwhelming New Deal majority to the
Congress. Most people, in and out of the Administration,

were confident that all was well. The President, the Congress, and the country were on the march.

But the Court was poised between two worlds. The older world of *laissez faire* was recognized everywhere outside the Court to be dead. Would the Court then hold any other world powerless to be born?

# Chapter IV

# THE COURT NULLIFIES

# THE NEW DEAL

## 1935

As the year 1935 opened, several statutes had come to judgment before the Supreme Court. It would be equally accurate to say that now the Supreme Court had come to judgment before the country. Where did it stand with reference to the general program of reform legislation? The answer was quick and unequivocal: In two blows the National Industrial Recovery Act was done to death; monetary legislation escaped, but barely; relief to farm debtors was set aside; railroad retirement pensions fell before a sharply narrowed definition of federal power over interstate commerce; and a new rule limiting the President's power of removal of his appointive officers was promulgated.

## I. STORM SIGNALS

### *" Hot " Oil*

On January 7, 1935, the Supreme Court held the legislation authorizing a code to govern the petroleum industry to be unconstitutional as delegating excessive power to the President.[1] The decision restored economic demoralization to the third largest industry in the nation and its constitutional doctrine prohibiting delegation of power, invoked for the first time to hold a law unconstitutional, introduced a new obstacle to effective government.

The oil industry had long been suffering from overproduction and wasteful competition. Several states had attempted in vain to regulate excessive exploitation of this precious and perishable natural resource. Some states had even enforced shut-downs in oil fields through the militia. But there was no uniformity of policy among them, and they were unable to act severally or to agree on a policy to pursue jointly. The states appealed for federal aid. Governor Landon of Kansas, as well as many other governors and industrialists, urged the President to initiate federal control.

Certainly the magnitude and interstate character of the industry made it an appropriate object of national concern. It employed a capital investment of twelve to fifteen

---

[1] *Panama Refining Co.* v. *Ryan; Amazon Petroleum Corp.* v. *Ryan*, 293 U. S. 389.

billions of dollars and the services of over a million men. Crude petroleum was produced in eighteen states, from over 325,000 wells. It was processed in about five hundred refineries and reached consumers everywhere through over 300,000 marketing outlets. At least ninety per cent of this production found its way through pipe lines, tank cars, or trucks into interstate or foreign commerce. Moreover, without its aid as fuel and lubrication, railroad, airplane, truck, and private automobile would cease to carry the trade between states.

The industry included some twenty huge integrated companies, each with complete production, refining, transportation, and marketing facilities. These, and many smaller unintegrated companies, were engaged in sharp competition. Peculiar operating conditions led owners to exploit fields in order to prevent oil from being drained out of their lands by adjoining owners. Vast surplus stocks overhung the markets, and costs of production exceeded prices, which had suffered utter collapse, wholesale gasoline falling to 2½¢ per gallon. Conditions of competition were notoriously cutthroat, and the industry was an old offender against the antitrust laws.[2] But antitrust suits had not remedied basic conditions, and independent operators were facing ruin.

Congress came to the rescue in two ways. The general provisions of the National Industrial Recovery Act au-

[2] *Standard Oil Co.* v. *United States,* 221 U. S. 1.

thorized codes of fair competition, and one was adopted for the oil industry. It prescribed production quotas for the various states, but it left to each state the allocation of its quota among its own operators. Also, Section 9(c) of the N.I.R.A. dealt specifically with the petroleum industry by authorizing the President to prohibit movement in interstate commerce of any oil produced in violation of the state laws which fixed production quotas, and to make interstate shipments thus prohibited a federal misdemeanor. Thus the federal power was used, not to interfere with, but to assist, the state governments. It seemed clear that the Federal Government could supplement state regulation by stopping movement of illegally produced oil into other states. A similar problem had arisen in connection with stolen automobiles, and it was met by the Dyer Act in the same way — by making it a federal crime to transport a stolen car into another state. But certain oil operators attacked both the code quotas and the prohibition of interstate shipments of " hot " oil as unconstitutional. The case produced some topsy-turvy results. The validity of the code was not passed on at all, but the President's order prohibiting interstate shipments of " hot " oil went down. So did crude oil prices.

The code was not passed upon because, to everybody's surprise, it turned out that the paragraph of the code which made violations a criminal offense had been inadvertently eliminated in a revision of the code. This curious incident led anti-Administration lawyers to charge that the New Deal was prosecuting citizens for violations of non-existent laws. Because the clamor over government-in-ignorance-of-the-law rested largely on a misunderstanding of what had happened, the incident deserves explanation.

One of the Government lawyers, in preparing the Government's brief, took the precaution of examining the originals of the President's Executive Orders promulgating and amending the code. It was the time-honored practice for Executive Orders to be deposited with the State Department. No regularized system for publication of such orders had been established. Copies could be obtained at nominal cost by writing to the Department. The meticulous Government lawyer who was interested in checking the punctuation in the original against that in the version distributed by the Interior Department made a discovery. He found that an Executive Order amending a section of the code read: " Section 4 of Article III is amended to read as follows," and then followed only the first paragraph of that section in amended form. The second paragraph, containing the criminal provisions, was not set forth. Of course the intention was to retain the second paragraph of the original without amendment, and both Government and industry had been acting on that understanding. But technically the amending order should have read: " *The first paragraph* of Section 4 of Article III is amended to read as follows." That would have made it plain that the second paragraph was retained in its original form. Someone had been careless in draftsmanship. The Government's brief candidly brought the matter to the Court's attention and announced that there would be no prosecutions for violations which had occurred before the error was discovered and rectified by a new Executive Order. At the argument, counsel for the Government was subjected to a raking fire of criticism from the bench because of the failure of the Government to publish Executive Orders in official and easily obtainable form. This would presumably have led to an earlier discovery of the error in draftsmanship.

The immediate result of the research and commendable candor which brought the situation to light was that the Court ruled there was no penal provision on which to base a prosecution for violation of the code when the case was begun, and the validity of the code could only be tested in a new lawsuit. And so the Government's hope for a helpful decision went glimmering. A further result was an end of the long-standing lack of an official publication for Executive Orders. A *Federal Register* was established, which publishes regularly official copies of all orders and regulations affecting the public.

The other branch of the litigation, concerning interstate shipments of " hot " oil, ended not in a fizzle but in a disaster. The decision of the Court struck down Section 9(c) of the law as unconstitutional. The oil industry was re-

manded to a state of uncontrolled competition. The industry soon ran afoul of the antitrust laws and was again
prosecuted.[3]

The legal consequences of this decision were as far-
reaching as the economic ones. The opinion by the Chief
Justice held the law void for unconstitutionally delegating too great and too undefined a power to the President.
It was the first time a federal statute was ever set aside on
this ground. This legal proposition was so little anticipated that the Government's brief of 227 pages and 200
more of appendix devoted only 13 pages to the subject.

This newly applied doctrine forbidding delegation of
power, which was to play an important part in rationaliz-
ing the Court's destruction of New Deal legislation, is a
doctrine not based on any express words of the Constitution itself. It was well settled by judicial decision that the
Constitution does not completely forbid delegation of
legislative power.[4] The early Court found delegation of
power even to a private corporation no obstacle to constitutionality when it held that governmental functions could
be delegated to the privately owned Bank of the United
States.[5]

It is plain that the Constitution contemplated a large

---

[3] *United States* v. *Socony-Vacuum Oil Co., Inc.; Socony-Vacuum
Oil Co., Inc.* v. *United States,* Nos. 346, 347 — October Term, 1939. Decided May 6, 1940.

[4] *United States* v. *Grimaud,* 220 U. S. 506.

[5] *McCulloch* v. *Maryland,* 4 Wheat. 316.

measure of delegation. For instance, it vests in Congress the power " to collect Taxes," " to borrow Money," " to coin Money," " to punish Piracies," " to raise and support Armies," and " to maintain a Navy." It is perfectly obvious that the Constitution-makers did not expect Congress itself to devote its own time to the performance of these functions, but that they expected they would be delegated to the President and his Executive agencies. There is no more reason to doubt that the Congress was expected to exercise its power over interstate commerce by similar delegation.

The makers of the Constitution were familiar with a degree of delegation of governmental power in colonial days which was extravagant as compared with any delegation ever attempted by the American Congress. Not only were the powers of government parceled out to public bodies, but all of the powers of government were actually vested in trading corporations. There is no better example than the Hudson Bay Company, chartered by Charles II in 1670, which was an important factor in the settlement of the North American continent. The complete lordship and entire legislative, judicial, and executive power was given to the company.[6] This governmental power was held and exercised until November 19, 1869, when the Hudson

---

6 See Willson: *The Great Company*. London: Smith, Elder & Co.; 1900, Vol. II, p. 318.

Bay Company returned its rights of government to the public authorities by a deed of surrender in which the consideration was more than nominal.

Virginia itself was settled by corporations exercising all of the powers of government under charters granted to " the London Company," and to " the Plymouth Company." [7] With such delegation of power entirely familiar, the makers of the Constitution never saw fit to place any restriction on it by any word or inference in the Constitution itself. But now a restriction was written into the Constitution to condemn New Deal legislation.

The anxiety created by the decision was profound. If the carefully limited power given to the President to prohibit interstate shipments of " hot " oil was unconstitutional, what was to become of the more general power to approve codes of fair competition for unspecified industries? Many thoughtful persons were unable to understand the decision except as a deliberate forewarning of what was to come — a straw tossed into the wind by the Court. They felt that Justice Cardozo had put the case in its true light in his dissent: [8]

" There is no fear that the nation will drift from its ancient moorings as the result of the narrow delegation of power permitted by this section. What can be done under

---

[7] Hockett, Homer C.: *Political and Social Growth of the United States.* New York: Macmillan Co.; 1937. Second edition, pp. 55–56.

[8] *Panama Refining Co.* v. *Ryan; Amazon Petroleum Corp.* v. *Ryan,* 293 U. S. 389, 443.

cover of that permission is closely and clearly circumscribed both as to subject matter and occasion. The statute was framed in the shadow of a national disaster. A
host of unforeseen contingencies would have to be faced
from day to day, and faced with a fulness of understanding unattainable by any one except the man upon the
scene. The President was chosen to meet the instant need."

The decision created a new obstacle to effective democratic government. It added a further perplexity in fram-
ing legislation. A rigid and inflexible law was in danger
of being held unconstitutional because, as applied to some
unforeseen situation, it might appear to the Court to be
arbitrary or capricious. Now it appeared that if legislators sought to avoid this risk and make for greater equity
by delegating discretion, such a law ran another risk
equally great. Of course some delegation would be permitted if adequate standards for the exercise of discretion
were laid down. But the Court that required Congress to
define standards to govern delegated power has, though
urged by the Solicitor General,[9] failed to set forth standards by which to define unconstitutional delegation. How
much delegation is constitutionally permissible, and under
what standards, cannot be learned from the Constitution
or from any Court decision.

Thus ended the Court's first round with the New Deal.

---

[9] See Brief for the Government, *Currin* v. *Wallace,* No. 275, October
Term, 1938.

## *Gold*

The day following the announcement of the oil decision a brilliant array of long-coated counsel began argument of the *Gold Cases*. The Court was reviewing the nation's monetary policy adopted by the Congress pursuant to the constitutional authorization to it to " coin Money," and " regulate the Value thereof." Not only were those powers confided by our Constitution exclusively to the legislative department but monetary policy the world over is a function of political government, an incident of sovereignty, and in no way a judicial function.

The new administration had faced a monetary and financial crisis. It was manifest in the collapse of the domestic price level and in the demoralization of the basis of foreign exchange. The disparity between the outstanding gold obligations and the supply of gold available to meet them was alarming, and the conventional processes of finance were threatened with panic.

England, in September 1931, suspended redemption in gold of its circulating notes, and sixteen countries followed the same year. Many nations had placed some kind of restriction on gold export; others had adopted some type of foreign-exchange control. When the new administration came into power the only commercially important currencies which had not been devalued or substantially depreciated were the United States dollar, the Swiss franc, and the Dutch guilder. Foreign commerce was demoralized, and United States exports dropped from $5,241,-000,000 in 1929 to $1,675,000,000 in 1933.

The domestic price level had so declined that a dollar would purchase on average one and a half times as many commodities in 1933 as during 1921-9. Our national income, estimated at over eighty billions in 1929, had shrunk fifty per cent by 1932. As the debt remained fixed while property values fell, and as interest charges were unyielding while income diminished, the burden of long-term debt became crushing to farmers, home owners, and borrowing corporations. Of the 1929 income produced, 9.2% was required to service long-term debt; by 1932 it required 21.1% of the national income to carry substantially the same debt.

The new administration moved with vigor to stop the run on the banks, to attack the causes of deflation, to relieve the relatively increasing debt burden, and to restore normal channels for foreign and domestic commerce. Immediately upon taking the oath the President exercised emergency power to deal with the banking crisis by closing all banks, reopening those found solvent and strengthening capital structures of those opened where necessary by government loans, and inaugurating a system of insurance for deposits.

The Emergency Banking Act of March 9, 1933 confirmed the President's authority to halt the run on banks, the export and hoarding of gold, and the flight of capital into foreign currencies.

An Act of May 12, 1933 authorized devaluation of the dollar by not to exceed fifty per cent in the discretion of the President. This power was exercised only in part, and the dollar was decreased in gold value on January 31, 1934 by 40.94%. The Gold Reserve Act of January 1934 gave more permanent form to these provisions. Devaluation was expected to restore our competitive position in the world markets and to help restore a pre-depression price level.

But in addition to a gold standard fixed by law a private gold standard had been created by contracts, and the advantage which this private contract standard gave to creditors over debtors was asserted to be above the nation's power to modify. For many years lawyers had used with the regularity of a ritual a clause by which their contracts and mortgages, even farm and home mortgages, simply declared in substance that they were immune from the effect of any use Congress might find it necessary or expedient to make of its constitutional power to regulate the value of money. " Gold clauses " were standardized by creditor demand and provided that principal and interest should be payable only in *gold* coin and that only at the standard of weight and fineness of the dollar at the time the bond was issued. Such gold obligations outstanding in the United States were estimated at about a hundred billion dollars, seventy-five billion of which were obligations of business corporations and private debtors and twenty-five billion of federal and state bonds in which market pressures had caused the same clause to be written. The total gold reserves of the country were only about four billion dollars, and of the whole world, something like eleven billion dollars. So one effect of the gold obligation was to create an artificial demand, threatening panic proportions at the moment, for gold. From February 1, 1933 to March 6, 1933 alone, $476,100,000 in gold was withdrawn from Federal Reserve Banks or the Treasury for export or earmarking or for domestic hoarding.

But there was another result. If, after the value of the legal tender dollar current in commerce was reduced, the holders of these bonds could refuse a dollar-for-dollar settlement in legal tender currency and insist on the old gold dollar or its equivalent, then in terms of current dollars they would collect more dollars than they had loaned. By legal tender standards they were unjustly enriched. Conversely, devaluation, expected to aid the debtor class, would actually accomplish its ruin, for every debt payable in gold would automatically be increased. It is not to be thought that all of the rich would profit and all the poor would suffer thereby; the effect of the gold clause was too capricious to operate according to amounts of wealth. Its effect depended on the character of property, not its extent. Many rich men and institutions had investments in equities, such as stocks or junior mortgage bonds of corporations that were heavy borrowers. Especially railroads and utilities were heavy borrowers on mortgage security. Many of the country's great corporations would be insolvent, embarrassed, or greatly injured, and many corporation stocks popular among big investors would be greatly impaired in value if the gold clause stood. But of course the most demoralizing social effects would be among borrowers on farm or home security.

On June 5, 1933, the Congress passed a joint resolution which declared such gold payment contracts to be against public policy and void, and made them dischargeable dollar for dollar in any legal tender currency, which of course meant the devalued dollar. By this simple act all the explosive injustices lurking in the private gold standard were swept away and gold-clause creditors were placed in the same position as others in the hardships of the deflation.

The constitutionality of this Act was challenged, and the cases which reached the Supreme Court illustrate the far-reaching effect of the policy on which the Court was asked to overrule the Congress. A holder of a railroad bond bearing an interest coupon payable in gold of face value of $22.50 demanded $38.10 in payment.[10] If he prevailed, the debt of already debt-ridden railroads would go up in like proportion, and their earnings be inadequate

---

[10] *Norman* v. *Baltimore & O. R. Co.,* 294 U. S. 240.

to the added interest charges. In another case the holder
of a gold certificate demanded redemption by the United
States Treasury in gold or its equivalent.[11] The effect on
public treasuries and on taxpayers was illustrated by the
third case in which the holder of a $10,000 government
bond demanded $16,931.25 of the new dollars in pay-
ment.[12]

Thus in the guise of private lawsuits involving a few
dollars, the whole American economy was haled before the
Supreme Court. Questions involving life or death to many
business enterprises, questions of justice to debtors whose
debt had grown because values had declined, questions of
adapting the United States's economy to a changing world
economy were argued by lawyers who as always relied less
on the right of the matter and less on the words of the
Constitution than on precedents. Some of these precedents, such as the argument based on the ancient custom
of kings to " clip " coins, were of no more real value to a
modern society than the ritual of Druid priests.

These cases were argued January 8–10, 1935. The
legislation had become effective a year and a half before.
While many lawyers had doubted its constitutionality, the
business world, which could not wait for lawyers' arguments to end, had accepted the whole monetary program
and gone ahead making settlements and commitments.

11 *Nortz* v. *United States,* 294 U. S. 317.
12 *Perry* v. *United States,* 294 U. S. 330.

Any decision that upset the law as Congress had enacted it, however sound in lawyer logic, could only breed widespread trade mischief, commercial confusion, and debtor disaster. The decisions were awaited with great concern. As several weeks passed without a decision, apprehension and conjecture grew. So intense was the excitement caused by the delay that on successive week ends the Court ordered its Clerk to announce that no decision in the cases would be forthcoming on the following Monday — announcements apparently without precedent in the history of the Court. But no such announcement was made just prior to February 18, and the public knew that the hour of decision was at hand.

The Court sustained the validity of the gold-clause resolution as applied to private contracts and as applied to the gold certificates, but it held that it was beyond the power of the Congress to modify the obligations of its own gold bonds. This decision would have increased the national debt some sixty per cent in the present legal tender, but the Court avoided such a result. It invoked technical rules of damage and held that the bondholder had not proved actual damage from his being required to accept 10,000 present dollars in settlement for his $10,000 bond, and so was not entitled to any greater sum. The opinions are a fascinating study in legalistic reasoning. To the layman they were a Chinese puzzle.

The victory for the Government, however, was against

the bitter dissent of four Justices. Mr. Justice McReynolds, Mr. Justice Van Devanter, Mr. Justice Sutherland, and Mr. Justice Butler united in an opinion which adopted the whole philosophy and terminology of the creditor class and assailed the Acts of the Government as " spoliation of citizens " and " repudiation " of government obligations, and concluded: ". . . the impending legal and moral chaos is appalling." [13]

Americans were shaken by this exhibition of confusion and anger in high places. But it was questions asked of me in Sweden shortly afterwards by Swedish lawyers and bankers who did not know our legal tradition that I left unsatisfactorily answered then and leave with the reader now:

" How could you Americans let your national monetary and economic policy be dependent on the outcome of a lawsuit between private parties over a difference of $15.60? "

" How could American business intelligently function over a year and a half while such basic questions were pending in the Court? Why could you not learn the answer earlier? "

" Why should within one of a majority of your Court hold that a private contract between two citizens should

---

[13] See dissenting opinion *Norman* v. *Baltimore & O. R. Co.; United States* v. *Bankers Trust Co.; Nortz* v. *United States; Perry* v. *United States,* 294 U. S. 361, 381.

deprive the nation of power to change its monetary policy? "

" And why, anyway, should lawyer-judges be supreme over the national parliament, the President, the Treasury, and the whole government in a matter so vital to economic life? "

## Railroad Pensions

Before the country had recovered from its confusion over the decisions in the *Gold Clause Cases* — decisions which the financial world found it very difficult to interpret as applied to government obligations — it received another shock.

In June 1934, the Congress passed the Railroad Retirement Act. The Act had not originated as an Administration measure, although in line with the social policy of the Administration.

On May 6, however, the Supreme Court held the Act to be wholly unconstitutional. Merely holding that this Act was unconstitutional might not have shocked and alarmed those in sympathy with social legislation such as the Retirement Act, but the Court went beyond all former restraints and cast aside the counsel of its Chief Justice, as well as that of Justices Brandeis, Stone, and Cardozo. The majority of the Court, in an opinion by Mr. Justice Roberts, sweepingly condemned the whole effort of the Act. The shocking thing about this decision cannot be better stated than in the language of Chief Justice Hughes himself in his dissenting opinion: [14]

" I am unable to concur in the decision of this case. The gravest aspect of the decision is that it does not rest simply upon a condemnation of particular features of the Railroad Retirement Act, but denies to Congress the power to pass any compulsory pension act for railroad employees. If the opinion were limited to the particular provisions of the Act, which the majority find to be objectionable and not severable, the Congress would be free to overcome the objections by a new statute. Classes of persons held to be improperly brought within the range of the Act could be eliminated. Criticisms of the basis of payments, of the conditions prescribed for the receipt of benefits, and of the requirements of contributions, could be met. Even in place of a unitary retirement system another sort of plan could be worked out. What was thus found to be inconsistent with the requirements of due process could be excised and other provisions substituted. But after discussing these matters, the majority finally raise a barrier against all legislative action of this nature by declaring that the subject matter itself lies beyond the reach of the congressional authority to regulate interstate commerce. In that view, no matter how suitably limited a pension act for railroad employees might be with respect to the persons to be bene-

[14] *Retirement Board* v. *Alton R. Co.*, 295 U. S. 330, 374.

fited, or how appropriate the measure of retirement allowances, or how sound actuarially the plan, or how well adjusted the burden, still under this decision Congress would not be at liberty to enact such a measure. That is a conclusion of such serious and far-reaching importance that it overshadows all other questions raised by the Act. Indeed, it makes their discussion superfluous. The final objection goes, as the opinion states, ' to the heart of the law, even if it could survive the loss of the unconstitutional features ' which the opinion perceives. I think that the conclusion thus reached is a departure from sound principles and places an unwarranted limitation upon the commerce clause of the Constitution."

## II. BLACK MONDAY, MAY 27

Up to this time the blows delivered by the Court had come at intervals — short, to be sure, but nevertheless with breathing spaces. At the close of the Court's term, however, on May 27, the Court struck three times.

### *Farm Debtors' Relief*

The first was a decision holding unconstitutional the Frazier-Lemke Act, directed particularly to relief of farm mortgagors.[15] The opinion was unanimous. The defects of the Act were not wholly incurable, as was later proved.

---

15 *Louisville Bank* v. *Radford*, 295 U. S. 555.

The decision denied prompt relief, however, to a great number of farm owners in acute distress. Whatever the legal merits of the decision may have been, it stripped of legislative protection those whose resources were fast being exhausted, and it brought home to those persons a knowledge and realization of the impact of judicial review upon the economic life of the country.

## *The President's Removal Power*

On the same day the Court decided that the President was without inherent power to remove a Federal Trade Commissioner.[16] The Federal Trade Commission had notoriously failed to carry out the expectations of President Wilson in its creation. President Roosevelt, after careful inquiry, became convinced that it could never function successfully without changes in its personnel. One of the most reactionary and dilatory of its members was William E. Humphrey, an appointee of President Hoover. He declined to resign, and the President removed him. But the President sought to base the removal on grounds that would not reflect on the Commissioner and assigned as its cause merely the disagreement between Humphrey's policies and those of the Administration in carrying out the Federal Trade Commission Act. This reason was ample as the Supreme Court decisions then stood.

---

16 *Humphrey's Executor v. United States,* 295 U. S. 602.

The President was following a decision of the Court which had held in substance that the power of appointment in the Executive carried the power of removal. Myers, a postmaster, was removed by President Wilson. The removal was upheld by the Court in 1926 in an opinion by Chief Justice Taft. That opinion had been based on the view that it was not only the President's privilege, but his duty as Chief Executive, to remove an appointee who was not performing his tasks wisely or intelligently. And Taft made no exception for members of commissions. He said: [17]

" Then there may be duties of a quasi-judicial character imposed on executive officers and members of executive tribunals whose decisions after hearing affect interests of individuals, the discharge of which the President can not in a particular case properly influence or control. But even in such a case he may consider the decision after its rendition as a reason for removing the officer, on the ground that the discretion regularly entrusted to that officer by statute has not been on the whole intelligently or wisely exercised. Otherwise he does not discharge his own constitutional duty of seeing that the laws be faithfully executed."

In Humphrey's case the Court " disapproved " its own statement on which the President had relied. The Court

---

[17] *Myers* v. *United States,* 272 U. S. 52, 135.

switched its doctrine and rebuked the President by holding the removal of Humphrey to be illegal. Within the Administration there was a profound feeling that the opinion of the Court was written with a design to give the impression that the President had flouted the Constitution, rather than that the Court had simply changed its mind within the past ten years. The decision could easily have forestalled this by recognizing the President's reliance on an opinion of Chief Justice Taft. But the decision contained no such gracious acknowledgment. What the Court had before declared to be a constitutional duty of the President had become in Mr. Roosevelt a constitutional offense. Small wonder that the decision became a political instrument. Those who saw executive dictatorship just round the corner had their fears confirmed: the President could be restrained only by the Court. Those who thought the ghost of dictatorship wore judicial robes had their fears, too, confirmed: the Court was applying to President Roosevelt rules different from those it had applied to his predecessors.

## N.I.R.A.

If the touch of malice that was thought to be in *Humphrey's* decision excited the most Administration resentment, the most far-reaching decision in its implication was the one which held the National Industrial Recovery Act unconstitutional.

This was one of the first and most extensive experiments of the New Deal. When President Roosevelt took office, production, trade, and living standards had been declining for over three years. Industry suffered a sharp fall in the prices of its goods and a greatly curtailed market. Overheads, such as interest and local taxes, remained fairly constant and, with shrinking business, became a relatively increasing burden. Pressure to reduce costs was directed toward one of the largest of its flexible items — labor. In the spring of 1933 industrial production was off 45%, employment was off 41%, but factory payrolls were off 63%. The number of unemployed in March 1933 was estimated at figures which varied from 13,000,000 to over 17,000,000, and unemployment had become a real menace to social stability.

The President called into conference many academic students of industry and public-spirited business men. The Act which he sponsored had widespread support of business interests, and one of its chief supporters was Henry I. Harriman, then President of the United States Chamber of Commerce. It also had the support of labor, and was finally enacted by a large Republican, as well as Democratic, vote.

On May 17, 1933, President Roosevelt initiated the Recovery Act in a message in which he asked Congress to provide " for the machinery necessary for a great co-operative movement throughout all industry in order to obtain wide re-employment, to shorten the working week, to pay a decent wage for the shorter week, and to prevent unfair competition and disastrous overproduction."

The Act which resulted provided that the President should have authority to approve codes of fair competition for a trade or industry if he found that the codes imposed no inequitable restrictions upon admission to membership, if they were proposed by a group truly representative of the trade or industry, and if they were not designed to promote monopolies or oppress small enterprises. The codes of fair competition, when adopted, required obedience by all those engaged in the industry, and criminal penalties for violation were provided.

Section 7(a) provided that every code should contain provisions giving employees the free right of collective bargaining; that no employee and no one seeking employment should be required to refrain from joining unions, and that employers should comply with maximum hours of labor, minimum rates of pay, and other conditions of employment approved and prescribed by the President.

This Act was approved June 16, 1933, to be effective for two years. It embodied generally the philosophy of self-government in industry. It permitted the majority of the industry to prescribe the methods by which it should be conducted and compelled the minority to comply.

It is probable that the original intention was to include, for a time at least, only basic industries. Soon, however,

nearly every industry and service trade demanded to be
allowed to come under the Act and to establish a way of
controlling its " chiselers." The Recovery Administration
probably yielded too readily, and its controls began to be
scattered beyond the reach of effective administrative supervision.

Meanwhile, irritations began to develop. Some large industrialists refused to comply with the Act. Threats of
" cracking down " aroused antagonism. The extension of
the code system to a great variety of small enterprises
afforded opportunity for the critics of the Act to arouse
a feeling that the Government was unduly interfering with
business. Moreover, employers who had sought the benefits of the Act began to develop resentment when they were
required to comply with its labor provisions. Had this Act
not been held unconstitutional, there is little doubt but
that it was in for a legislative examination and overhaul-
ing upon its expiration in June 1935.

Concededly the N.R.A. was an experiment. Nothing
like it had been undertaken before, and there was no body
of experience or tradition to guide it. There seems to be
little doubt that at least in its early stages it was effective
psychologically, if not otherwise, and that the N.R.A. did
a substantial emergency service in arresting the deadly
downward spiral that was driving America to ruin. There
seems to be as little doubt that some of the self-governing
businesses were developing a tendency to promote their

own interests at the expense of the general public. We were not permitted to know what the true value of the experiment would have been. The experiment was struck down by the Court before such conclusions could justly be reached.

The law came to test in a case which involved the Live Poultry Code. The Schechter brothers, of Brooklyn, were indicted and convicted for violating the labor provisions and the trade-practice provisions of the Code. The Circuit Court of Appeals for the Second Circuit unanimously upheld the conviction as to the trade-practice violations, but not as to the wage and hour violations. The commerce power of Congress was held to extend to trade practices but not to labor conditions. The Schechters and the Government both petitioned the Supreme Court for review. The case was far from ideal as a test case. The industry was not a major one, and the fair trade provisions, which related to selling sick chickens, selecting chickens from the coop, and the like, were hardly calculated to electrify any Court to the need of federal regulation. Nevertheless, the Court of Appeals had decided the case in part for the Government, and as the Schechters were carrying it to the Supreme Court, there was no real choice but to make it the test case there.

The Supreme Court decided that the N.I.R.A. delegated power to the Executive in violation of the Constitution. Those who had read this conclusion in the stars of the

" hot " oil case were sound diviners. This conclusion was enough to release the Schechters from jeopardy, and to end the case. Had it ended here, Congress could have amended its defects and salvaged the general plan of " self-government in industry " if it so desired.

But the Court, having thus killed the N.R.A., proceeded to deal its corpse a second blow. The opinion went on to declare that the statute was beyond the power of Congress under the commerce clause. Thus the Court not merely decided the case before it but drew into doubt the capacity of the Federal Government by use of the commerce power to accomplish many other things that the emergency seemed to require. The decision on the commerce power was not only unnecessary but, by the test of later decisions, was highly questionable at the very least.[18] The Court was not only making doubtful constitutional law but was doing it in the teeth of the first principle of constitutional adjudication; namely, that a court will not decide a constitutional question unless such a decision is absolutely necessary to dispose of the case. The implications of this new expansiveness on the part of the Court were even more disturbing than the fate of the N.R.A. itself.

---

[18] See *Labor Board* v. *Jones & Laughlin,* 301 U. S. 1; *Mulford* v. *Smith,* 307 U. S. 38; *Labor Board* v. *Fainblatt,* 306 U. S. 601.

### III. SOWING THE WIND: THE LOWER COURTS

Meanwhile, " hell broke loose " in the lower courts.  Sixteen hundred injunctions restraining officers of the Federal Government from carrying out acts of Congress were granted by federal judges.[19]  At this time a single district judge could grant an injunction nullifying a federal law passed by a House of Representatives and a Senate, and approved by the President.  That was stopped after the court fight in 1937 by requiring a three-judge court to pass upon applications for such injunctions.[20]  But in 1935–6 over a hundred district judges each had assumed the power to nullify acts of Congress.  Most of these judges were conscientious and impartial.  Some among them were known partisans, and to their doors business flowed.  Their manner of utterance left little hope that the Government could defend with any chance of success before them.

It has been put mildly by Messrs. Frankfurter and Fisher: [21]

" Friction between Congress and the judiciary was intensified by the atmosphere which enveloped some of the opinions of the lower court judges.  There were utterances

---

19 See Sen. Doc. No. 42, 75th Cong., 1st sess., p. 1: Injunctions in Cases involving Acts of Congress.

20 Judiciary Act of August 24, 1937.

21 Frankfurter and Fisher, " The Business of the Supreme Court at the October Terms, 1935 and 1936," 51 Harv. L. Rev. 611 (1938).

more appropriate to the hustings than to the bench, reminiscent of political harangues by early Federalist judges which involved the federal judiciary for the first time in the conflict of politics."

In Kentucky, District Judge Dawson, who was soon to resign and represent the coal companies in contesting federal legislation, granted an injunction to the Hart Coal Corporation to restrain the enforcement of the National Recovery Act to the accompaniment of this language: [22]

" It is the boldest kind of usurpation — dared by the authorities and tolerated by the public only because of the bewilderment of the people in the present emergency."

In another case he charged Congress with knowingly resorting to subterfuges to circumvent constitutional limitations.[23]

The Duke Power Company obtained a decision against the Federal Administrator of Public Works, and others, from Judge H. H. Watkins, holding that loans could not be made by the Federal Government for the construction of hydroelectric plants. In language more gallant than judicial Judge Watkins stated: [24]

" It is due to the gallant members of the American Legion, and to their comrades in arms who made the supreme sac-

---

[22] *Hart Coal Corporation* v. *Sparks,* 7 F. Supp. 16, 28.
[23] *Penn* v. *Glenn,* 10 F. Supp. 483.
[24] *Duke Power Co.* v. *Greenwood County,* 10 F. Supp. 854, 865.

rifice, that America should see to it that their struggles and sacrifices were not in vain."

And so the power companies must be protected from competition.

District Judge Otis of Missouri, in denouncing the Labor Relations Act, subsequently sustained by the Supreme Court, included among his grounds: [25]

" The individual employee is dealt with by the act as an incompetent. The government must protect him even from himself. He is the ward of the United States to be cared for by his guardian even as if he were a member of an uncivilized tribe of Indians or a recently emancipated slave."

Judge Otis also gave a clue to his attitude toward the effort to abolish child labor by saying of Congress: [26]

" It cannot prohibit the movement in commerce of harmless things because, forsooth, they were manufactured by child labor, or by vegetarians, or by teetotalers. . . ."

District Judge Symes had to " resist the temptation to write a general dissertation upon this section or the economics of the New Deal." [27]

---

25 *Stout* v. *Pratt*, 12 F. Supp. 864, 867.
26 *United States* v. *Sutherland*, 9 F. Supp. 204, 210.
27 *United States* v. *Gearhart*, 7 F. Supp. 712, 714.

District Judge Akerman, admitting that in the pending case he had no jurisdiction over the Secretary of Agriculture, nevertheless scored the Government for not coming to him anyway, saying: [28]

" This Act was undoubtedly passed at the request of the Department of Agriculture. It was undoubtedly drawn by counsel representing the Department of Agriculture. Congress used to write its own Bills, but it cannot do that any more. It undoubtedly had the okey of the Attorney General before it was approved and if there is any constitutional authority for this setup as we have it here, it seems to me that those two departments would welcome the opportunity to come into a Court and furnish the Court with the authority for such action."

Lawyers bent on destruction of acts of Congress were quick to find out responsive judges and to use sharp legal devices to test constitutionality, usually obstructing enforcement while doing so.

One of these was the procedure by which a stockholder would sue his company to enjoin it from obeying the law. Of course neither of them wanted to obey it, and in that neat way they had a lawsuit in which both sides wanted the same thing. There was no real issue between them; the " issue " between them was only feigned, and the apparent

---

[28] *Hillsboro Packing Co.* v. *Wallace,* Opinion of Judge Alexander Akerman, delivered Jan. 30, 1934, U. S. Dist. Court for the Southern District of Florida.

adversaries were not in real controversy. They framed the issues to suit themselves. At that time even though such an action threatened to set aside an act of Congress, the Government could only be heard as a matter of grace. That was remedied — but not until after the court fight.[29]

Also, inventive lawyers had just devised an even more exclusive method of lynching a Congressional enactment without fair trial. Some lawyer who had in his hands a receivership or a trusteeship in reorganization proceedings would apply to a federal judge for " instructions " as to whether he should obey the law. Of course he did not want to, or he would not ask. Even the President could not obtain an advisory opinion as to his duty, but corporation lawyers got such advisory opinions for their clients.

The use of a federal trusteeship in reorganization to obtain an opinion striking down the entire Public Utility Holding Company Act of 1935 deserves to rank as the leading example of lawless use of the law. It occurred in the District Court at Baltimore before Judge Coleman.

The counsel for the trustees and for two creditors at the same time filed three petitions in the district court. The trustees asked that the Act be held to be unconstitutional. One of the creditors came to be represented by distinguished counsel, a former Solicitor General of the United States, John W. Davis, although the creditor did not know it and supposed that Mr. Davis was represent-

[29] Judiciary Act of August 24, 1937.

ing the company. Mr. Davis, however, was counsel for the
Edison Institute, the trade alliance of the utility interests
which had announced that the law was unconstitutional
and had retained him to have it held so. The Institute
counsel had agreed to represent any creditor in the case
that counsel for the trustees might find for him. It was
evidently not well explained to the creditor, who thought
Mr. Davis was to represent the company, and not him
personally, but when the Government subpoenaed the
creditor to come to the hearing he was for the first time
introduced to his counsel and in answer to questions asked
in the presence of the court agreed to allow this counsel
to represent him.

In order to give the appearance of a controversy, counsel for another creditor asserted that the law was constitutional. It was interesting that the attorney who was
thus undertaking to uphold the law had been opposed to
its enactment. When the Government was notified of the
proceeding, this array of counsel had already made the
statements and admissions of their pleadings on which
the court would act. The court rebuked government counsel for even suggesting that the case was collusive, and proceeded to advise that the entire law was unconstitutional.
On the basis of this decision utilities throughout the country refused to comply with the Act.

When it was sought to carry this fantastic case to the
Supreme Court, the Government objected that such a

record in such a case presented no fit basis upon which the constitutionality of the Utility Holding Company Act should be decided. The Supreme Court declined to hear the case.[30] Hostile as the Court then was to Administration measures, it could not stomach such procedures as this. Nor would all district courts approve such procedures. Judge Nields of Delaware promptly dismissed a petition for instructions in a similar case and said:

" Far more than instructions as to the administration of a trust is asked for. A body created by an act of Congress is sought to be destroyed and stripped of its powers without being a party to the proceeding and without having its day in court. Such a course violates accepted canons of legal procedure." [31]

Another instance of extraordinary district court procedure was presented by the maneuvers of the utility interests in relation to the Tennessee Valley Authority. The Georgia Power Company brought suit against the Tennessee Valley Authority and asked for an injunction, which Circuit Judge Sibley denied on May 28, 1936. The next day the Georgia Power Company joined with others and went into another district in Tennessee and raised the same issues of law and fact which had been decided against it in the Georgia case the day before. Notwithstanding the

[30] See *In Re American States Public Service Co.*, 12 F. Supp. 667; *Burco* v. *Whitworth*, 81 F.2d 721; certiorari denied, *Burco* v. *Whitworth*, 297 U. S. 724.

[31] In Re *Central West Public Service Co.*, 13 F. Supp. 239.

decision of the case against them, District Judge Gore, on December 22, 1936, granted their petition and enjoined the Tennessee Valley Authority from proceeding in the State of Georgia with the construction of transmission and distribution lines, negotiation of contracts, or the sale of power to customers other than those served at the date of the injunction.

The Tennessee Valley Authority then went back to the district court in Georgia which had refused to give the company an injunction in the first place and obtained an injunction to stop the enforcement of Judge Gore's injunction within the State of Georgia. The Court held that the second court owed respect to the decision of the first court and said of the company: [32]

" It is not equity to seek relief in this court and then, after a full hearing and an adverse decision, to hasten to two other courts on the very next day and pray of them substantially the same relief sought and denied in this court. Such conduct is not only inequitable, but is vexatious and productive of a multiplicity of suits and should be enjoined."

Thus, there were district judges who not only would not respect the acts of Congress, but who would not respect the prior decisions of other judges.

---

[32] *Georgia Power Co.* v. *Tennessee Valley Authority*, 17 F. Supp. 769, 771.

Such was the picture of judicial supremacy at work in the district courts of the United States, the point of its most reckless, partisan, and irresponsible manifestation. District courts were sowing the wind — the Supreme Court would reap the whirlwind.

# Chapter V

# LAW AND POLITICS

## 1936

The year 1936 was one of increasing tensions. The President must stand for re-election. Each judicial decision which denounced or undid his legislative policy would tend to discredit his administration. His enemies were counting among their best assets the pronouncements already made by a majority of the Supreme Court, and they anticipated others equally useful. The words of the Justices carried political as well as legal significance. None knew that better than the Justices themselves. It was unfortunate, if the majority felt compelled to strike blow after blow at the President's policy, that this compulsion was concurrent with political preparations for the campaign. The coincidence left an uneasy suspicion that the law and politics were not as fully separated as juristic tradition would indicate.

## AGRICULTURE: A " LOCAL " PROBLEM

The year began with a crushing disappointment to the Administration. On January 6, the Supreme Court, by a vote of six to three, held unconstitutional the essential provisions of the Agricultural Adjustment Act of 1933.[1]

This law embodied one of the most important recovery plans of the Administration, and it had been in process of execution since May of 1933 — almost three years. Concurrent with its operation, whether attributable to it or not, there was considerable improvement in conditions among farmers and among trades dependent on them.

The new administration had found it both politically and economically necessary to attend to farm distress. About forty-four per cent of the entire population lived in rural areas, while our six and a fourth million farms were both dwelling place and means of living of over thirty million people. From 1929 to 1932 available cash income from farming operations — that is, cash income minus cash production expenses — dropped from five billion to barely one and a half billion dollars. Relatively, farm prices reached their lowest point since the Civil War.

The effect on rural life was devastating. Taxes and interest did not fall with farm prices, and there were wholesale foreclosures, tax sales, and bankruptcies. In

---

[1] *United States* v. *Butler,* 297 U. S. 1.

some sections they were accompanied by ominous disorders. Farmers boycotted forced sales and brought various pressures, some none too gentle, against buyers of distress-goods or farms. In some cases judges who granted foreclosures were threatened, and in a few instances actual violence occurred. The countryside was neglected. In 1931–2 depreciation of farmer-owned buildings and equipment was estimated at $1,648,000,000, but repairs and replacements were only $782,000,000. Deterioration was only half made good.

The secondary effects were grave. Tax delinquency undermined the solvency of rural states and local governments. Heavy withdrawals from banks caused a wave of rural bank failures. Forced economies in the use of fertilizers, feed, and machinery led to sharp contraction of industrial production of farm-consumed goods.

The farmers had no voluntary mechanism for co-operation in reducing acreage to offset decrease in foreign demand, or in avoiding the large surpluses which depressed their prices and income. But industrialists, from whom the farmer must buy, had so organized as to reduce production rather than price.[2] The farmer sold in a highly competitive market, but he bought at " managed " prices. For example, agricultural implements decreased only six

---

[2] G. C. Means: *Industrial Prices and their Relative Inflexibility*, letter from Secretary of Agriculture in response to Senate Res. No. 17 (Senate Doc. No. 13, 74th Cong., 1st sess.) ; also O. M. W. Sprague: *Recovery and Common Sense*. Boston: Houghton Mifflin Co.; 1934, p. 80.

per cent in price, but decreased eighty per cent in production, and motor vehicles went off sixteen per cent in price and off eighty per cent in production.

The need for nation-wide action to better balance production with consumption of agricultural products was universally recognized. William Jardine, Secretary of Agriculture in the Coolidge administration, had reported in 1925 that: " This is one of the major economic problems of the Nation. It is well known that small surpluses exercise a depressing effect on prices altogether disproportionate to their amount," and again in 1928 he reported: " The surplus problem is of vital importance not only to agriculture but to the Nation as a whole."

In 1929, the Hoover administration established the Federal Farm Board and gave it power to purchase commodities for stabilization purposes.[3] These purchases exerted some sustaining influence on market prices, while they were being made, but they had practically no effect in adjusting production to consumption, and the existence of vast surplus stocks overhung the market and depressed prices. At one time the Board controlled over two hundred fifty million bushels of wheat and three and a half million bales of cotton. The stocks were finally disposed of at a heavy loss to the Farm Board. In late 1932, the Farm Board, after acknowledging its inadequacy to the problem, recommended specifically that it be given power to provide

---

[3] 46 Stat. 11, c. 24.

some means of elevating the returns to farmers and to provide an effective system for regulating acreage or quantities sold, or both.[4] Thus the outgoing Republican administration recognized the necessity for the effort which the incoming administration made.

The constitutional difficulties in the way of direct and effective regulation of the farm surplus were recognized, and the new administration sought to avoid them in the Agricultural Adjustment Act which was promptly passed. It declared a purpose " to relieve the existing national economic emergency by increasing agricultural purchasing power." It aimed to restore the relative level of farm income to that which prevailed from 1909 to 1914. To do so it provided for the making of rental or benefit payments to farmers in return for which the farmers would agree to reduce acreage or marketings of basic agricultural products, of which there was a gross oversupply. The funds to make benefit payments were raised by a tax on processing of farm commodities, which tax was of course passed on in the price of the processed goods. A cotton mill resisted the tax, and the whole plan was crushed at its demand.

But hope did not die until the actual decision was announced, for the need for some program was imperative, and the results from the particular plan were presented

---

4 See Special Report Federal Farm Board, House Document 489, 72d Cong., 2d sess., p. 3.

to the Court in its vindication. The operation of the Act was tested in the cotton program of 1933, the wheat program of 1934–5, and the corn-hog program of 1934–5, while the Act was still believed to be constitutional. In each of these programs the great majority of producers voluntarily contracted to readjust production. Acreage diverted from these crops was devoted to certain other crops, chiefly soil-building crops. Between 1932 and 1935 the movement of farm prices was an advance in wheat from 38½¢ to 81½¢ per bushel, in corn from 30.2¢ to 80.8¢ per bushel, in cotton from 6½¢ per pound to 11½¢ per pound, and in hogs from $4.06 per hundred to $10.22 per hundred. In addition to improved prices farmers received payments and obligations in connection with the adjustment programs for 1933, 1934, and 1935 of $1,350,616,379.

This increased farm purchasing power spread activity into other industries. Between 1932 and 1935 the level of mail order sales increased fifty-four per cent. Farmers' expenditures for machinery and buildings increased ninety per cent, and new car registration in typical agricultural states more than doubled. Shipments of industrial products from industrial states to agricultural states increased thirty-nine per cent from 1932 to 1934.

The benefit spread to industrial workers. From 1932 to 1934 the purchasing power of employees in the farm machinery industry increased 136%; in automobiles, 77%; in fertilizers, 56%; in cotton goods, 61%. The increase in farm incomes was a very important factor in the general business recovery which took place between 1933 and 1935. The National City Bank of New York, a source from which no gratuitous compliments to the New Deal could be expected, said in October 1935, in its business survey:

" It is hardly deniable that the impetus to the general business improvement originated on the farms, in the improved relationship between farm and industrial prices, which gave farm products a greater value in exchange for the products of industry. . . .

" All the farm markets have had a vast improvement, through the reduction or elimination of the surpluses accumulated even before the depression. Balanced relationships between supply and demand have been restored, and buyers are no longer afraid of the markets, or unwilling to carry the stocks that accumulate during the season of production."

This was what the Supreme Court destroyed on that first January Monday of 1936. Moreover, its decision was upon grounds which made reconstruction impossible.

The case had been argued against the Government by George Wharton Pepper, former Republican Senator from Pennsylvania. He rivaled in emotionalism Joseph H. Choate's appeal to the Court to invalidate the income tax to stop the march of communism. As in the income tax case, the Government had pointed to the economic evils and the urgency of remedy. But Mr. Pepper, with much show of feeling, swept all this aside and concluded on behalf of the cotton mill: [5]

" But I do not want your Honors to think that my feelings are not involved, and that my emotions are not deeply stirred. Indeed, may it please your Honors, I believe I am standing here today to plead the cause of the America I have loved; and I pray Almighty God that not in my time may ' the land of the regimented ' be accepted as a worthy substitute for ' the land of the free.' "

To judge from the opinions, the stirring of emotions within the Supreme Court building was not confined to the counsel table.

The perplexing thing about the decision was the ground taken by the majority. The tax was invalid, they ruled, because the benefit payments were invalid; and the benefit payments were invalid because Congress had no power under the Constitution to expend money to encourage farmers to help themselves by voluntarily avoiding production of surpluses.

The Constitution gives Congress the power to tax and spend for the general welfare. Could it be that the welfare

---

5 *United States* v. *Butler*, 297 U. S. 1, 44.

of the farming population is not a lawful object of solicitude on the part of Congress? The Federal Government
had for many years been attempting to assist agriculture,
however ineffectually, and we had long maintained a Department of Agriculture with a head of Cabinet rank.
What was there, then, in the New Deal measure that
caused its downfall? Counsel for the cotton mill argued
that the lure of benefit payments served to coerce the
farmers into reducing production, and that such coercion
went beyond the spending power of Congress. This solicitude for the independence of the farmers was truly touch-
ing, coming as it did from the cotton mills. As a matter of
fact, the farmers used their own judgment in deciding
whether to come in under the benefit payment plan or not,
and the owners of about one-fourth of the cotton acreage
decided to stay out. These non-cooperators guessed that
they would fare better by planting without limit, trusting
that prices would rise as a result of the reduction by their
neighbors. There was nothing that the Government could
do under the law to force this one-fourth to conform to
the plan. This hardly looked like coercion to a non-
judicial world that knows the real thing when it sees
it. And yet the majority of the Justices did accept the
argument of coercion so magnanimously advanced by
the mill.

But the opinion did not stop there. As if unsure of its
ground, the opinion went on to announce:

" But if the plan were one for purely voluntary co-operation it would stand no better so far as federal power is concerned."

Why not? Because, apparently, the overproduction of farm products is not a matter of the " general welfare " but a purely local problem. The majority said:

" Congress has no power to enforce its commands on the farmer to the ends sought by the Agricultural Adjustment Act. . . . It does not help to declare that local conditions throughout the nation have created a situation of national concern; for this is but to say that whenever there is a widespread similarity of local conditions, Congress may ignore constitutional limitations upon its own powers and usurp those reserved to the states."

Did this mean that, after all, the welfare of the farmers was not a proper object of federal expenditure? If so, every package of seed sent to a farmer by his Congressman and every bag of fertilizer furnished by the Department of Agriculture carried the taint of unconstitutionality. Perhaps the trouble was that under the Agricultural Adjustment Act the farmer was asked to do something in return for the money he got; he was asked to help relieve his plight by adjusting his acreage. Surely this was good business on the part of Congress — like asking the banks and insurance companies and industrial corporations to pay back the money that was being advanced to *them*. If conditions of this sort could not be attached to federal handouts, the result would be that Congress could pour the public money down the sink as freely as it pleased, but could do nothing to get an equivalent for its money — and all because the Constitution, in one of its invisible clauses, was said to say so.

A fiscal plan to encourage adjustment of production: was that a revolutionary step? It was just as revolutionary as the protective tariff. It is constitutional to make us all pay to maintain industrial prices and enable domestic manufacturers to increase their output. It is constitutional, though one could not be too sure, to make consumers pay a tariff to encourage domestic farmers to *increase* their output. Perhaps it is constitutional to make us pay to keep farmers from starving as a result of the industrial prices and the agricultural overproduction we have thus encouraged. But it is unconstitutional to use taxpayers' money to help the farmers lift themselves out of their predicament.

Such a gospel, spoken in the name of the Constitution, did not go unchallenged in the Court. The dissenting opinion of Justice Stone, which was joined in by Justice Brandeis and Justice Cardozo, called this a " tortured construction of the Constitution." The opinion of these three members of the Court is hardly paralleled in the century and a half of the Court's existence for its scathing rebuke to the majority. Something of the temper of the Court's deliberations can be gathered from the biting admonition of the dissenters to their brethren " that while unconstitutional exercise of power by the executive and legislative branches of the government is subject to judicial restraint, the only check upon our own exercise of power is our own sense of self-restraint." And that for the removal of unwise laws from the statute books " appeal lies not to the courts but to the ballot and to the processes of democratic government." The opinion concluded:

" Courts are not the only agency of government that must be assumed to have capacity to govern. Congress and the courts both unhappily may falter or be mistaken in the performance of their constitutional duty. But interpretation of our great charter of government which proceeds on any assumption that the responsibility for the preservation of our institutions is the exclusive concern of any one of the three branches of government, or that it alone can save them from destruction is far more likely, in the long run, ' to obliterate the constituent members ' of ' an indestructible union of indestructible states ' than the frank recognition that language, even of a constitution, may mean what it says: that the power to tax and spend includes the power to relieve a nation-wide economic maladjustment by conditional gifts of money."

What Mr. Justice Stone was saying, in measured words, was that the decision of the majority was not a legal judgment, but a political and an economic judgment, which the Court had no constitutional authority to make.

It is doubtful whether any judicial tribunal anywhere at any time has rendered a decision of such far-reaching and disastrous economic implications. Denunciation of the decision was immediate and pretty general. Promptly political leaders of all parties began the consideration of what Congress should do next about the farm program, utterly refusing to accept the logic of the Court's opinion that Congress should and could do nothing about a farm program. The basic assumption of the opinion that agricultural conditions rooted in surplus of production were too local to be any affair of the Federal Government was repudiated immediately and on all hands.

The disaster of this decision by a sharply divided Court must be measured, not only in its effect upon the farming community and the traders, industries, and labor that supply its needs, but it also must be measured in its disorganization of government finances. Never before had a blow of such force been struck at the federal budget, and this at a time when the legislative and executive branches of the government were striving against overwhelming odds to balance expenditures with income. Nearly a billion dollars had been collected from processors under a law which was now held to be unconstitutional, and the over-

burdened Treasury faced immediate demand for refunds
in this amount.

Nor was this the worst. Those who technically could
claim the refund of these taxes had in many, perhaps in
most, instances already collected the tax from consumers
by passing it on in the price of their products. Those who
stood to collect a billion in refunds from the United States
Treasury were those who had not actually borne the burden of the tax. Processing companies stood to be unjustly
enriched to the tune of a billion dollars. Having collected
the taxes once out of their customers, to re-collect them
from the government was a clear windfall. It was this
which led to the denunciation of the decision as promoting
the "biggest steal in history." The problem of tax refunds thrown upon the Government by the Supreme Court,
in the magnitude of the sums involved and in the number and conflicting equities of the persons affected, was
without precedent in the history of any nation. What
could Congress do? There were four possibilities.

1. Congress could have permitted a full refund upon
mere proof of payment. But the Government could not
recall the payments already made to farmers even if the
Court said they were unconstitutional. To raise by general taxation moneys to distribute in such unjust enrich-
ment of processing companies could not be done by any
government with conscience.

2. Congress could have tried to refund to the consumer

who had actually borne the burden of the tax. But practically it was impossible to determine from possibly a hundred million consumers, most of whom had kept no books or accounts, the amount of tax burden which each had borne.

3. Congress could have refused to make any refund of the taxes by resorting to its sovereign immunity from suit. This would have achieved a certain rough justice. To keep the money for the taxpayers as a class would probably more closely than any other plan return the benefit to those who had actually borne the burden, for the great majority of American taxpayers are American consumers.

4. A fourth plan was adopted, however. It provided for refund of the taxes to the extent that the processors actually bore the burden of the taxes, and required them to prove before they could obtain a refund that they had not shifted or passed on the burden of the tax. Undoubtedly this plan fulfilled every obligation of a government anxious to deal fairly with its citizens, for it would restore any funds it had unlawfully collected to any person who had himself been harmed by the collection and who could identify himself as a taxpayer. Nevertheless, there was a billion dollars in the jack pot, and some of the most enterprising high pressure lawyers in the land had taken contingent fee contracts by which, if they could succeed in forcing the Government to refund the tax, they would split the windfall with the client. The effort of the Gov-

ernment to restrict refunds and limit them to amounts not passed on was promptly challenged.

On May 17, 1937, after the elections had returned President Roosevelt to power and after he had demanded reorganization of the courts, the same Supreme Court, with Justice McReynolds a lone dissenter, sustained this Act by which Congress had sought to minimize the disaster.[6] But the original *Butler* decision, more than any to that date, had turned the thoughts of men in the Administration toward the impending necessity of a challenge to the Court.

## NO TAXATION WITHOUT LITIGATION

Since 1867 our law had contained the substance of Section 3224 of the Revised Statutes [7] which provided:

". . . no suit for the purpose of restraining the assessment or collection of any tax shall be maintained in any court."

Preceding administrations had pleaded this section with almost unvarying success to prevent judicial interference with the regular process of revenue collection and fiscal administration. The taxpayer was provided remedies to recover taxes illegally paid, and the judiciary proceeded

---

6 *Anniston Mfg. Co.* v. *Davis,* 301 U. S. 337.
7 26 U. S. C. A. sec. 3653. (a).

on the policy of pay first and litigate afterward. Thus litigation delays would not stall the government. As late as 1921 the Supreme Court sustained the Harding administration in urging through its Solicitor General, James M. Beck, that even though the child labor tax were to be held unconstitutional, as indeed it was, no injunction could issue to restrain its collection in view of this Section 3224. Chief Justice Taft said: " The averment that a taxing statute is unconstitutional does not take this case out of this section." [8]

But, in disregard of this provision sixteen hundred injunctions had been granted by district judges to restrain collection of the processing tax under the Agricultural Adjustment Act, and denied in only one hundred sixty-six cases.[9] The inequity of these, as well as their effect on the revenues, stood out in bold relief. Those who had paid the tax would get it back ultimately only if they had not already collected it out of customers. But those who had not paid the tax because judges had issued injunctions in their behalf could keep the tax if they could keep the injunctions, even though they had collected it from customers. They would thus have the advantage over other taxpayers and over the Treasury if those injunctions stood. This advantage would disappear, all would be treated alike, and what had been collected from unidentifiable

---

[8] *Bailey* v. *George,* 259 U. S. 16.
[9] See Sen. Doc. 42, 75th Cong., 1st sess., p. 1.

consumers would go to the public treasury instead of to private profits, if the Supreme Court dissolved those injunctions and gave the Roosevelt budget the protection of Section 3224, as it had given it to the Harding budget.

But it did not. On the Monday following the *Butler* decision it upheld the injunctions and also held that the 1935 amendments to the A.A.A. of 1933 were unconstitutional.[10] Section 3224 was dead, though it was an Act of Congress, never held unconstitutional. Professor Corwin says of this decision:

" The gradual strangulation of this provision in recent years makes a most extraordinary chapter in the history of judicial power, the latest phase being the award by the Court of some $200,000,000 to people most of whom were probably not entitled to it." [11]

Confusion and resentment were the aftermath of these decisions, increased by the feeling that they foreshadowed other difficulties with the judiciary yet to come.

There was wisdom as well as wit in a cynical wag's remark that the lawyers had transformed the ancient principle of " No taxation without representation " into a doctrine of " No taxation without litigation."

10 *Rickert Rice Mills* v. *Fontenot,* 297 U. S. 110.
11 Corwin, Edward S.: *The Commerce Power vs States Rights.* Princeton: Princeton University Press; 1936, p. 264.

THE POWER COMPANY AND " US FOLKS IN
FLORENCE ": T.V.A.

Cheap and plentiful energy — once coal, but now
chiefly electric power — is as essential to an industrial
civilization as fertile land is basic to an agricultural civilization. Great financial interests had not overlooked this
fact. As land speculators early sought to anticipate many
years of profits of agriculture, so power speculators had
sought to anticipate and get the profits which the growth
of power resources would bring to modern life. Holding
company systems, fancifully capitalized, had bought stra-
tegically located hydroelectric sites and distributing
systems, and through dividend policies, management contracts, and other devices of exploitation had skimmed fortunes from their enterprise. The great progress of the art,
which owed little to financiers and much to operating men,
had reduced costs fast enough to pretty well cover the
manipulations of the holding companies. Public regulation failed to reach them, and public ownership of power
sites and systems had been advocated and established to
protect the public from the vast holding companies. The
Tennessee Valley had been made the site of such an experiment. Federal flood control and navigation improvement
dams were the source of energy which the Government desired to distribute at low cost to the industries and inhabit-

ants of that region. The threat to private interests was obvious. The private interests were organized and their warfare against the Administration rang out on many fronts.

A part of the project under control of the Tennessee Valley Authority was Wilson Dam at Muscle Shoals which had been constructed pursuant to the National Defense Act of June 1916 to assure abundant electric energy for the manufacture of munitions. Ever since the war private interests had been trying to get control of it and had come near to doing so. Since 1925 the Alabama Power Company, a subsidiary of the great Commonwealth and Southern holding company system, had been buying power from the Government at Wilson Dam and reselling it at a good profit to its customers. Now the T.V.A. proposed to sell power directly to a number of towns in the vicinity. For this purpose the Authority had contracted to buy from the Alabama Power Company for $1,000,000 certain transmission lines and equipment. It had also agreed not to sell power in competition with the private power company for a stated period, except in the area served by those lines — about a tenth of the company's business in the state.

This contract to buy the lines was attacked as unconstitutional. The suit was not brought by the power company, but by a few of the owners of its preferred stock, to restrain the company from selling. It was a grave question whether a government undertaking should be brought to judgment in such a suit. The contract had been approved by the State of Alabama, the common stockholders of the company, the management of the company, and the directors. The possible injury to these preferred stockholders was at best conjectural and remote. The directors were admitted to have acted in good faith for the best interests of the company. " These directors," said counsel for the suing stockholders, " are my friends." There was no real adverse interest — the company as well as the stockholders wanted the Government to be defeated. To entertain the suit would be to ignore the tradition that a court will not interfere with corporate management on far-fetched suppositions of minority stockholders. And if historic practice counted for anything, the Court would not review such an act of corporate management when to do so would also require it to review an act of Congress. But the Court entertained the stockholders' suit.

It is one of the little understood characteristics of the judicial process that while small issues are in the spotlight great issues lurk in the background. It was so now. Former Solicitor General James M. Beck on behalf of the power interests struck at the very heart of government power policy. It was admitted that under war powers or in aid of navigation and flood control the Government could spend its money to build and operate dams. But it could not, he argued, convert this stored-up water power into electric energy for sale to the people. It could, however, lease hydrogenerators and permit the lessee to sell power to the public. In short, any power produced must be turned over to private utilities to be resold by them.

The case was argued for two days. The evidence taken had been voluminous. The briefs were elaborate and learned. But to the detached observer, one curious fact stood out. The Power Company itself had been buying power from the Government at Wilson Dam at very low rates since 1925 and had been reselling it to its customers. When the smoke of argument cleared away and the eloquence of the leaders of the bar was stilled, the simple statement of the issue by the attorney for the little town of Florence remained in the memory:

" For ten years the Alabama Power Company has been buying power from the Government at Muscle Shoals and selling it to us folks in Florence — and now when we want to buy it from the Government ourselves, the Power Company says it's unconstitutional."

On February 17, the Court handed down its decision.[12] It was a carefully limited government victory, and held that the water power at the dam and the right to convert it into electric energy constituted property of the United States which it might dispose of and that the power companies had no constitutional right to insist that the energy

---

[12] *Ashwander* v. *Valley Authority*, 297 U. S. 288.

should be sold to them at the dam or go to waste. But the decision was limited to the dam at Muscle Shoals, the Wilson Dam, which had been constructed pursuant to the National Defense Act. Whether the Tennessee Valley plans, which did not have the same war-power origin, were constitutional was not decided.

Justices Brandeis, Stone, Roberts, and Cardozo joined in an opinion denying the right of the Court to entertain the suit. They urged that the Court follow its traditional rules limiting the right of litigants to challenge the constitutionality of legislation. Mr. Justice McReynolds disagreed with both opinions and adopted the entire theory of the utility interests.

There was gratification in Administration circles that the threatened annihilation of its power policy had been at least postponed. But there was no assurance of the future of projects other than the Wilson Dam, and every transaction by a corporation with the Government was now subject to the risk of a lawsuit by a stockholder, whether as a stalking-horse or otherwise.

" SANGUINARY SIMILES " OR STOCK FRAUDS —
S.E.C.

On April 6, in deciding a relatively simple question of statutory construction, the Court, against sharp protest of a minority of the Justices, made an attack of unprecedented intemperance on the Securities and Exchange Commission.[13]

The Securities and Exchange Commission, with the basic Securities Act and the Exchange Act which it administered, was a favorite of the Administration. It was the outgrowth of the brilliant exposé by Ferdinand Pecora of the abuses, frauds, and deceits of the market place.[14] It represented a determined effort to make our system of finance and industrial capitalism honest. The Commission personnel had been chosen with great care and included such eminent men as Joseph P. Kennedy, later our Ambassador to the Court of St. James; James M. Landis, later Dean of Harvard Law School; Ferdinand Pecora, later Justice of the Supreme Court of the State of New York; and William O. Douglas, later a Justice of the Supreme Court of the United States. But it had encountered both open and under-cover resistance from the brokers, investment bankers, and money powers. The Court gave aid and comfort to them — went outside the necessities and even the proprieties of the case to do so.

Jones was engaged in selling oil royalties, and filed a registration statement with the Securities and Exchange Commission. The Commission questioned the truth and sufficiency of his statement and issued its subpoena to require Jones to appear and testify and bring his books and

[13] *Jones* v. *Securities Commission*, 298 U. S. 1.
[14] Pecora, Ferdinand: *Wall Street Under Oath*. New York: Simon & Schuster; 1939.

papers. Jones then withdrew his statement and insisted
that the power of the Commission to examine into the
manner in which he did business was thus cut off. The
Commission persisted in its investigation, and the simple
question before the Court was whether, after an issuer of
securities had initiated a proceeding before the Commission, he could stop the entire machinery upon finding that
his statement was going to be investigated.

The Court decided, six to three, that the statute gave
Jones the right to protect himself from investigation by
withdrawing. There would have been no very serious
ground for complaint had the Court simply decided this
question of statutory construction. But the Court's opinion went on to a bitter attack upon the Securities and Exchange Commission. The majority opinion by Mr. Justice
Sutherland was written with what Justice Cardozo termed
" denunciatory fervor." It assailed the action of the Commission in trying to find out whether Mr. Jones had filed
a false statement, saying: [15]

" The action of the commission finds no support in right
principle or in law. It is wholly unreasonable and arbitrary. It violates the cardinal precept upon which the
constitutional safeguards of personal liberty ultimately
rest — that this shall be a government of laws — ," and
much more of the same tenor. It dismissed the Commis-

---

[15] *Jones* v. *Securities Commission,* 298 U. S. 1, 23.

sion's claim that it had indications that Jones was a violator of the Act by saying:

" The fear that some malefactor may go unwhipped of justice weighs as nothing against this just and strong condemnation of a practice so odious."

It even suggested that the law establishing an administrative tribunal to supervise securities issues was of doubtful validity, saying:

" The federal courts are open to the government; and the grand jury abides as the appropriate constitutional medium for the preliminary investigation of crime and the presentment of the accused for trial."

It compared the Commission's continuance of the investigation which Jones himself had started with the " intolerable abuses of the Star Chamber."

However, the persistence of the Commission in trying to find out what Jones was really doing in the securities market, which the majority found so arbitrary and unreasonable, appealed to Justices Cardozo, Brandeis, and Stone as not only reasonable but within the plain duty of the Commission. " Recklessness and deceit do not automatically excuse themselves by notice of repentance," said Mr. Justice Cardozo. He did not let the reference to " Star Chamber " proceedings go unanswered. He wrote:

" The argument for immunity lays hold of strange analogies. A Commission which is without coercive powers, which cannot arrest or amerce or imprison though a crime has been uncovered, or even punish for contempt, but can only inquire and report, the propriety of every question in the course of the inquiry being subject to the supervision of the ordinary courts of justice, is likened with denunciatory fervor to the Star Chamber of the Stuarts. Historians may find hyperbole in the sanguinary simile."

Other portions of Justice Cardozo's opinion, which show the lines of division in the Court, deserve quotation:

" An investigator is not expected to prove or charge at the beginning the offenses which he has reason to suspect will be uncovered at the end. The petition in behalf of the Commission enumerates one by one the false statements and the omissions imputed to the registrant. Some at least are of such a nature that if chargeable to him at all, they can hardly have been made otherwise than with criminal intent. To give the investigating officer an opportunity to reach down into the hidden wells of knowledge and the more hidden wells of motive is the very purpose of the Regulation by which the proceeding is kept open after the registrant has tried to end it.

" The opinion of the court reminds us of the dangers that wait upon the abuse of power by officialdom unchained. The warning is so fraught with truth that it can

never be untimely. But timely too is the reminder, as a
host of impoverished investors will be ready to attest, that
there are dangers in untruths and half truths when certificates masquerading as securities pass current in the market. There are dangers in spreading a belief that untruths
and half truths, designed to be passed on for the guidance
of confiding buyers, are to be ranked as peccadillos, or
even perhaps as part of the amenities of business. When
wrongs such as these have been committed or attempted,
they must be dragged to light and pilloried. To permit
an offending registrant to stifle an inquiry by precipitate
retreat on the eve of his exposure is to give immunity to
guilt; to encourage falsehood and evasion; to invite the
cunning and unscrupulous to gamble with detection. If
withdrawal without leave may check investigation before
securities have been issued, it may do as much thereafter,
unless indeed consistency be thrown to the winds, for by
the teaching of the decision withdrawal without leave is
equivalent to a stop order, with the result that forthwith
there is nothing to investigate. The statute and its sanc-
tions become the sport of clever knaves.

" Appeal is vaguely made to some constitutional immunity, whether express or implied is not stated with dis-
tinctness. It cannot be an immunity from the unreasonable search or seizure of papers or effects: the books and
documents of the witness are unaffected by the challenged
order. . . . If the immunity rests upon some express pro-

vision of the Constitution, the opinion of the court does
not point us to the article or section. If its source is to
be found in some impalpable essence, the spirit of the
Constitution or the philosophy of government favored by
the Fathers, one may take leave to deny that there is anything in that philosophy or spirit whereby the signer of
a statement filed with a regulatory body to induce official
action is protected against inquiry into his own purpose
to deceive. . . .

" The Rule now assailed was wisely conceived and lawfully adopted to foil the plans of knaves intent upon ob-
scuring or suppressing the knowledge of their knavery."

Those in, or sympathetic to, the Administration felt
that the opinion of the majority struck a foul blow. Seiz-
ing a case in which the Securities and Exchange Commission had, at the worst perhaps, misunderstood the law,
though three of the most respected of the Justices insisted
that the Commission had not even done that, the majority
used the occasion to write an opinion which did all that a
court's opinion could do to discredit the Commission, its
motives, its methods, and its existence. It had declared a
hostility to the whole philosophy of preventing frauds by
publicity and a preference for only the grand jury secret
investigation and criminal trials which had long proved
futile to reach the subtler kinds of fraud at all, and able to
reach grosser frauds only rarely. Every tricky knave in

the investment business hailed the opinion, and the enemies of the Administration seized it to drive home the charge that the New Deal was destroying old liberties.[16]

## ADDING FUEL — COAL

After a breathing spell of a month the Court majority struck again, invalidating the entire Act for regulating the bituminous coal industry.[17] But the majority was diminished. This time its excesses had alienated Chief Justice Hughes, who protested sharply.

The case itself was one of those curious stockholders' suits. James W. Carter sued the Carter Coal Company, of which he was president and a large stockholder. His company, he complained, was going to obey the law, although he demanded it should disobey. He asked for an injunction that would make his company mind him instead of Congress. In this strange way the Court took upon itself to decide whether Congress had acted constitutionally. And in this way it again reached the clumsy hand of legalism into the economic policy of the country with disastrous effect.

The Bituminous Coal Conservation Act of 1935 was the result of more than twenty years of Congressional study of

---

16 For the practical effect on the work of the Commission, see James M. Landis: *The Administrative Process*. New Haven: Yale University Press; 1938, pp. 136–140.

17 *Carter* v. *Carter Coal Co.*, 298 U. S. 238.

an industry that supplied the nation with an essential source of energy. It may safely be said that Congress had given more attention to this than to any other industry. In the twenty-three years between 1913 and 1935 there were no less than nineteen investigations or hearings by Congress or by specially created commissions with respect to conditions in this industry which were of grave national concern.

A number of these investigations had dealt with bitterly contested strikes arising from failure of producers in certain areas to recognize the right of employees to bargain collectively. There had been serious disorders in West Virginia in 1913 and in 1920–1; in Colorado in 1914–5; and in West Virginia, Ohio, and Pennsylvania between 1925 and 1927. These disorders frequently resulted in bloodshed and martial law, and on at least four occasions were restrained only by the intervention of federal troops.

Other investigations were concerned with coal shortages and high prices. For a time lack of coal became a limiting factor in the military program of the nation during the World War, and Congress authorized control of distribution and fixing of maximum prices. In 1919, mines which employed 415,000 men were closed, and wartime powers were again invoked to establish maximum prices and to control distribution, and the United States Bituminous Coal Commission was appointed to arbitrate the issues. When maximum limits were removed, prices again rose to an all-time peak and protests from consumers led to further Congressional investigations. A strike in 1922 closed down seventy-three per cent of the mining capacity of the nation. It forced many industries to shut down for lack of fuel and raised prices again to exorbitant heights. Congress once more provided for federal control of distribution. These investigations had uniformly revealed a surplus capacity in the industry, cutthroat competition, including price cutting and wage cutting, a breakdown of the machinery of collective bargaining, heavy financial losses for operators, and violence and disorder in mining communities. They also disclosed serious waste of coal resources.

Bituminous coal production and distribution is a national industry. Most of the production is sold in interstate commerce or for use in interstate commerce. Over fifty per cent is shipped to consumers outside the state of production, and twenty-three per cent to railroads engaged in interstate commerce. Commercially important deposits of bituminous coal are found in twenty-six states, but the four states of Pennsylvania, West Virginia, Kentucky, and Illinois produce seventy per cent of the national production.

An item of exceptional importance to the industry is labor cost, the remaining items offering little leeway for variations. In 1929, wages were about sixty per cent of the total value of coal at the mine. The general average of such wages for four other large mining industries was only twenty-one per cent, and for the forty-eight largest manufacturing industries, only eighteen and two-tenths per cent of the value of the product. This heavy ratio of wages to the total value of the product had an important bearing on the labor difficulties that had beset the industry from time out of memory. The competition not only had been bitter between separate companies but it had become the most bitter kind of competition between different producing areas in some of which collective bargaining prevailed and in some of which it did not.

Even before the depression the bituminous coal industry was suffering heavy losses, and from 1923 to 1929 the wage payments of the industry dropped over thirty per cent, brought about both by drastic wage reductions and by a large decrease in the number of persons employed. Not only was the industry suffering from internal disorders but it had come upon bad days from external competition. Hydropower, fuel oil, and other substitute fuels, such as natural gas, had deprived it of a good deal of its original market, and more efficient utilization of coal itself had restricted the tonnage required.

After 1929, the decline in the soft coal industry was catastrophic. Production dropped from 535,000,000 tons in 1929 to 310,000,000 tons in 1932. Operators lost money, the deficit for the entire industry in 1933 being

$47,549,000. Labor costs were about the only flexible costs, and wages were slashed. The calculated average earned income for a miner in 1933 at the rates enforced before the N.R.A. for the average number of days worked was $561.00, clearly less than a living wage. Under N.R.A. annual earnings were increased in some fields by as much as fifty per cent, still not up to decent living levels. After N.R.A. was struck down, the wages declined again.

This state of affairs presented more than merely an economic problem. In the coal mining states, whole communities were blasted. Miners and their families, and those who had lived by servicing them, reduced their standard of living almost to the vanishing point. The problem in terms of human misery and demoralization alone was one which challenged the government.

Congress felt that the long history of stoppages and interruptions to commerce from the difficulties within the industry, the destructive price fluctuations to which interstate commerce was subjected, the reliance of interstate transportation upon coal as a fuel, and the diversions and dislocation of interstate commerce which had resulted from conditions in the industry had made its problems preeminently national problems.

In this it was justified in believing it would have the approval of the Supreme Court. In 1933, the Court had refused to find the efforts of coal operators to improve conditions by creating a collective marketing agency to be a violation of the Antitrust Act.[18] It had recognized the " deplorable " state of the industry and had not questioned that it was so interstate in character as to be subject to federal regulation. In fact, while the Court dismissed the complaint, it directed that jurisdiction of the operators be retained to prevent abuses if any should occur. Probably it never occurred to Congress that an industry within federal judicial power would be held to be outside of federal legislative power.

It was clear that no state or group of states could improve these competitive conditions or stabilize this delirious industry. States had tried and abandoned the effort and pleaded for federal intervention. The National Industrial Recovery Act had answered this prayer, and the soft coal industry was one of the first to submit a code under it. That code governed it from September 1933 to May 1935, when the N.R.A. was held to be unconstitutional. Among its efforts to repair the economic damage from that decision was Congressional consideration of the Bituminous Coal Conservation Act. Whatever criticism was directed at the operation of other codes, there was substantial unanimity of opinion during the hearings on the new Guffey Coal Bill that conditions in the bituminous coal industry had been greatly improved under the scheme of regulation which its N.R.A. code provided.

[18] *Appalachian Coals, Inc.* v. *United States,* 288 U. S. 344.

The Act which Congress finally passed declared that the production and distribution of bituminous coal directly affected interstate commerce and that regulation of production and of prices was necessary to promote interstate commerce, and created the National Bituminous Coal Commission. It imposed a tax on the sale of coal of fifteen per cent on its sale price at the mine, but gave any producer a drawback of ninety per cent of this tax if he became a code member. It authorized the formulation of a code which provided for the election by producers of district boards in twenty-three coal-producing districts for the establishment of minimum prices and, under certain circumstances, maximum prices and a specification of trade practices to be deemed unfair methods of competition. The minimum prices were to be determined by a rather elaborate procedure necessitated by the diversity of the industry, but the basis was to be cost of production and did not provide any profit margin in calculating such cost. No code member was allowed to sell coal at prices below the minimum or above the maximum established.

The Act then contained a separate part or title which dealt with labor relations. It gave employees the right to organize and bargain collectively through representatives of their own choosing without employer interference, and forbade any requirement that employees join any company union. It gave employees the right to select checkweight men, to check the weights which formed the basis of their pay, and provided that employees should not be required to live in company houses or to trade at company stores. It made certain provisions with reference to maximum hours and minimum wages and provided for the establishment of a bituminous coal labor board to administer labor provisions and to mediate or, upon request of the parties, arbitrate labor disputes in the industry.

The Act provided for judicial review of all important orders of the Commission, and it provided distinctly that if any provision of the Act should be held invalid the remainder of the Act should not be affected thereby.

It was recognized that there might be a constitutional distinction between the labor provisions of the Act and the price-fixing provisions, and they were carefully segregated in separate titles, so that each might stand on its own footing.

Mr. Justice Sutherland, for a majority of the Court, read a states' rights opinion which would have done credit to the talents and sentiments of Roger Taney in his last years. He spoke bitterly of the states' being " despoiled of their powers." This must have assumed that the states did not know when their rights were invaded, because Illinois, Indiana, Kentucky, New Mexico, Ohio, Pennsylvania, and Washington filed briefs urging the Court to sustain the Act, and not a single state claimed that its rights were invaded. Carter won the states' rights plea against the states themselves. Justice Sutherland held that the labor provisions were utterly beyond the power of the Federal Government. It would have been pretty difficult to hold the price provisions beyond federal power, because the Federal Government had long been fixing rates for transportation. A majority of the Court conveniently ignored this phase of the Act and expressed no opinion as to whether it was constitutional or unconstitutional. But because these provisions were included in the same Act with the unconstitutional labor provisions, the Court simply struck the whole thing down, notwithstanding that Congress had by most explicit terms provided that each provision was separate and should not be affected by the fate of any other.

At this point Chief Justice Hughes broke sharply with the majority of the Court.[19] He agreed that the labor provisions were invalid, but he found that the price-fixing provisions were within the power of Congress, and he found in the Act " a flat declaration against treating the provisions of the Act as inseparable." He pointed out that: " The purpose of Congress, plainly expressed, was that if a part of that aid were lost, the whole should not be lost," and that on this issue the intention of Congress was controlling on the courts. He was therefore opposed to holding the entire Act invalid.

Mr. Justice Cardozo, Mr. Justice Brandeis, and Mr. Justice Stone united in an opinion in which they reviewed

---

[19] *Carter* v. *Carter Coal Co.*, 298 U. S. 238, 317.

the long and troubled history of the industry and concluded that the Act was within the power of the central
government, in so far as it provided for the fixing of prices
of coal in interstate commerce, and thought it unnecessary
to consider the other questions at that time, since only the
price provisions were yet in effect. They said, as to the
labor provisions, that " the complainants have been crying
before they are really hurt," and as to the other provisions,
that Congress was not " condemned to inaction in the face
of price wars and wage wars so pregnant with disaster."

Why were the labor provisions held to be beyond the
power of Congress? Because, in the view of the majority,
labor practices in a mining industry do not " directly affect " interstate commerce. Congress thought they did,
and so did the experienced trial judge who heard the very
extensive testimony of experts on the subject. But the
majority found it unnecessary to consider the evidence.
To the majority the question was not the extent to which
interstate commerce was actually affected by strikes, competitive wage-cutting, and the like; the question was not
one of fact but of words: Was the effect, however catastrophic, " direct " or " indirect "? These words are not
in the Constitution. The majority, asking this non-consti-
tutional question, was able to answer it by simply observing that labor practices in mining must necessarily affect
production first, and then interstate commerce. Since
there was an intervening effect, the effect on commerce was

" indirect." And so a national government that has power, through the Federal Trade Commission, to prohibit the giving of prizes with penny candy shipped by the manufacturer from one state to another,[20] was powerless to deal with the causes of critical stoppages in the gigantic bituminous coal industry.

Another fatal objection to the labor provisions of the law was found by the majority. The statute provided that maximum hours of labor for the industry, and minimum wages for the several producing districts, were to be established by agreements reached between a stated majority of the producers and of the employees. This method was denounced by the majority as delegation of legislative power " in its most obnoxious form; for it is not even delegation to an official or an official body, presumptively disinterested, but to private persons whose interests may be and often are adverse to the interests of others in the same business." [21] The power of some individuals to bind others who have not agreed to be bound does indeed present a thorny problem of law and government. But it is hardly to be solved by dubbing it delegation in its most obnoxious form. Many rights, in fact, that the law protects come down to just this power to bind others against their will, on pain of legal punishment or coercion.[22] The employer who

20 *Federal Tr. Comm'n* v. *Keppel & Bro.,* 291 U. S. 305.
21 298 U. S. 238, 311.
22 For an illuminating discussion, see Jaffe, " Law-Making by Private Groups," 51 Harv. L. Rev. 201.

could bring the powers of the state to bear upon those who attempted to persuade his employees to strike has had sovereign power delegated to him. And what of the manufacturer who can go into court to prevent a retailer from selling an article below the price that the manufacturer has announced as the minimum resale price? That certainly is a delegation of the power to fix prices and to bind others who have not agreed. Yet six months after the Coal Act was held invalid, the resale-price maintenance laws passed by a state were sustained,[23] and it was Mr. Justice Sutherland who wrote both opinions. Taken together, the decisions suggest that the labor provisions of the Coal Act were " obnoxious " not so much to the Constitution as to the judicial sense of what was good for the business community.

This decision affected the fortunes of hundreds of thousands of families engaged in mining. The Court had held that while Congress might perhaps validly pass a law that would guarantee to the operators a fair price for coal, Congress has no power to see that a just portion of such an increase should go to labor. The decision aroused deep animosities in a labor group that was highly organized. The majority of the Court was also building up a bad case for itself among students of the law and, perhaps most important, the majority was building up a body of sharp and

---

[23] *Old Dearborn Co.* v. *Seagram Corp.,* 299 U. S. 183.

well-reasoned criticism of its own excesses from within the Court itself.[24]

### HANGING SEPARATELY — MUNICIPAL BANKRUPTCY

On May 25, 1936, the Court, by a vote of five to four, held the Municipal Bankruptcy Act wholly unconstitutional.[25] This law, enacted May 24, 1934, authorized municipal corporations and other political subdivisions of states, unable to pay their debts as they matured, to resort to federal courts of bankruptcy to effect readjustment of their obligations. Plans scaling down or compromising debts could be enforced by the federal courts if approved by creditors holding sixty-six and two-thirds per cent of the indebtedness, even though opposed by minority creditors. No city or municipality could apply for the relief unless authorized by the laws of the state in which it was situated.

The Court held, however, that this invaded the rights and interfered with the fiscal affairs of the states and their subdivisions.

Mr. Justice Cardozo wrote a sharp dissenting opinion in which Chief Justice Hughes and Justices Brandeis and

---

[24] Congress re-enacted in substance the marketing provisions of the Act and it was sustained by the Supreme Court as constitutional in 1940. It thus took over four years to make effective provisions never held in themselves to be beyond the power of Congress. See *Sunshine Anthracite Co.* v. *Coal Commission,* No. 804 October Term 1939, decided May 20, 1940.

[25] *Ashton* v. *Cameron County Dist.,* 298 U. S. 513.

Stone joined. He pointed out that the Act was purely permissive, could never be invoked by a city unless the state law authorized it and, hence, it could not invade the rights of the states.

This case illustrated the reckless extent to which the Court was interfering with the economic affairs of the country. The Act to relieve municipal corporations, where their states authorized it and the creditors consented, was a recovery measure and gave no power whatever to the Administration. It was administered only by the courts, to which it gave a power to relieve distressed and debt-ridden public corporations similar to the power they had long exercised to relieve private corporations.

In January 1934, when hearings on the proposed bill were held, some 2,019 municipalities, improvement districts, and other taxing agencies were known to be in default on their obligations. Including smaller districts not covered in this study, the estimates ran as high as four thousand defaulting taxing units. Those in default included such large cities as Detroit, Miami, Asheville, and Mobile, as well as a host of small communities and local improvement districts. They were located in forty-one of the forty-eight states. The defaulted bonds were estimated as high as $2,800,000,000.

Many of these smaller units were hopelessly insolvent. For example, a Florida city in 1925 paved streets and installed sewers for a population of fifteen to twenty thousand people. After the collapse, only a half dozen families remained, and the per capita indebtedness was $11,000. A Texas water improvement district had a bonded debt of $100 per acre to be paid by assessments against land valued at only $75 per acre. Not only were many communities demoralized in their taxing structures and blocked in their growth, but bondholders had no effective remedy and were utterly unable to collect their obligations. Communities which might have paid a readjusted obligation were paying nothing because they were at an impasse with creditors. Both debtor and creditor interests wanted, and were benefited by, the law.[26] State law could afford no remedy because the Constitution prohibited any state from impairing the obligation of contracts. Only the national government may provide a bankruptcy procedure.

In this state of affairs, the majority of the Supreme Court closed the door to readjustment through the federal courts, the privilege and benefit of which, for years, every private corporation had enjoyed. The law was not one extending federal power. The Federal Government could not institute proceedings against municipalities, nor was the Federal Government particularly concerned in the plight of these localities, except as it affected the credit structure of the country and retarded sound recovery.

---

26 Hearings before Subcommittee, Committee on the Judiciary, S. 1868 and H. R. 5950, 73d Cong., 2d sess.; Hearings, Senate Committee on Banking and Currency, S. 3255, 75th Cong., 3d sess.; Hearings before Subcommittee on Bankruptcy and Reorganization, Committee on the Judiciary, H. R. 2505, 2506, 5403, 5969, 75th Cong., 1st sess.

Here, then, was another example of the states' being
" protected " against their will. In the Coal Act case, the
states signified their approval of the federal law as the
only method of coping with the problem. In the Municipal
Bankruptcy case the states went further and legislated to
enable their subdivisions to take advantage of the federal
law; the states could withdraw their authorization at any
time and so make the federal law inoperative. But active,
even eager, cooperation by the states was held to involve
an invasion of the states' rights. Apparently the federal
and state governments would have to hang separately, for
they were not permitted to hang together.

The truth is that the states were being hamstrung, along
with Congress. To the discerning, this had been made
plain at the end of 1935, as a result of an unspectacular
but significant case involving the income tax law of Vermont.[27] That state exempted from income tax the interest
on loans secured by property taxed in Vermont and also
the interest on unsecured loans made in Vermont at not
more than five per cent interest. The reason for the ex-
emptions was made clear. The basic reason was to relieve
from a kind of double taxation, where the security was already taxed. But to exempt only secured loans while taxing unsecured loans would have forced up the interest rates
on the latter, and this the legislature wanted to avoid;
hence the exemption for unsecured loans also. Objection

_____

[27] *Colgate* v. *Harvey*, 296 U. S. 404.

was raised by Vermonters who lent money to borrowers outside of Vermont; the income from those loans was not exempt, but the lenders said that the Constitution required it to be exempt if purely local loans were exempt. A majority of the Court agreed with this astonishing argument. Compelled to point to some pertinent constitutional provision, the majority fixed on the " privileges and immunities of citizens of the United States " which, the Fourteenth Amendment provides, no state may abridge.

Now for half a century that provision had been held to apply only to rights of purely national citizenship, such as the right to petition Congress and the right of diplomatic protection abroad. Otherwise there would be no end to the restraint on state legislation. What right of national citizenship was Vermont abridging? Mr. Justice Stone, who spoke also for Justices Brandeis and Cardozo, could discover none unless it be a new right not to pay taxes. These are his words: [28]

" To gain the benefits of its shelter the citizen has only to acquire, by a transaction wholly intrastate, an investment outside his state. I can find in the language and history of the privileges and immunities clause no warrant for such a restriction upon local government and policy. Citizens of the United States are given no privilege not to pay taxes."

---

[28] *Colgate* v. *Harvey,* 296 U. S. 404, 449.

Mr. Justice Stone also observed that:

" Since the adoption of the Fourteenth Amendment at
least forty-four cases have been brought to this Court in
which state statutes have been assailed as infringements of
the privileges and immunities clause. Until today none has
held that state legislation infringed that clause."

So the Court was not only making bad law, it was making new law. The revolutionary character of the majority's decision was exposed to view. A whole new line of
attack on state legislation was opened up by the decision.
Because the case did not involve any great political or
social cause, its import escaped the general public. But for
that very reason, no case more clearly illumined, for the
initiated, the actual direction of the Court's march. It was
not simply anti-Congress, to protect the states; it was anti-
Government, and it was anti-Government with arms newly
forged for the occasion. Vermont, hardly an arch radical
among the states, could have learned from its own defeat
what the Constitution meant in 1935–6.


### THE FREEDOM OF THE SWEAT SHOP

The Court closed its year's labors and crowned its
achievements by striking down another, and a more fundamental, item of state legislation: the New York Minimum

Wage Law for Women.[29] The vote was five to four, but the majority opinion in the breadth of its language was calculated to prohibit any state, at any time, from passing legislation of this kind in any form.

The Court had previously held that the Federal Government was without power to enact legislation of this character for the District of Columbia,[30] although in that case Chief Justice Taft and Justices Sanford and Holmes dissented, and Mr. Justice Brandeis took no part in the case. Chief Justice Taft then warned the majority of the Court:

". . . it is not the function of this Court to hold congressional acts invalid simply because they are passed to carry out economic views which the Court believes to be unwise or unsound."

But the Chief Justice had been overruled by his Court, and Justices Van Devanter, McReynolds, Sutherland, and Butler participated in the decision that the Federal Government was without power to enact minimum wage laws to protect women in industry. These same Justices now participated in the decision which denied the states this power.

The New York Minimum Wage Law had been prepared with great care. It prohibited the employment of a woman

29 *Morehead* v. *Tipaldo*, 298 U. S. 587.
30 *Adkins* v. *Children's Hospital*, 261 U. S. 525.

in certain industries at a wage which is " both less than the fair and reasonable value of the services rendered and less than sufficient to meet the minimum cost of living necessary to health." It empowered a commissioner to fix fair wages, which it defined as " fairly and reasonably commensurate with the value of the service or class of service rendered."

This Act was now stricken down by the Supreme Court, and the opinion by Mr. Justice Butler contended that the Act interfered with " freedom of contract " and announced this philosophy:

" In making contracts of employment, generally speaking, the parties have equal right to obtain from each other the best terms they can by private bargaining."

This, of course, meant that the weak must bear the consequence of their weakness, and the strong may drive the best bargain that their strength and labor's necessities make possible. Labor relations were to be governed by the law of the jungle, and the state might not protect even women and children from exploitation.

The decision was challenged in a ringing dissent by Chief Justice Hughes and in another by Mr. Justice Stone, in which Justices Brandeis and Cardozo joined. These four, in the opinion of the Chief Justice, " can find nothing in the Federal Constitution which denies to the State the power to protect women from being exploited by over-reaching employers through the refusal of a fair wage as defined in the New York statute and ascertained in a reasonable manner by competent authority."

Notwithstanding this, the majority opinion held that " the State is without power by any form of legislation to prohibit, change or nullify contracts between employers and adult women workers as to the amount of wages to be paid."

Justice Stone had this to say of the majority theory of freedom of contract:

" There is grim irony in speaking of the freedom of contract of those who, because of their economic necessities, give their services for less than is needful to keep body and soul together. But if this is freedom of contract no one has ever denied that it is freedom which may be restrained, notwithstanding the Fourteenth Amendment, by a statute passed in the public interest."

The conservative majority recklessly overshot its mark in the minimum-wage decision. Within two weeks the Republican National Convention met in Cleveland, and its platform strategy was to echo the Court majority's criticisms of the Roosevelt program, except for one thing: To say that neither the state nor the Federal Government could take any step to stop sweatshop use of women was more than the opposition was willing to say — in a campaign. Even the Republican Convention repudiated the Court on that. It pledged itself and its candidate to

" Support the adoption of State laws and interstate compacts to abolish sweatshops and child labor, and to protect women and children with respect to maximum hours, minimum wages and working conditions. *We believe that this can be done within the Constitution as it now stands.*" [Italics supplied.]

As the Court adjourned, a review of its term's work showed that it had more than halted the principal measures in the New Deal recovery and reform program. The Court had struck at the Constitution itself by denying to it the capacity of adaptation to " the various crises of human affairs." The greatest expounders of the Constitution, from John Marshall to Oliver Wendell Holmes, have always insisted that the strength and vitality of the Constitution stem from the fact that its principles are adaptable to changing events.

Although it is difficult, on sober reflection, to regard the measures which the Court upset as being wholly outside the scope of traditional constitutional power or as being wholly arbitrary, capricious or unreasonable exercise of governmental power, I have no doubt that many of these measures were imperfectly conceived and crudely executed. Had the decisions of the Court been confined to the limited issues actually involved in the immediate controversies and the way left clear for the Congress to improve and perfect its remedies, no irrepressible conflict would have arisen.

But in striking at New Deal laws, the Court allowed its language to run riot. It attempted to engraft its own nineteenth century *laissez-faire* philosophy upon a Constitution intended by its founders to endure for ages. In overthrowing the A.A.A. the Court cast doubt upon all federal aid to agriculture; in laying low the N.R.A., the Court struck at all national effort to maintain fair labor standards; and in outlawing the New York Minimum Wage Law which had been carefully drawn to overcome the objections raised by the Court in the first minimum-wage case, the Court deliberately attempted to outlaw any form of state legislation to protect minimum-wage standards. The Court not merely challenged the policies of the New Deal but erected judicial barriers to the reasonable exercise of legislative powers, both state and national, to meet the urgent needs of a twentieth-century community.

The community, however, was about to speak for itself. The election of 1936 was at hand.

# Chapter VI

# THE CHALLENGE

Never had the nation been so aroused as by the elections of November 3, 1936. Over 45,646,000 votes were cast, — almost six million more than in 1932 and almost nine million more than in 1928. The Roosevelt popular vote swelled from 22,800,000 to 27,751,612. Translated into electoral votes, the President had 523 out of 531, representing the electors of every state in the Union except Maine and Vermont.

The conservative opposition to the President, however, had neither dissolved nor relented. In fact, supported by an estimated eighty-five per cent of the newspaper circulation of the country, supported by probably a similar percentage of the country's financial power, the opposition actually gained. Landon received nearly a million popular votes more than Hoover had received in 1932.

The President had said almost nothing about the Court during the campaign. His strategy was not of defense but of pressing forward with the unfinished legislative program of the New Deal, but the path he was mapping out led squarely into conflict with the philosophy of a majority of the Court. Nor was the issue a silent one. The opposition charged in its platform and on the stump that Mr. Roosevelt was using unconstitutional methods and seeking forbidden ends, and always it called to witness — the Supreme Court. The Republicans lost no opportunity to identify themselves with the Court and the Court with themselves. Although the Court was helpless to prevent being thus publicly embraced, it had, as I have pointed out, at least encouraged the advances. The claim later made that the Supreme Court had not been an issue in the campaign is unfounded. It was merely an issue on which the President had no need to speak — one which his enemies could not win even by his default. The election had gone against the Court quite as emphatically as against the Republican Party, whose bedfellow it had been.

Before the votes were all counted the opposition sounded the call again to rally round the Supreme Court as an " obstacle " to the President's leadership and program.[1] There was no evidence that the President's enemies were misjudging the disposition and potentialities of the Court.

As the President returned to the Capital after the elec-

---

[1] The *New York Herald Tribune,* spokesman of the opposition, said that the result is a " rising vote of confidence in a man. If that man interprets it as a grant of power to lead the nation where it seems to him best to lead it, we do not see how those who voted for him can complain," and comforted the opposition which had not voted for him as follows: " Two obstacles still interpose. They are the Constitution and the Supreme Court. These two safeguards of American freedom, these historic guardians alike of the national structure and of minority rights, held fast against the presidential will to power during the last four years." *New York Herald Tribune,* November 4, 1936.

tion, the Court was beginning work on a calendar heavy with cases vital to his program of reform and recovery. Of the New Deal laws that had not already been stricken down, few had escaped being involved in some kind of legal cloud by opposition lawyers. Attacks were pending on such legislation as old-age benefits, unemployment compensation, railway pensions, the Labor Relations Act, the Public Utility Holding Company Act, and many others. The social order was already badly torn by sit-down strikes. It was becoming difficult to explain to discontented men and women why they should respect the decrees of the courts when the courts did not respect laws duly enacted by the legislature, or to urge that they rest on the ballot for a satisfaction of their grievances if the officials they elected were to have so little weight in the ultimate policy of the government.

At the turn of the year the tension was great. The President's Annual Message to Congress on January 6, 1937 encouraged public anticipation of a Court reform program of some kind. It reminded the people of some of the unsolved problems that faced him. He said: " The vital need is not an alteration of our fundamental law but an increasingly enlightened view in reference to it." And he warned that " means must be found to adapt our legal forms and our judicial interpretation to the actual present national needs of the largest progressive democracy in the modern world." And there could be no doubt that the man who had just received the votes of 27,000,000 of his fellow citizens spoke for them when he added: " The judicial branch also is asked by the people to do its part in making democracy successful." But he announced no plan and deferred to another day the search for the means.

The evil was easy to identify; the remedy had baffled generations of statesmen. The President's hesitation in the choice of a course is understandable. Many ways were open, each offering some advantage and some disadvantage, and each plan had a following of its own.

Amendment was an obvious legal possibility, but hardly a practical remedy. The delay must be counted in years at best in coming to agreement on a formula, getting it through Congress, and obtaining ratification by the required three-fourths of the states, many of whose legislatures meet only every second year. And since, to defeat an amendment entirely, it was necessary to block it in only one-fourth of the state legislatures, the interests opposed could concentrate publicity, influence, and money on the most reactionary and venal spots with good hope of success. Meanwhile, the Roosevelt program was on the judicial chopping block, and the nation was stirred with unrest.

What amendment could be chosen in any event? The most radical of all proposals to come before the Congress was the proposal of Senator Burton K. Wheeler to allow the Congress virtually to overrule a Supreme Court decision of unconstitutionality by re-enacting the questioned statute by a two-thirds vote.[2] This would end judicial supremacy except as a retarding force in government. But neither the President nor his advisers were prepared to go to such lengths. Deep as was their dissatisfaction, they felt it was men, not the institution, that needed correction.

Another amendment had been proposed to require a two-thirds vote of the Justices to set aside an act as unconstitutional.[3] Specific amendments were also suggested in reference to specific problems to follow the pattern of the long-pending Child Labor Amendment. But there was no preponderant sentiment for any particular proposal. Moreover, it was difficult to frame any amendment which, since it would be interpreted by the same court, could be sure of accomplishing its intent. Amendments — as well as constitutions — are what the Judges say they are.

It was apparent that the immediate difficulty was with the Justices, not the Court or the Constitution. It was only a bare majority of them whose hostility to the Administration was so fixed and extreme that they were counted on by interested groups to continue to nullify social legislation. A minority of the more moderate Justices had sought to protect their records by recording sharp protests against the decision of the overriding majority. The persistent and stubborn split made the functioning of the Court dif-

---

2 See Appendix, p. 352.
3 See Appendix, p. 353.

ficult and discredited the public weight of its conclusions. The vote of the Court in constitutional cases preceding hearings on the Court reorganization proposal follows:

### On Federal Statutes

| | | |
|---|---|---|
| Hot Oil (Sec. 9c, N.I.R.A.) | void | 8–1 |
| Gold Clauses | valid | 5–4 |
| Railroad Pensions | void | 5–4 |
| Farm Mortgages | void | 9–0 |
| N.R.A. | void | 9–0 |
| A.A.A. | void | 6–3 |
| T.V.A. | valid | 8–1 |
| Bituminous Coat Act | void | 6–3 |
| Municipal Bankruptcy | void | 5–4 |
| Silver Tax | valid | 9–0 |
| Second Gold Clause Case | valid | 5–4 |

### On State Statutes

| | | |
|---|---|---|
| Mortgage Moratorium | valid | 5–4 |
| Milk Price Act | valid | 5–4 |
| Minimum Wage | void | 5–4 |
| Washington Utility Regulation Fund Case | void | 5–4 |
| New York Unemployment Compensation | No decision | 4–4 |

The Court, rent asunder, came to a standstill and was unable to reach a decision as to the validity of the New York Unemployment Compensation Act, Justice Stone being absent from illness. A petition for rehearing before the full Court had been pending undecided for months.[4] This left a cloud on the Social Security program of both the states and the Nation, and the repute of the judicial process as a reasonable one was not helped by the fact that the constitutionality of a law had come to depend on the health of a Justice.

Over the years the conservatives had shown a more intelligent appreciation of the importance of each Justiceship than had the liberals. Preoccupied with getting popular support and legislative action for reform, the liberals had not been so alert to the menace of a hostile Court. Property interests were better advised. They had come to regard the Supreme Court as their own House of Lords and to believe they had a moral right to control its sheltering veto. When Woodrow Wilson named Louis D. Brandeis, a mild reformer, to the Court, they assembled unprecedented forces to fight his confirmation and predicted that only ruin for the country could follow their own failure. Wilson had an opportunity to appoint only three Justices in his eight years of Presidency. That was not wholly accidental. William H. Taft revealed the spirit of

---

[4] *Associated Industries* v. *Dept. of Labor,* 299 U. S. 515 (Nov. 23, 1936). Rehearing denied, 301 U. S. 714 (May 24, 1937).

the Court, no doubt, as well as himself, as he turned the White House over to the liberal Wilson after he and his own conservative party had been driven from power:

" Above all other things," President Taft told newspaper men, " he was proudest of the fact that six of the nine members of the Supreme Court, including the Chief Justice, bore his commission. ' And I have said to them,' Taft chuckled, ' Damn you, if any of you die, I'll disown you.' " [5]

Most of them took the hint and stuck it out until the tide had a chance to turn and appointments again would come from a conservative source.

The voluble Taft revealed at the end, as he did at the beginning, the Court strategy of his conservative crowd and their concept of the Court's function in society. In the campaign of 1920 to elect a successor to Mr. Wilson, Taft charged that the Administration was " subservient to labor-union domination " and had appointed " many persons of socialistic tendency to office and power " and said: " Mr. Wilson is in favor of a latitudinarian construction of the Constitution. . . ." He concluded: [6]

" Four of the incumbent Justices are beyond *the retiring age of seventy*, and the next President will probably be called upon to appoint their successors. There is no

---

[5] Pringle, H. F.: *The Life and Times of William Howard Taft*. New York: Farrar & Rinehart; 1939. Vol. II, pp. 853–4.

[6] Taft, William H.: " Mr. Wilson and the Campaign," 10 Yale Rev. 1.

greater domestic issue in this election than the maintenance
of the Supreme Court *as the bulwark to enforce the guaranty that no man shall be deprived of his property without
due process of law.*" [Italics supplied.]

The election of Mr. Harding introduced further manipulations of the Court, which we had suspected but
which, until the Taft biography was published, we lacked
the means to prove. Taft as President had appointed as
Chief Justice, Edward Douglass White, a nominal Demo-
crat. Taft informed Harding that White " had said he
was holding the office for me and that he would give it back
to a Republican administration." [7] But when Taft called
on the aging White, the old gentleman did not renew his
offer to retire and so " Taft's anxious appraisal of the
jurist's health was a degree ghoulish." [8] Soon the Chief
Justice died, but a new complication arose. " The President, he learned, had promised to elevate Senator George
Sutherland of Utah to the Supreme Court at the first opportunity." [9] The circumstances of this promise are not
disclosed. But a fellow Ohioan of Taft, Attorney General
Harry Daugherty, influenced Harding to make the Taft
appointment at once.[10] The promise to Senator Sutherland was kept later, and he became the most scholarly of

---

[7] Pringle, H. F.: *The Life and Times of William Howard Taft.* New
York: Farrar & Rinehart; 1939. Vol. II, p. 955.

[8] Id., p. 956.

[9] Id., p. 957.

[10] Id., p. 959.

the bloc that destroyed the Roosevelt program.

We have seen how, by holding on after the " retiring age of seventy," four Justices had kept Wilson from naming as many new and younger men to the Court. Now Taft confesses to using the same strategy against the Republican President, Hoover, whom he suspected of liberal intervals. He wrote: [11]

" I am older and slower and less acute and more confused. However, as long as things continue as they are, and I am able to answer in my place, I must stay on the court in order to prevent the Bolsheviki from getting control. . . ."

". . . the only hope we have of keeping a consistent declaration of constitutional law is for us to live as long as we can. . . ."

When the Roosevelt administration opened in 1932, this conservative bloc in the Court had been holding on for four years in fear of that radical Hoover! It continued the same strategy against Roosevelt and had prevented any vacancy during his first four years. It had become on average the most aged Court in our history. But there was little doubt that the conservatives had determined that so long as they were able to answer in their places they would give neither Mr. Roosevelt nor the rising generation

---

[11] Id., p. 967.

a chance at the judgment seat before which the policies of a democracy were to be arraigned.

In this majority were those who had outdone even Taft as a conservative. They had encouraged the enforcement of the " yellow dog " contracts against labor.[12] But Taft, as a member of the War Labor Board, took a stand against that.[13] Taft dissented warmly from the decision holding the District of Columbia minimum-wage law unconstitutional,[14] but this Court held firmly to that decision, and in fact extended it.[15]

Woodrow Wilson had clearly perceived the coming of the conflict that must result from such a course. When Justice John H. Clarke, one of his appointees, resigned from the Court in 1922, Mr. Wilson wrote to him: [16]

" Like thousands of other liberals throughout the country, I have been counting on the influence of you and Justice Brandeis to restrain the Court in some measure from the extreme reactionary course which it seems inclined to follow. . . . The most obvious and immediate danger to which we are exposed is that the courts will more and more outrage the common people's sense of justice and cause a revulsion against judicial authority which may seriously

---

[12] *Hitchman Coal & Coke Co.* v. *Mitchell,* 245 U. S. 229.

[13] Pringle, H. F.: *The Life and Times of William Howard Taft.* New York: Farrar & Rinehart; 1939. Vol. II, p. 920.

[14] *Adkins* v. *Children's Hospital,* 261 U. S. 525.

[15] *Morehead* v. *Tipaldo,* 298 U. S. 587.

[16] Baker: *Woodrow Wilson.* New York, Doubleday, Doran & Co.; 1937. Vol. VI, p. 117.

disturb the equilibrium of our institutions, and I see nothing which can save us from this danger if the Supreme Court is to repudiate liberal courses of thought and action."

Life tenure was a device by which the conservatives could thwart a liberal administration if they could outlive it. The alternations of our national moods are such that a cycle of liberal government seldom exceeds eight years, and by living through them the Court could go on without decisive liberal infusions. So well has this strategy worked that never in its entire history can the Supreme Court be said to have for a single hour been representative of anything except the relatively conservative forces of its day. It had worked to prevent Mr. Roosevelt from getting a single vacancy in four years, although six Justices had passed " the retiring age of 70." It seemed likely to work for four more and, as a matter of fact, but for retirement, Mr. Justice Van Devanter and Mr. Justice Sutherland would still be on the Court, and the only changes by death would be a replacement of the liberal Cardozo and the conservative Butler. The Court seemed to have declared the mortality table unconstitutional. And a nation was waiting for the President to move.

On February 5, 1937, the President sent to Congress his anxiously awaited Court message [17] with a supporting

[17] See Appendix, p. 328.

letter by Attorney General Cummings.[18] This message
made no reference to the Supreme Court's course of decision or its reactionary attitude. It pointed out the heavy
burden on the Supreme Court and the many petitions for
review it denied. It discussed the infirmities of age and the
need for " constant infusion of new blood." It contained
only one proposal directly affecting the Supreme Court.
The President asked authority to appoint a new Justice
or judge in any federal court where an incumbent judge
reached the retirement age of seventy and failed to retire
as he might do on full salary for life. There were other
proposals affecting lower courts.

The proposal for additional judges might have enlarged
the membership of the Supreme Court in theory by as
many as six Justices. But this consequence would have
been avoided if those over seventy retired, which the message was something of an invitation to do. It is hard to tell
what the effect of the plan over the years would have been.
Of course it was no permanent or positive protection
against bad constitutional doctrine. It probably would
have resulted in retirement at seventy as a pretty consistent custom. That would have prevented to some extent
the kind of maneuvering that the Taft biography reveals.
It would have shortened the real service of most of the
Justices, and would have kept it on average a younger
Court fresher from the people. Both the merits and de-

---
[18] See Appendix, p. 337.

fects of the plan were, because of the tension of the time, exaggerated a thousand fold, and the debate touched some low levels on both sides. I shall not trace the play of politics, ambition, animosities, and personalities which featured the court battle. The struggle did little to clarify the underlying issues of Judicial Supremacy, for both sides evaded it.

The President's message was so generalized in order to relate to all courts that it failed to focus attention on the real judicial offending. The fighting issues, ready-made for the President, were not seized. There was not a word about the usurpation, the unwarranted interferences with lawful governmental activities, and the tortured construction of the Constitution, all of which could be proved against the Court from the words of some of its most respected members. It lacked the simplicity and clarity which was the President's genius and, to men not learned in the procedures of the Court, much of it seemed technical and confusing.

Much of the support for the plan was accompanied by reservations which clouded the issue in the public mind. While George Norris, a symbol of liberal sentiment and veteran critic of the Court, supported the plan, he did not conceal his dislike of its indirection. Senator Wheeler, author of a far more radical plan of his own, led the attack on this. Many other liberals who disliked some features of the proposal came to its support on the theory of Theodore

Roosevelt who said: " I may not know much about law, but I do know one can put the fear of God into judges." [19]

Perhaps the most serious consequence of the form of the proposal was its alienation of those Justices who had been critical of the Court themselves — such as Brandeis, Stone, Cardozo, and to some extent the Chief Justice. It would have been wise to capitalize their dissents in support of the plan. Instead of accusing some Justices of being stubbornly and wrongly reactionary, which the other Justices could hardly deny, the message in effect charged the Justices collectively with inefficiency and inadequate discharge of duty. The charge alienated Brandeis, oldest of the Justices, and, in a sense, the original New Dealer. He joined with the Chief Justice in a letter hotly denying the whole thesis of the message so far as the Supreme Court was concerned. They were, of course, silent as to any defense of the Court's course of decision against which both had at times protested. Had the attack been on the Court's doctrine, there would have been no excuse and, of course, no basis for their counterattack.

On March 9, the President spoke to the nation and supplied the frontal attack which the message had lacked.[20] Two days later testimony before the Judiciary Committee was concentrated on the causes which had produced wide-

---

[19] Quoted in Frankfurter: *Law and Politics.* New York: Harcourt Brace and Company; 1939, p. 15.

[20] See Appendix, p. 340.

spread dissatisfaction with the Court. But it was all too late — the plan never lived down its initial indirection.

Had the plan been put forth expressly to curb the tortured interpretations of the Constitution imposed on the country by the personal predilections of an honest but misguided majority of the Court, it would have been obvious to everyone that by April 12, 1937 the President had won his court fight.

As early as March 29, there were indications that something had happened within the Court. There had been pending before the Court a case involving the constitutionality of the Minimum Wage Act of the State of Washington which was substantially identical with the New York Act declared unconstitutional only the year before. It was taken for granted that the Washington Act would be unceremoniously scrapped by the Court, probably without even an opinion. But, to the amazement of lawyers and laymen, on March 29, 1937, the Chief Justice rendered an opinion upholding the Washington law and expressly overruling the *Adkins* case. Mr. Justice Roberts had shifted from the reactionary to the liberal side of the Court.

If doubt persisted whether the Court had really reformed or only become as expedient as the Republican Party in its 1936 platform, that doubt was resolved on April 12, 1937. For on that day the Court handed down a series of decisions on the National Labor Relations Act which clearly foreshadowed a full retreat by the Court from the untenable positions it had taken the year before. The majority opinions in the Labor Board cases were so sweeping that there could be little doubt that the most serious grievances which had provoked the court plan would be redressed by the Court itself.

Reform of any institution like the Supreme Court about which traditional loyalties cluster is difficult of accomplishment except under the immediate spur of grave abuse and extreme provocation. Many who had felt obliged to support the plan " to save the Constitution from the Court and the Court from itself," had done so with sadness in their hearts. As soon as the Court began to show contrition and to do penance for its sins, sentiment grew for forgiveness.

The Court's abuse of its powers had called forth the Court plan; an awakened sense of judicial self-restraint and self-discipline removed its urgent need. And the Court fight became a shadow fight on both sides to save face. Each side tried to justify the stand it had taken before the Court had yielded, and the time was not opportune to work out dispassionately the extremely difficult and possibly insoluble problem of providing permanent safeguards against a possible recurrence of the irresponsible exercise of judicial power.

In June, at the close of the Court term, came the retirement of Justice Van Devanter. What planning preceded it has never been revealed, but it was so perfectly timed as a strategic move that it seems unlikely to have been accidental. It threw onto the President the task of a new appointment, and from then on the fate of the court plan became interwoven with the ambition of Senator Robinson to become a member of the Court. Fate settled it. Senator Robinson died. A token settlement of the court plan followed. Relatively minor lower court reforms were embodied in the somewhat anemic Judiciary Act of August 24, 1937.

When we glance back over the hearings, we find that of those who were opposed to the plan few denied that the Court of 1936 was in urgent need of reform. The opposition was generally directed to the President's method rather than to his objective. While opponents were united against the President's proposal, they were hopelessly divided among themselves as to what would be a proper one, so that it was fairly clear that the practical choice was to accept in some form the method proposed by the President, or none. Those who followed closely observed that scarcely one whose name carried weight in the world of scholarship was willing without qualification to sustain the Court.[21]

But the Report of the Senate Judiciary Committee not only failed to recognize, but denied that there existed, any

---

21 For example, Young B. Smith, Dean of Columbia University Law School, said to the Senate Judiciary Committee: ". . . I fully realize that the interpretations of the Constitution by a majority of the Supreme Court in certain cases have created a situation that is manifestly unsatisfactory and calls for corrective action." But he opposed the Court proposal. See Hearings S. Judiciary Committee, S. 1392, 75th Cong., 1st sess., 1937, p. 716.

real problem. It is a document without precedent in recent state papers for the savagery of its attack on the President and for its bitter treatment of a problem that called for dispassionate consideration.

Asserting that the plan " was presented to the Congress in a most intricate form and for reasons that obscured its real purpose," it turned to the President's speech of March 9 as a statement of its real objective and said: [22]

" These words constitute a charge that the Supreme Court has exceeded the boundaries of its jurisdiction and invaded the field reserved by the Constitution to the legislative branch of the Government. At best the accusation is opinion only. It is not the conclusion of judicial process."

It is hard to make sense of this unless it means that the President would have no right to conclude that the Supreme Court had usurped power unless the Supreme Court had entered a judgment against the Supreme Court that it had usurped power. Strange as it may seem, even before the Senate Committee had made its report the Supreme Court had rendered just that judgment against itself and was to render a similar judgment again and again.[23]

---

[22] S. Report No. 711, 75th Cong., 1st sess., pp. 23 and 9.

[23] For example see *West Coast Hotel Co.* v. *Parrish,* 300 U. S. 379; *Erie R. Co.* v. *Tompkins,* 304 U. S. 64; *Graves* v. *O'Keefe,* 306 U. S. 466; *O'Malley* v. *Woodrough,* 307 U. S. 277; *United States* v. *Bekins,* 304 U. S. 27.

The report declared that " from the very beginning of our Government to this hour, the fundamental necessity of maintaining inviolate the independence of the three co-ordinate branches of government has been recognized by legislators, jurists and presidents." It cited authorities to show that each department " shall be free from the remotest influence, direct or indirect, of either of the other two branches." It then devoted a section to proving that both the executive and legislative departments must be not only influenced, but actually governed, by the opinions of the Court on constitutional matters, and it must also be governed by the Court's opinions as to what constituted constitutional matters, and that the Court in deciding what were constitutional questions, could have recourse to its own notions of delegation of power, liberty of contract and due process of law, although their notions were found nowhere in the language of the Constitution itself.

The President had met the dilemma posed by the judicial power by avoiding both horns; the Senate Judiciary Committee met it by choosing both. The country asked, " Is the Judicial Department or the will of the people supreme in America? " The Senate answered, " Yes." The President had said, " Let younger men constitute the Judicial Department." The question was then left for another generation.

So the court reorganization debate came to an inconclusive end. But even as the Senators and lawyers shouted ringing defenses of the old and changeless order, the Court made certain that the old order should yield rapidly and decisively. In politics the black-robed reactionary Justices had won over the master liberal politician of our day. In law the President defeated the recalcitrant Justices in their own Court.

# Chapter VII

# THE COURT RETREATS

# TO THE CONSTITUTION

## 1937

Returning to pick up the threads of constitutional doctrine which we dropped to review the legislative battle, we
find the Court resuming work after the election of 1936
on a calendar which included many important New Deal
cases.

### I. HALTING STEPS

Between the election and the presentation of the court
plan there was little opportunity for the Justices to indicate their response, if any, to the elections. Government
attorneys felt a less hostile attitude in arguments, but
whether it was more than superficial was not disclosed by
any opinions rendered.

The Court, on December 7, gave the Government relief
from a barrage of injunction suits filed by utility holding

companies to prevent enforcement of the Public Utility Holding Company Act of 1935. The Administration had made a long and bitter legislative fight for this Act. As its effective date approached, substantially the whole utility holding company group announced that it would refuse to register as required. Forty-eight comprehensive injunction suits were brought in thirteen district courts, five of them in the District of Columbia, to set aside the Act and to restrain government officials from enforcing it. So great a number of suits involving extensive issues of fact and law was beyond the capacity of the government staff to handle at once, and the many big law firms which had filed suits were clamoring for immediate trials.

The Government had brought suit in the Southern District of New York to compel the three billion dollar Electric Bond and Share holding company system to register as required by the Act. The Government contended that this case would test the constitutionality of the Act and asked the District Court of the District of Columbia to stay the trial of all cases in that court to await the decision of this test case. The District Court had granted that relief, but the District of Columbia Court of Appeals had set aside its order.

The Supreme Court now reversed the Court of Appeals and reinstated, with slight modification, the order staying the trial of the vexatious batch of cases.[1]

---

[1] *Landis* v. *North American Co.,* 299 U. S. 248.

But it neutralized this victory on the following Monday. Electric power interests had brought a number of injunction suits to prevent municipalities from constructing and operating electric power plants with the aid of federal funds and to prevent the loaning of federal funds for that purpose.

The Congress had authorized the President to create a Federal Emergency Administration of Public Works,[2] and the Secretary of the Interior, Harold L. Ickes, was named as Administrator. The Act required him to prepare a comprehensive program of public works including, among other things, projects for development of water power, transmission of electricity, and for constructing publicly owned buildings, parks, facilities, or instrumentalities. Two kinds of projects were undertaken, federal projects and nonfederal. In the latter, financial aid was given by loan or grant to states, cities, and other public agencies. These projects were initiated and executed by local municipal corporations. As of May 1936, allotments of federal funds were made for 8,010 of these nonfederal projects aggregating $1,427,905,556. These included 3,074 school and library buildings for $279,061,000; 883 sewer systems, $228,264,071; 741 streets and highways, $65,967,570; 363 hospitals, $70,140,647; 134 non-water power electric plants, $27,642,427; and 10 water power development projects, $44,327,000. Many of these power

---

2 National Industrial Recovery Act, Title II, c. 90, 48 Stat. 200.

projects were additions to existing systems, but allotments had been made for ninety-three new electric power projects.

These last caused a storm of utility opposition, and the Duke Power Company led the fight in its suit to stop the construction of the hydroelectric plant and distribution system at Buzzard's Roost in South Carolina, which it regarded as its private domain. It alleged that the federal statute authorizing the loans was unconstitutional and asked an injunction to stop the undertaking. The Power Company contended that because the municipal plant would sell power at less than the prevailing rates of the Duke Company, it was in effect " constituting the rates of the municipally owned project a yardstick to regulate and bring about a reduction of the rates of the privately owned utility." The district court granted the injunction, but the circuit court of appeals reversed, and the Duke Company went to the Supreme Court. Meanwhile, most of the other electric projects were held up pending the outcome.

But after deliberating for five weeks the Court found the record below technically — very technically, many felt — defective, and it sent the case back to the lower court with no decision on the vital questions involved.[3] It was felt that the procedural difficulties would not have prevented a decision on the merits, had the Court been so disposed. To

---

[3] *Duke Power Co.* v. *Greenwood Co.,* 299 U. S. 259.

send the case back seemed unnecessary to settle whether the company had any standing to object to municipal competition or to raise the question of the constitutionality of federal financing. The Court decided nothing about this, though it had been argued at length. Did the action of the Court in sending the case back for further trial mean that the company had a right to raise the constitutional question? Ultimately, when the case wended its weary way up to the Supreme Court once more, the Court decided unanimously that the company never had a right to attack the constitutionality of P.W.A., because it had no right to be free of municipal competition, however financed. Only those in the counsels of the Court itself know whether the decision in December 1936 saved the P.W.A. from a fate worse than delay. Maybe wise heads thought delay a fair price to pay to avert an adverse decision.

The Court also, on December 21, made a Christmas present to the President of a power over foreign affairs larger than the Government had really contended for.[4] In sustaining the embargo on the shipment of arms to the Chaco, the Court said:

". . . the powers of external sovereignty did not depend upon the affirmative grants of the Constitution. The powers to declare and wage war, to conclude peace, to make treaties, to maintain diplomatic relations with other sover-

---

[4] *United States* v. *Curtiss-Wright Corp.,* 299 U. S. 304.

eignties, if they had never been mentioned in the Constitution, would have vested in the federal government as necessary concomitants of nationality."

Moreover, it held that in this field:

". . . with its important, complicated, delicate and manifold problems, the President alone has the power to speak or listen as a representative of the nation."

And it said that it was dealing:

". . . not alone with an authority vested in the President by an exertion of legislative power, but with such an authority plus the very delicate, plenary and exclusive power of the President as the sole organ of the federal government in the field of international relations — a power which does not require as a basis for its exercise an act of Congress, but which, of course, like every other governmental power, must be exercised in subordination to the applicable provisions of the Constitution."

The Court opened the new year by interpreting the power over interstate commerce to be broad enough to allow Congress to exclude from transportation goods made by convict labor where the laws of the state to which they were consigned prohibited the receipt, possession, or sale of such goods.[5] The opinion by the Chief Justice distin-

---

[5] *Ky. Whip & Collar Co.* v. *Illinois Central R. Co.*, 299 U. S. 334.

guished and laid aside as inapplicable, without overruling,
those cases that had been most restrictive of the federal
power, such as the *Child Labor* case. It was an important
victory for the Government if it foreshadowed a changed
attitude toward the commerce power. But this was
doubted.

On the same day the Court held the Criminal Syndical-
ism Law of Oregon to be a violation of the right of free
speech and peaceable assembly,[6] and released **De Jonge**, a
member of the Communist Party, who had been held by the
Oregon courts to have violated the Act as they construed it.

On January 11, the Court upheld the constitutionality
of the Silver Purchase Act of 1934,[7] which imposed a tax
of fifty per cent of the profits over cost and allowed expenses on transfers of any future interest in silver bullion
and made the tax retroactive to May 15, a period of thirty-
five days. The effect of this was to tax heavily profits from
transactions consummated while the statute was in course
of enactment.

The law represented a frank use of the taxing power for
non-revenue purposes. The background was this: In 1934
the monetary silver stocks of the Government stood, in
relation to gold, at the lowest point in recent history. On
May 22, 1934, the President sent a message to Congress
recommending a policy " to increase the amount of silver

---

6  *De Jonge* v. *Oregon,* 299 U. S. 353.
7  *United States* v. *Hudson,* 299 U. S. 498.

in our monetary stocks with the ultimate objective of having and maintaining one-fourth of their monetary value in silver and three-fourths in gold." He also said: " There should be a tax of at least 50 per cent on the profits accruing from the dealing in silver."

A bill, authorizing the silver purchases but omitting the tax, was introduced in the Senate. Government purchases might amount to as much as 1,300,000,000 ounces. The silver market on that day saw sales of over 7,500,000 ounces; and the following day, sales of 6,275,000 ounces. This two-day turnover was about five times the estimated amount of free silver in the United States at that time. Speculators were at play with the nation's market. The following day the House Bill was introduced containing the tax feature. Wall Street had forgotten that tax bills can originate only in the House. It thought the tax had been abandoned. Sales at once settled down again to a normal volume and remained there.

" It is plainly evident that the determination of the Administration to tax profits on silver speculation 50 per cent is killing trade in silver futures,"

said the *Journal of Commerce* on May 26, 1934.

Of course it was — and that was its chief purpose. As a revenue measure it was not important.

But was it constitutional to make it take effect as of May 15, when it was not enacted until June 19? The Supreme Court had held that the federal gift tax could not be made retroactive.[8] The Court of Claims unanimously held this silver tax invalid.

The issue was whether Congress could protect the Treasury against speculative manipulation of the market while Congress was deliberating. Congress must act publicly, and it takes time. Meanwhile, its policies are subject to pretty accurate forecast. Before the Treasury could be authorized to act, speculators could have their own way with the markets in which the Treasury must later buy.

This was the reason the Administration wanted to win the silver tax case: to establish a device to protect the Government against those who would gain from manipulating markets while the public policy was being settled.

This was what the Court in effect conceded in its decision which held the Act constitutional, but with no intimation in its opinion of such significance of the case.

On February 5 came the President's bombshell message proposing reorganization of the Supreme Court.

The first decision of importance to Administration policy after the President's message was another *Gold-Clause* case.[9] The question concerned the application of the Joint Resolution of June 5, 1933. It declared that every obligation " payable in money of the United States "

---

[8] *Untermyer* v. *Anderson,* 276 U. S. 440; cf. *Milliken* v. *United States.* 283 U. S. 15.

[9] *Holyoke Power Co.* v. *Paper Co.,* 300 U. S. 324.

should be discharged upon payment, dollar for dollar, in any coin or currency which was legal tender, irrespective of any provision whereby the creditor was given a right to require payment in gold or in a particular kind of coin or currency. Did it apply to a contract which required the payment as rent of a quantity of gold which should be equal in amount to a stated number of dollars of the gold coin of the United States of the standard of weight and fineness of the year 1894? The Court held that this amounted to a contract for the payment of money and that the Joint Resolution did apply, as the Government contended. While Justices Van Devanter, McReynolds, Sutherland, and Butler dissented, as they had in the earlier *Gold-Clause Cases*, they merely noted their dissent. Bitter denunciation or lectures to the Administration about morals and economics were significantly omitted this time.

Hearings before the Senate Judiciary Committee on the proposal to reorganize the Court opened on March 10. One of the most advantageous points of Administration attack was the Court's minimum-wage decision.[10]

A case was pending which renewed this question.[11] Disregarding the decision of the Supreme Court, the State of Washington since 1913 had an Act providing for the establishment of minimum wages for women in certain indus-

---

[10] Hearings, Committee on the Judiciary, S. 1392, 75th Cong., 1st sess., p. 49.

[11] *West Coast Hotel Co.* v. *Parrish,* 300 U. S. 379.

tries. The Act was challenged and the case had been argued before the Supreme Court in December, before the President's court plan was announced. The Act, if precedents governed, was certain to be set aside, for it was substantially identical with the New York Act which the Court, made up of the same Justices, only the previous June had condemned when it had declared that no state had power by any form of legislation to establish minimum wages. But forces more potent than precedents were at work.

## II. WHITE MONDAY, MARCH 29, 1937

There are few days in the story of the Court so dramatic as March 29, 1937. The President's proposal had focused the attention of the nation on the Supreme Court. The room was crowded with spectators, and a long double line of those who could not get in extended through the majestic corridors to the outer portals of the building. The distinguished visitors' seats were filled with important personages. The wives of most of the Justices betrayed by their presence and gravity that something unusual was to happen. Many Senators were present, aware, it seemed, that what the Court might do that day would powerfully influence the fate of the court reorganization bill then in the balance.

To one who sat at the government counsel table the spec-

tacle of the Court that day frankly and completely reversing itself and striking down its opinion but a few months
old was a moment never to be forgotten. The Chief Justice
read the opinion confessing error. But his voice was of
triumph. He was reversing his Court, but not himself. He
was declaring in March the law as he would have declared
it the previous June, had his dissent been heeded. What
had made the June 1936 minority a June 1937 majority
was the changed vote of Mr. Justice Roberts.

The Chief Justice moved swiftly through the statement
of facts and announced that attempts to distinguish this
case from the *Adkins* case, in which the Court held the
District of Columbia Act void, were futile. He then disposed of the New York case by asserting that the New
York attorneys had not asked the Court to reconsider the
constitutional questions decided in the *Adkins* case and
that, therefore, those questions were closed to the Court's
inquiry in the case of the previous June. This doctrine
that the Court would apply bad constitutional law to a
case unless the lawyers asked it specifically to correct itself was a bit of face-saving for the Court which it soon
abandoned, when it changed a century-old doctrine on its
own motion without even hearing argument of the point.[12]
However, coming to the question at issue in the minimum-
wage case, the Chief Justice stated that:[13]

---

[12] *Erie R. Co.* v. *Tompkins,* 304 U. S. 64.
[13] *West Coast Hotel Co.* v. *Parrish,* 300 U. S. 379, 390.

" The importance of the question in which many States having similar laws are concerned, the close division by which the decision in the *Adkins* case was reached, and the economic conditions which have supervened, and in the light of which the reasonableness of the exercise of the protective power of the State must be considered, make it not only appropriate, but we think imperative, that in deciding the present case the subject should receive fresh consideration."

It will be remembered that a few months before the majority of the Court had said that a minimum-wage law for women interfered with the constitutional freedom of contract of the women themselves. " What is this freedom? " asked the Chief Justice, and answered:

" The Constitution does not speak of freedom of contract. It speaks of liberty and prohibits the deprivation of liberty without due process of law."

and continued:

" In prohibiting that deprivation the Constitution does not recognize an absolute and uncontrollable liberty. Liberty in each of its phases has its history and connotation. But the liberty safeguarded is liberty in a social organization which requires the protection of law against the evils which menace the health, safety, morals and welfare of the people. Liberty under the Constitution is thus necessarily subject to the restraints of due process, and regulation which is reasonable in relation to its subject and is adopted in the interests of the community is due process."

He reviewed the history of minimum-wage legislation in the courts and quoted Chief Justice Taft's dissent in the *Adkins* case, and said:

" We think that the views thus expressed are sound and that the decision in the *Adkins* case was a departure from the true application of the principles governing the regulation by the State of the relation of employer and employed."

He found it impossible to reconcile that case with previous law, and he reviewed recent economic experience with the exploitation of workers. He said: " The community is not bound to provide what is in effect a subsidy for unconscionable employers." And he reached the climax of his opinion with the declaration: " Our conclusion is that the case of *Adkins* v. *Children's Hospital, supra,* should be, and it is, overruled."

Justices Sutherland, Van Devanter, McReynolds and Butler dissented in an opinion by Mr. Justice Sutherland. He denied that the judicial function included the power of amendment under the guise of interpretation.

" If the Constitution, intelligently and reasonably construed in the light of these principles, stands in the way of desirable legislation, the blame must rest upon that instrument, and not upon the court for enforcing it according to its terms. The remedy in that situation — and the only true remedy — is to amend the Constitution."

The Constitution, it seems, must be wrong; the judges could not be! And he referred to the *Adkins* and *Tipaldo* cases for a more complete discussion.

The effect of this decision was far-reaching in law and in economics, but its immediate repercussions were political. The Administration forces had to like the decision, for it was what they had long contended the law to be. It stimulated the movement in both state and nation to " put a floor under wages " and a " ceiling over hours," and a law to prescribe minimum wages and maximum hours in interstate commerce was soon proposed to Congress. But the liberals had a good deal to say about judicial strangling for fifteen years of such legislation in both state and nation by what was now conceded to be a blunder of the Court. And they contended that we now had in substance a one-man Supreme Court, before which laws were constitutional or unconstitutional, as Mr. Justice Roberts voted.

The conservatives liked the decision. They knew the former one took ground too reactionary to be held. The timing of the yielding was a boon to them. It removed a great deal of pressure for reform of the Court, and they made much of the argument that the Court did not need reforming, but could and would reform itself. At any rate the Court had made a bold turn in direction. The doctrine of " freedom of contract," which had menaced all types of legislation to regulate the master and servant relation, had been uprooted so definitely that it could hardly be expected to thrive again. Labor was free from the shackles of a fictitious freedom.

On the same day this Court held to be constitutional the National Firearms Act, which required dealers in firearms to register and pay an annual tax. It represented a use of the taxing power for the purpose of regulating the traffic in firearms. Mr. Justice Stone upheld the power of the Congress to lay the tax and said, for a unanimous Court: [14]

" Inquiry into the hidden motives which may move Congress to exercise a power constitutionally conferred upon it is beyond the competency of courts."

At the same time the Court with no dissent sustained the constitutionality of the amended Railway Labor Act,[15] which sought to avoid interruptions in interstate commerce by the promotion of collective bargaining and by mediation and arbitration between the railroads and their labor. The Act had been assailed as unconstitutional in its en-

---

[14] *Sonzinsky* v. *United States*, 300 U. S. 506.
[15] *Virginian Ry.* v. *Federation*, 300 U. S. 515.

tirety. While railway labor had a more definite identification with interstate commerce than industrial labor, the government victory raised the hope that the more general labor relations act might be sustained.

Nor did the Court stop here on that 29th day of March. It sustained as constitutional a revised Frazier-Lemke Act for the relief of farm debtors.[16] After the first Act was held invalid the pressure continued for some plan by which federal power could aid an insolvent farmer to readjust his debt load without giving up his farm, which was not only a business but a home. The Congress attempted to cure the defects in the prior Act and, while it re-enacted substantially the same plan, it modified details to meet the Court's criticism. Its validity was still challenged and doubted by many. Its fate seemed to depend on the strictness or liberality of the Court. Despite the little difference between the earlier and later statutes, the second was upheld. The opinion referred to the earnest effort of Congress to cure the constitutional defects. A collegiate wag remarked that Congress was given an " A " for effort.

What a day! To labor, minimum-wage laws and collective bargaining; to farmers, relief in bankruptcy; to law enforcement, the firearms control. The Court was on the march!

---

[16] *Wright v. Vinton Branch,* 300 U. S. 440.

### III. LABOR, FARMERS, CIVIL LIBERTIES

April 12 saw the Wagner Labor Relations Act upheld in the most far-reaching victory ever won on behalf of labor in the Supreme Court. Probably no act of the New Deal was more widely misunderstood or more actively misrepresented than the National Labor Relations Act. Its purpose was to set up machinery for the peaceful settlement of industrial disputes through collective bargaining. It aimed to end or reduce strikes by eliminating their chief causes. In no year from 1916 to 1936 did the number of industrial disputes in the United States fall below six hundred — about two every day — and in some years the number rose to four thousand, or an average of over ten every day. In 1933, over 812,137 workers were drawn into strikes; and in 1934, the number rose to 1,277,344. In this two-year period over 32,000,000 working days were lost because of labor controversies.[17] These strikes had affected a large number of industries, and the gravity of this strife was illustrated by frequent federal intervention in times past by dispatching troops to areas of dispute.

The National Labor Relations Act, known as the Wagner Labor Act,[18] was an exercise of the power of Congress

---

[17] Sen. Rep. 573, 74th Cong., 1st sess., pp. 1 and 2.
[18] Act of July 5, 1935, U. S. C., Sup. I, Title 29, Sec. 151 *et seq.*, c. 372, 49 Stat. 449.

over interstate commerce to prevent strikes that would affect the flow of such commerce.

The Act recited the injuries to commerce resulting from denial by employers of the right of employees to organize and from the refusal of employers to accept the procedure of collective bargaining. It created the National Labor Relations Board and then set forth the right of employees to self-organization and to collective bargaining through representatives of their own choosing, and it defined unfair labor practices. It laid down rules as to the representation of employees for the purpose of collective bargaining. The Board was empowered to prevent the unfair labor practices defined by the Act where they affected commerce and to petition designated courts to secure the enforcement of its orders. Court review was permitted, but findings of the Board as to facts, if supported by evidence, were to be conclusive. The Board had broad powers of investigation. The Act did not interfere with the right to strike, nor did it compel employers to accept employees' terms, but only to bargain in good faith.

This Act aroused the deep resentment of many employers who, because of it, entertained fears as extravagant as the hopes of labor. Its underlying philosophy, while accepted by a few of the more enlightened employers, was rejected by most of them as the rankest kind of radicalism. Their legalists had advised them that the Act was unconstitutional and, while the Act was under test in the courts, many employers had made a special drive to destroy organized labor. Employees took possession of plants by sit-down strikes in retaliation for the refusal to recognize their rights as declared by the law. Courts had granted injunctions which could not be enforced without bloodshed.

The Act came to judgment in the Supreme Court in an atmosphere of strife and bitterness. Not only did it present a question of great consequence to the industrial interests of the country and to organized labor, but everyone was conscious that it would be of very substantial consequence in determining the fate of the President's court reform proposals.

On April 12, 1937, the Court sustained the Labor Relations Act against all of the constitutional objections that lawyers had raised.[19]

The prevailing opinion in the key case was read by the Chief Justice. Speaking of the right of labor to organize, he declared: [20]

" That is a fundamental right. Employees have as clear a right to organize and select their representatives for lawful purposes as the respondent has to organize its business and select its own officers and agents. Discrimination and coercion to prevent the free exercise of the right of

---

[19] *Labor Board* v. *Jones & Laughlin,* 301 U. S. 1; *Labor Board* v. *Fruehauf Co.,* 301 U. S. 49; *Labor Board* v. *Clothing Co.,* 301 U. S. 58; and *Associated Press* v. *Labor Board,* 301 U. S. 103.
[20] *Labor Board* v. *Jones & Laughlin,* 301 U. S. 1, 33.

employees to self-organization and representation is a proper subject for condemnation by competent legislative authority. Long ago we stated the reason for labor organizations. We said that they were organized out of the necessities of the situation; that a single employee was helpless in dealing with an employer; that he was dependent ordinarily on his daily wage for the maintenance of himself and family; that if the employer refused to pay him the wages that he thought fair, he was nevertheless unable to leave the employ and resist arbitrary and unfair treatment; that union was essential to give laborers opportunity to deal on an equality with their employer."

He further said:

" Experience has abundantly demonstrated that the recognition of the right of employees to self-organization and to have representatives of their own choosing for the purpose of collective bargaining is often an essential condition of industrial peace. Refusal to confer and negotiate has been one of the most prolific causes of strife. This is such an outstanding fact in the history of labor disturbances that it is a proper subject of judicial notice and requires no citation of instances."

and

" The Act has been criticised as one-sided in its application; that it subjects the employer to supervision and

restraint and leaves untouched the abuses for which employees may be responsible; that it fails to provide a more
comprehensive plan, — with better assurances of fairness
to both sides and with increased chances of success in
bringing about, if not compelling, equitable solutions of
industrial disputes affecting interstate commerce. But we
are dealing with the power of Congress, not with a particular policy or with the extent to which policy should go. We
have frequently said that the legislative authority, exerted
within its proper field, need not embrace all the evils
within its reach. The Constitution does not forbid ' cau-
tious advance, step by step,' in dealing with the evils which
are exhibited in activities within the range of legislative
power."

He gave to the interstate commerce power of the Federal Government a scope which rejected the narrow philosophy of the child-labor decision and the N.R.A. case
and relied upon the precedents which gave to the interstate
commerce power its maximum sweep.

Mr. Justice McReynolds read a dissenting opinion, in
which Justices Van Devanter, Sutherland, and Butler
joined, accusing the majority of departing from the principles followed in the N.R.A. case and the bituminous coal
case. He protested that under the majority's interpretation: " Almost anything — marriage, birth, death — may
in some fashion affect commerce." This minority of the

Court insisted that an employer's will to hire upon any terms and to fire for any cause he chose could not be regulated or interfered with by Congress.

In the *Associated Press* case the dissenting opinion on behalf of the same Justices was prepared by Mr. Justice Sutherland. He contended that to require news agencies to practice collective bargaining was an interference with the freedom of the press and if the employees organized it might lead to " suppression or coloration of unwelcome facts " in press dispatches! But the majority saw no issue of freedom of the press which required the organized newspapers to be on a different labor basis than other employers.

The impression which these decisions made upon Congress, the Administration, and the country was profound. Temporarily, even those who were opposed to these decisions accepted them rather cheerfully because they felt that the decisions moderated the force behind the demand for reorganization of the Court.

On April 26, the Court held unconstitutional, as the state court had applied it to the activities of a Negro Communist, an ancient statute of Georgia, designed to make insurrection criminal.[21] There was a strong dissent, but the decision added to that left wing support of the Court which was based on its protection of civil rights.

On May 3, the Government won an important victory

---

21 *Herndon* v. *Lowry*, 301 U. S. 242.

for the farm interests. The Court unanimously, in an opinion by Justice Sutherland, upheld the constitutionality of a processing tax on cocoanut oils.[22] The Congress in 1934 had laid a tax upon the first domestic processing of a number of oils, including cocoanut oil.[23] Much cocoanut oil was of Philippine origin and as to such oils it had been claimed in Congress that the tax would violate, at least in spirit, the Philippine Independence Act in which the United States had stipulated that for ten years there might be imported duty free two hundred thousand long tons of Philippine cocoanut oil. To avoid any bad faith the proceeds of this tax on such oil were to be turned over to the Philippine Treasury.

It was claimed that the law was unconstitutional because its purpose was to raise prices of domestic oils and fats by what was an economic equivalent of a tariff. Undoubtedly protection for the farmer had been a motive for the Act, and farm interests had strongly supported it. The tax had proved to be an unexpectedly fruitful source of revenue, and there was in the Treasury to January 31, 1937, $44,336,506.19, which the Philippine Government claimed. It was a windfall to that government. The soap makers, who were the chief users of cocoanut oil and in whose processes of manufacture it had superseded domestic farm-produced fats, contested and lost to the farmers.

---

[22] *Cincinnati Soap Co.* v. *United States,* 301 U. S. 308.
[23] Revenue Act of 1934, Sec. 602½, c. 277, 48 Stat. 680.

On May 24, the Court gave union labor another victory. It upheld the Wisconsin Labor Code which declared picketing to be legal and prohibited injunctive interference with it.[24] The case had asserted the right to picket against a tile layer who took small contracts and did his own work, sometimes employing a helper. The purpose was to force him to join the union and make his own labor subject to union conditions. It had been feared by some of labor's friends that the case was not a good one in which to test the validity of the Labor Code. But it was sustained in a strong opinion by Mr. Justice Brandeis. Justices Van Devanter, McReynolds, and Sutherland joined Mr. Justice Butler in the latter's opinion, sharply dissenting. But these diligent dissenters could no longer rally a majority.

## IV. SOCIAL SECURITY

The end of the term was approaching, and two important New Deal laws were in the shadow of death. The Circuit Court of Appeals for the First Circuit, sitting at Boston, had held both the unemployment compensation and the old-age benefit provisions of the Social Security Law to be wholly unconstitutional. These laws represented the most forward step of the Administration in its effort to forestall further crises in unemployment and to end the neglect of the aged. Both laws were passed in response to

---

[24] *Senn* v. *Tile Layers Union,* 301 U. S. 468.

depression conditions; both projected the Federal Government into concerns that were until lately generally thought to be local, and both embodied principles of social insurance. There was great anxiety as to their fate. There had been no change in the membership of the Supreme Court. If these cases could be won in such a court, the main items of the New Deal would be on solid ground. If they were lost, it would set the movement for social security back a generation.

Unemployment had been the major problem created by the depression. From 1930–6 the number of involuntarily unemployed had much of the time been up to 10,000,000 and at times was estimated at 16,000,000. The effects had been devastating. From 1930–4 over thirteen million depositors closed their savings accounts, their withdrawals totaling more than $7,000,000,000. In 1932–3, 11,654,-000 industrial insurance policies having a face value of over $24,000,000,000 were surrendered, while 32,410,000 of such policies were allowed to lapse. By June 1933, city dwellers were losing equities in their homes at the rate of a thousand houses per day. Private charities did heroic, but wholly inadequate, work. Local governments exhausted their taxing resources or reached their debt limits and passed the burden to the states. Many of the states exhausted their limited revenues, and the national government was forced to use its taxing power to aid local relief and to provide jobs through public works.

But unemployment had become more than a depression problem — it had become a permanent and fairly common characteristic of our industrial economy. From 1920–9 when the country was unusually prosperous, the industrial unemployed fluctuated between 1,400,000 and 4,000,000 and was over 1,800,000 in the boom year of 1929.[25] Harry L. Hopkins, Works Progress Administrator, said that " it is reasonable to expect a probable minimum of 4,000,000 to 5,000,000 unemployed, even in future ' prosperity ' periods." [26] This unemployment was often a symptom of progress, as well as of depression, in an industry. Technological advance and improved processes, as well as seasonal fluctuation, style changes, and shifting markets, contributed to the permanent burden. The disaster involved more than the personal misfortune of the worker. It reduced living standards of the family, discouraged marriage and offspring, reacted unfavorably on health, and too often drove younger members of a family to become vagrants or criminals.

Not only the social structure but the economic structure was sapped by it, for unemployment sharply curtails consumer demands, which in turn reduces production, which again increases unemployment.

The average worker, if he were not caught in any of these causes of unemployment, would live through several

---

[25] Report of President Hoover's Committee on *Recent Social Trends,* Vol. II, pp. 478–498.
[26] *The New Republic,* February 10, 1937.

typical cycles of depression, during which employment would fall off and his earnings be curtailed. His wages, even with thrift and good management, would not make him secure against this. Bank accounts, insurance policies, and equities in a home had all proved illusory plans of saving. It was one of the great tragedies that both the spendthrift and the prudent came to the same end when unemployment overtook them. Many will remember the cartoon of the ragged man on a park bench who, on being asked why he didn't save for a rainy day, answered simply, " I did."

The states hesitated to act separately to set up systems of unemployment compensation. Most were unable to finance them without special taxes upon industry. If a state imposed special taxes upon its own industry, it handicapped its competitive position in the national markets and discouraged the coming of new industries.

The national government sought a system that would anticipate the drain on the public treasury and create a store of consumer purchasing power to sustain the living standards of the unemployed and level out the peaks and valleys in the national economy.

For this purpose the Congress invoked its power to tax for the general welfare, feeling that unemployment had reached the magnitude of a general welfare problem. This the circuit court of appeals denied, maintaining that it was only local.

An excise tax on employers' payrolls was imposed, not applicable, however, to agricultural labor, domestic service, or certain other groups, and not applicable to those who employed less than eight persons. The rate for 1936 was one per cent of wages.

Each employer, however, was entitled to a credit against the tax of not to exceed ninety per cent thereof on account of any contributions paid by him into any employment fund under a state law, provided the state law met certain minimum requirements of a real unemployment compensation statute. Each state was free to determine within certain limits what system, if any, of unemployment compensation it would adopt. The result was that the Federal Government said to the citizens of each state: " If you will establish and administer a suitable unemployment compensation law, the state may have the revenue from a payroll tax. If any state leaves that burden to be carried by the Federal Government, the Federal Government will collect the tax." The imposition throughout the nation of the uniform payroll tax did not affect the competitive position of industries in different states, but the means were really made available to the states which desired to establish unemployment compensation systems.

Thus the system required action by both the state and the Federal Government. The federal unemployment compensation law did not operate directly upon the citizens of any state. The federal tax was really a plan to enable the state to set up its own system without fear of competition from states which chose to do nothing. Thus enabled, the states promptly acted to set up systems according to their several ideas of wise policy.

It will be seen that those who were opposed to the plan had two avenues of attack. They could contend that the state's power was inadequate to the establishment of a compensation system, or they could contend that the federal power was inadequate to authorize its tax and credit plan. They did both. The Alabama state statute was assailed on all of the conventional constitutional grounds.

The Court's answer was delivered by Mr. Justice Stone, with Justices Butler, Van Devanter, McReynolds, and Sutherland dissenting.[27] It sustained the state tax against all of the charges that it was arbitrary and discriminatory and took money from one class for the benefit of another. But it went further and held that relief of unemployment was a proper public purpose and that a law to raise revenue for that end did not transgress constitutional limitations. Its review of the economic and social aspects of the problem pointed out the permanency of some substantial unemployment and the manner in which the evil permeated the entire social structure. The Court held that the federal statute had not been " coercive " upon the state legislature and showed the propriety of a federal interest in Alabama's own problem by the fact that

---

27 *Carmichael* v. *Southern Coal Co.*, 301 U. S. 495.

while, from 1933–5, emergency relief in Alabama had cost $47,000,000, only $312,000 of that came from state funds and $2,243,000 from local sources, leaving the overwhelming part of the burden on federal shoulders. Thus was put at rest all doubts about the right of states to extend aid based on the mere fact of unemployment, as distinguished from poor relief based on destitution. The decision allowed the states to put unemployment insurance on the basis of a right instead of a charity.

On the same day the Court sustained the federal Act in an opinion by Mr. Justice Cardozo.[28] The division of the Court was again in evidence. Mr. Justice McReynolds dissented, protesting that the principles of our federal system were being obscured by a " cloud of words " and an " ostentatious parade of irrelevant statistics." To define those principles he recited the whole message from President Franklin Pierce to the Senate dated May 3, 1854, in which he vetoed a grant of public lands to the several states for the benefit of indigent insane persons. Pierce expounded the political philosophy that the Federal Government was not concerned with the fate of the local insane. It was unusual for a Justice of the Court to base his judicial judgment upon the political philosophy of an Executive, even one who had been off the political scene for over three-fourths of a century. Mr. Justice Butler, who agreed on the general proposition that the federal Act was

---

[28] *Steward Machine Co.* v. *Davis*, 301 U. S. 548.

an invasion of states' rights, was unwilling to identify the source of his philosophy with the pro-slave politician of 1854. He wrote a separate opinion. Mr. Justice Sutherland in a fourth opinion, with the concurrence of Justice Van Devanter, questioned only certain administrative provisions of the law.

The majority of the Court, however, through Mr. Justice Cardozo, upheld the purposes of the law and of the tax and upheld the Government's argument that the separate sovereignty of the state and nation did not prevent the two sovereigns from uniting in a common endeavor to combat a common evil, and that each might contribute to the common enterprise such of power as it possessed so that the two would be equal to the problem involved.

Thus the Court placed unemployment compensation upon solid constitutional ground. It could henceforth be validly enacted by the action of the states alone, or it could rest on the action of the nation alone, or it could rest upon a combination of the two.

The Court term was fast drawing to a close when the validity of the old-age benefit titles of the Social Security Act came into litigation. The tax for that purpose first became due on March 1, 1937. The Government exerted every effort to obtain an early decision of the questions which lawyers eagerly raised about it. It was upheld by the Supreme Court on May 24, 1937, which perhaps establishes something of a record for speed in constitutional litigation.

The decision itself presents a paradox resulting from the effort to get a quick determination of the validity of the law. The Government carried up a lower court decision rendered on the petition of a stockholder to restrain his corporation from paying the tax. Mr. Justice Cardozo and Justices Brandeis, Stone, and Roberts agreed at the outset that the stockholder had no standing to enjoin his corporation from paying the tax, and so they voted to dismiss the suit without passing upon the merits. The paradox consists in the fact that these Justices were all in favor of sustaining the Act on the merits. Mr. Justice McReynolds and Mr. Justice Butler were against the Act on the merits. But if either of them had joined with the four liberal Justices on the procedural point, they would have thrown the case out of court. But these two dissenting Justices would not give up their previously expressed views on procedure, with the result that they forced the making of a decision with which they disagreed.

An adverse decision on this procedural question would have been a grave disaster to the Administration. Revenue of over $253,000,000 for the fiscal year 1937, and over $621,000,000 for the fiscal year 1938 was anticipated, and collection had begun. Congressional appropriations and government fiscal policies had been made in reliance on that revenue. The old-age benefit tax was the largest collection task ever attempted by the United States Treasury. It required over two and a half million returns per month to be made by employers covering their own and their employees' taxes. If the tax were unconstitutional, refunds of taxes already collected and interest thereon would have to be made to over twenty-six million employee taxpayers and approximately two and a half million employers. This was the hazard under which Government counsel moved in such haste and at such a risk to their own reputations as lawyers.

The economic story of dependent old age which formed the background for the Act is well known. There were in the United States nearly eight million persons aged sixty-five and over, constituting approximately six per cent of the population. In 1870, that age group had constituted only three per cent of the population. In other words, in less than seventy years, while the population slightly more than tripled, the aged increased over sevenfold, and their ratio to the total population approximately doubled. It was even more significant that population experts anticipated an increase in the ratio of aged persons in the future, and a projection of vital statistics indicated that by 1980 those aged sixty-five and over might become fourteen per cent of the total population, or three times the proportion of 1930.

Urbanization of population and the industrialization of

the country had worked hardships to the aged. On the farms and in small villages men grew old in their occupations by slowing their pace or doing lighter chores. But the increasing efficiency of the great economic machine called for the services of industrial workers only during the short part of life when they were at maximum productivity. While science had lengthened the span of life, during all of which a man is a consumer, growing efficiency had narrowed the span of life in which he could be a wage earner. That was the real crux of the old age dependency problem. Older employees were first to be laid off in many industries, and once out of work the man over forty found it increasingly difficult to get re-employment.

The result was that a growing percentage of aged were dependent and fell back upon the aid of younger persons who, being generally of the same economic class, extended relief, if at all, only by depressing the living standards of the family and denying educational opportunities to children.

Industrial pension systems and group retirement plans had been set up in particular industries, but all told their coverage was so limited as to leave the problem virtually untouched. State old-age benefits were not only difficult to finance but were subject to several inherent difficulties because of the migration of population. States, of course, did not dare to set up systems that would attract a movement of the aged to them. The population structure varied between the different states, some having a higher percentage of aged than others. If old-age assurance were to be based on contributions from the worker himself, it could only be operated by the Federal Government, which would have jurisdiction to collect his contribution in whatever state the worker migrated. The Federal Government, therefore, did not enter into combination with the states on old-age benefits. The system was solely federal, the Federal Government making all collections and distributing all the benefits. Its validity, therefore, rested entirely upon the power of Congress to collect and appropriate revenues for the general welfare.

During almost one hundred and fifty years of the Federal Government's history there had never been a case before the Supreme Court which required it to interpret the general welfare clause. As late as 1935, after observing that there had been a question about its interpretation, the Court said: " This court has noticed the question, but has never found it necessary to decide which is the true construction." [29] Although the power to tax for the general welfare equally with the common defense was the first power which the Constitution conferred upon the Congress, the philosophy had grown up, as stated by President Pierce in his message of 1854, so impressive to Mr. Justice McReynolds, that the Federal Government had nothing to do with matters of individual local concern

[29] *United States* v. *Butler,* 297 U. S. 1.

even if multiplied so as to affect the whole population. The Roosevelt administration had repudiated that philosophy and had acted upon the doctrine that unemployment and old-age dependency had come so to permeate society as to become problems of general welfare.

The much criticized opinion in the *Butler* case had helped to lay a foundation for victory in the Social Security cases. It had conceded that government expenditures for the " general welfare " need not be limited to objects embraced within the specifically enumerated powers of the Federal Government. Only if the spending amounted at the same time to a regulation was it required to rest on other grants of power. It thus established the " general welfare " clause as an independent grant of a power of expenditure, not requiring other constitutional justification.

In the closing days of the term of the Court, Mr. Justice Cardozo led the Court in holding the general welfare clause applicable and ample authority for the system of old-age benefits. He pointed out [30] that the depression of 1929 had taught the solidarity of interests that may once have seemed to be divided and in lucid and sweeping language upheld the exercise of the general welfare power to relieve dependent old age. The decision met with only two dissents, which was a low record for a case of that novelty and importance.

---

[30] *Helvering* v. *Davis*, 301 U. S. 619.

The Court not only validated old-age benefits as enacted but cleared the way for Congress to select other types of social insurance needful in the relief of the hardship and cruelty which seem inseparable from the operation of our economic machine. It had long been doubtful whether the trend of judicial decision in the United States would not make us the one great nation powerless to adopt such measures. Indeed there was fear, and an examination of the grounds of dissent shows the fear to have been well grounded, that unemployment insurance and old-age benefits might meet the same fate as had minimum wages and be held to be beyond reach of either states or nation. It is probable that few decisions in constitutional history will be more significant over the years than this decision with which the Court closed the term.

### V. JUDICIAL SECURITY

At this time many in the Administration felt that there was no longer urgency about a reconstruction of the federal judiciary and that the President's plan might prudently be withdrawn. The Court by its avalanche of liberal decisions had greatly reduced the pressure originally back of the revolt against judicial supremacy as practiced in 1935–6. Other counsels prevailed, and the plan was not withdrawn.

Mr. Justice Van Devanter did not retire until after the

work of the term was finished. All of these government victories were won before a single Justice was appointed by President Roosevelt. While the next two years saw four new appointments which considerably changed the personnel of the Court, it is worth while to bear in mind that many of the old precedents which so restricted the Constitution were overruled by the identical Court which had previously invoked them. There was no change in its personnel until after it provided new precedents that were an adequate basis for much that the newer judges were later to decide.

Thus the Court, with no change of its Justices, had ridden out of the storm and when it closed the books for the term it had rewritten the law of the Constitution. But more than this, it had convinced the Court of Public Opinion that the sentence of reorganization proposed by the court bill might safely be suspended, at least during a period of probation.

# Chapter VIII

# CONSOLIDATING THE

# NEW POSITION

## 1938–40

The Court in a series of great decisions had adopted a more respectful, or at least tolerant, attitude toward government by representatives of the people. It was now, in the succeeding terms, to consolidate the new position and withdraw even further from the cross-fire of economic philosophies and interests.

### AGRICULTURE AND THE COMMERCE POWER

In the field of federal regulation of commerce among the states, three decisions were rendered which cemented the Court's position on federal power in line with the vigorous and historic conceptions of Marshall. In the first of these cases the power of the Federal Government to require federal inspection and to establish standards for the grading of tobacco at auction markets and to prohibit tobacco from being offered for sale at auction until it is inspected and certified was upheld.[1] It is true that these auction sales were held wholly within the state and for some purposes might be subject to some degree of state regulation. But auction markets constitute the throat of a great interstate commerce in tobacco, and the Court held that federal inspection could be imposed at that point, notwithstanding the tobacco had not yet moved across state lines.

The second case upheld the Agricultural Adjustment Act of 1938 which authorized the Secretary of Agriculture to determine the total amount of tobacco that the market for the year would absorb and to apportion that among the states and within each state prescribe a marketing quota for each producer in proportion to his previous production.[2] A heavy penalty was levied upon sales in commerce in excess of the quota so established. The opinion of the Court was written by Mr. Justice Roberts and it sustained the validity of this regulation of interstate commerce notwithstanding the fact that practically it would accomplish a substantial regulation of tobacco production. Mr. Justice Roberts had written the decision in the *Butler* case striking down the first Agricultural Adjustment Act, and the dissenting opinion by Mr. Jus-

---

[1] *Currin* v. *Wallace,* 306 U. S. 1.
[2] *Mulford* v. *Smith,* 307 U. S. 38.

tice Butler now urged that earlier decision as a basis for holding the later act unconstitutional. The Court would not go along with Justice Butler. His dissenting opinion served to emphasize the broad sweep which, as in the days of Marshall, is again attributed to the federal power over interstate commerce.

The decision was followed by a good deal of uninformed comment to the effect that Mr. Justice Roberts had reversed his position and that the Court had reversed itself on the subject of control of agricultural production by the Federal Government. This was certainly untrue. The first Agricultural Adjustment Act rested on the power to tax for the " general welfare." The latter Act rested on the power to regulate interstate commerce. The regulation of marketing was all that the latter Act attempted, and while regulation of marketing undoubtedly would have the effect of regulating production, nothing in the Constitution requires Congress to avoid such effects; were this not so, many a tax and tariff would be unconstitutional. The two opinions by Mr. Justice Roberts are not legally inconsistent, since they are not concerned with the same power of Congress. I would agree, however, that the latter opinion indicates a broader and more tolerant approach to the constitutional problem than did his first opinion.

The third group of the cases involving interstate commerce likewise arose in the field of agriculture and involved the validity of milk marketing orders made by the Secretary of Agriculture fixing the price that handlers must pay to producers in the Boston and New York milk sheds.[3] This Act was an exercise of the interstate commerce power, and it dealt in a general way with the same surplus problem that the tobacco quota act dealt with. Both industries were demoralized by surplus production. In the case of tobacco, the interstate commerce power attempted to deal with the surplus by making all producers share it. They were all assigned quotas which reduced the amount of tobacco that they could market, leaving on the hands of each producer his proportion of the unmarketable surplus. The problem of surplus control of the milk industry was met by a complicated technique evolved within the industry itself for the blending of several use prices to obtain a uniform price and equalization of that price between producers.

Instead of each producer having to take care of his own surplus, as in the case of tobacco, his total milk was marketed, but the depreciation caused by the surplus was distributed among all producers equally in the price. The mechanism for the accomplishment of uniform and equalized prices was complicated and of interest, probably, only to students of the particular industry. The essential constitutional question was whether the power to regulate interstate commerce included the power to fix the price of

---

3 *United States* v. *Rock Royal Co-op.*, 307 U. S. 533; *H. P. Hood & Sons* v. *United States*, 307 U. S. 588.

a commodity moving in interstate commerce, a question which had not been squarely decided theretofore. The Court sustained the orders of the Secretary and settled the law so that henceforth the constitutional power to regulate interstate commerce does include the fixing of prices and does authorize the equalization device to equalize market advantages among those engaged in such commerce.

Whether and in what circumstances the price-fixing power should be employed to stabilize an industry is now a question that can be decided, as it should be decided, by the Congress on the basis of economic and administrative considerations. Congress is no longer powerless in the face of a demoralized industry engaged in interstate commerce.

### MUNICIPAL DEBTS

The Court sustained the constitutionality of a municipal bankruptcy law [4] in all essentials the same as one it had held unconstitutional two years before.[5] This opinion was by the Chief Justice and, while it recognized a distinction between the two statutes, it must be admitted that the distinction was pretty thin and was not visible to Mr. Justice McReynolds or Mr. Justice Butler, who dissented. Be that as it may, the decision enabled the Federal Government to extend the bankruptcy powers to the aid of munici-

---

[4] *United States* v. *Bekins,* 304 U. S. 27.

[5] *Ashton* v. *Cameron County Dist.,* 298 U. S. 513. (See discussion supra pp. 165–168.)

palities which, with the consent of two-thirds in amount of their creditors, desired to reorganize their municipal finances. The importance to the financial structure of the country of extending to public debtors the benefit of a law long available to private debtors, but until now denied to municipalities, has already been pointed out.

### TAXATION — IMMUNITY V. EQUALITY

In the important field of taxation the Court was even more forthright in abandoning old positions that had grown untenable. The Court had long been vexed by questions concerning immunity of state officers from federal taxation and of federal officers from state taxation. Marshall had held that the state had no power to tax the Bank of the United States, upon the ground that an instrumentality of the United States was immune from state taxation. After many years and many intervening decisions this doctrine was inverted in *Collector* v. *Day*,[6] and extended to hold that the Federal Government could not apply its income tax to the salary paid to an officer of a state — even though the representatives of the states in Congress set up no such exemption in the law.

This latter decision of 1870 completed the process by which the Court took the immunity which Marshall had held belonged to the Federal Government and transposed

[6] 11 Wall. 113.

it to state governments and, more than that, extended the governmental immunity to those private individuals who happened to be deriving their incomes from government service. However persuasive the argument for governmental immunity, there was little reason in law and none at all in sound government for holding that officeholders shared the government's immunity from tax.

This decision led to innumerable difficulties and fine-spun distinctions. As the states extended their activities and went into the distribution of liquor or into the operation of municipal electric or water plants or transportation systems, questions arose as to the extension of immunity to employees in such enterprises. The decisions of the courts became a confusing maze by which some gained immunities and others were subject to tax by technical distinctions, often without a substantial difference. Taxes " on " income from government were distinguished from taxes " measured by " such income; " proprietary " activities of the states were distinguished from " governmental "; " employees " of states were distinguished from " independent contractors." Of course the Constitution said nothing about such distinctions or about tax immunity at all.

We had been waiting for some time for a favorable opportunity in which to present to the Court a clear-cut challenge to the whole doctrine of immunity as applied to government officeholders. That opportunity came in *Graves* v. *O'Keefe*.[7] The State of New York asserted a right to tax the income received by an attorney for services to the Federal Home Owners' Loan Corporation. New York based its claim to a tax, not on a challenge to the immunity doctrine, but on a wholly untenable argument for an exception to the immunity. It asserted that the Home Owners' Loan Corporation employees were to be differently treated from employees of the United States because " the Home Owners' Loan Corporation has all the earmarks of a regular private business corporation."

The Government was not a party to the suit, but it afforded an opportunity to urge the Court to overthrow the whole doctrine of immunity and to do that in a case in which we would be conceding to the state a power to tax rather than asserting a broader scope to federal power. The Government intervened as *amicus curiae* and presented a challenge to the whole basis of the immunity of officeholders, both state and federal. The state, mindful of its own employees and sensing in our intervention a gift from the Greeks, characterized the Government's argument as " wholly impertinent "; but the Court took occasion to sweep out the entire doctrine of inter-governmental tax immunity in so far as it protected public officers from taxation. The Court said:

---

7 306 U. S. 466.

" The theory, which once won a qualified approval, that a tax on income is legally or economically a tax on its source, is no longer tenable, . . ."

and it concluded that:

". . . *Collector* v. *Day* [and other cases which followed in its steps] are overruled so far as they recognize an implied constitutional immunity from income taxation of the salaries of officers or employees of the national or a state government or their instrumentalities."

## TAXATION AND AN INDEPENDENT JUDICIARY

Judges of the United States courts were enjoying complete immunity from income tax on their salaries as a result of a judicial decision. A majority of the Justices had declared that federal income tax could not apply to the salary of a judge of the United States because it diminished his compensation in violation of the Constitution.[8] The Constitution protects the independence of the judiciary by providing that the compensation of judges shall not be reduced during their term of office. Its obvious purpose was to restrain the other branches of the government from coercing the judiciary by striking at their compensation. Mr. Justice Van Devanter had written a

---

[8] *Evans* v. *Gore*, 253 U. S. 245.

labored opinion to show that this prevented the judges from being taxed. Mr. Justice Holmes had vigorously dissented and, after quoting Hamilton as saying that " a power over a man's subsistence amounts to a power over his will," he continued:

" That is a very good reason for preventing attempts to deal with a judge's salary as such, but seems to me no reason for exonerating him from the ordinary duties of a citizen, which he shares with all others. To require a man to pay the taxes that all other men have to pay cannot possibly be made an instrument to attack his independence as a judge. I see nothing in the purpose of this clause of the Constitution to indicate that the judges were to be a privileged class, free from bearing their share of the cost of the institutions upon which their well-being if not their life depends."

Mr. Justice Brandeis concurred with Mr. Justice Holmes, but they were as a voice crying in the wilderness, and the entire federal judiciary was exempted from taxation on its salaries.

Bowing to this decision as immunizing judges appointed before the income tax became effective, Congress then attempted to tax newly created judges by providing in advance that their salaries should be subject to income tax, thereby attempting to avoid making the tax a diminution of their salaries " during their term of office." The judges, however, challenged even this as unconstitutional, and the Supreme Court was confronted with the question as to whether it would apply the self-serving *Evans* v. *Gore* opinion, as it had done once before,[9] to protect the newly appointed judges. The Government was in the awkward position of asking the Justices to vote themselves to be taxable.

The Court in *O'Malley* v. *Woodrough*[10] not only refused to extend the immunity to new judges, but it overruled the basis of immunity even as to all judges already in office. Mr. Justice Frankfurter, speaking for the majority, said:

" To suggest that it makes inroads upon the independence of judges who took office after Congress had thus charged them with the common duties of citizenship, by making them bear their aliquot share of the cost of maintaining the Government, is to trivialize the great historic experience on which the framers based the safeguards of Article III, § 1. To subject them to a general tax is merely to recognize that judges are also citizens, and that their particular function in government does not generate an immunity from sharing with their fellow citizens the material burden of the government whose Constitution and laws they are charged with administering."

---

9 *Miles* v. *Graham,* 268 U. S. 501 (1925).
10 307 U. S. 277.

Mr. Justice Butler dissented, as he had dissented from the decision denying immunity to public officers. He held to the older doctrine and said:

" For one convinced that the judgment now given is wrong, it is impossible to acquiesce or merely to note dissent. And so this opinion is written to indicate the grounds of opposition and to evidence regret that another landmark has been removed."

## THE UTILITY REBELLION

The Court greeted the year 1938 by declaring on January 3 that privately owned power companies had no standing to question the validity of federal loans and grants to aid the construction of municipally owned power plants.[11] It held that whatever injury resulted to the private power companies was the damage of lawful competition. This ruling was deemed of great importance by the Administration and by municipal ownership advocates and had been sought for from the beginning, as we have seen, in the case of *Duke Power Co.* v. *Greenwood County*,[12] but the Supreme Court had sent the case back without a decision because of technical defects in the record. Now, more than four years after Congress had embarked on a

11 *Alabama Power Co.* v. *Ickes,* 302 U. S. 464.
12 299 U. S. 259; see the discussion *supra,* pp. 199–201.

public works program, it was unanimously decided that the power companies, which had succeeded in holding up by injunction virtually all the proposed municipal electric projects, had no legal standing to question the source of the funds for financing the projects. And so at long last the injunctions were dissolved, and the courts withdrew from this area of economic conflict.

Also awaiting termination by the Court was one of the most bitter and spectacular battles of the Administration, likewise involving the utility industry. The Public Utility Holding Company Act of 1935 had been one of the most important acts of the New Deal. At the height of the Congressional struggle a campaign of telegrams to Senators and Congressmen threatened it with defeat. But the utility lobby overplayed its hand and brought on an investigation. It was then disclosed that telegrams were largely sent by employees of interested utility companies who promiscuously signed the names of persons taken from such sources as telephone directories, and without their knowledge or permission.

After the Act passed, the far-flung utility holding company systems of the country united their efforts and flatly refused obedience to the Act until it should be enforced by the courts. It was pointed out to them in vain that the Act was presumed to be valid until found otherwise and that it was their duty to obey until relieved by the courts, instead of to disobey until compelled by the courts. Many of the utility industry regarded its " sit-down strike " against the Government as bad strategy and doubtful citizenship.[13] However, the industry was dominated by narrow and stubborn financial adventurers who had built up great utility empires with other people's money. Under the advice of their lawyers they had organized the Edison Electric Institute, and it had participated in the highly questionable proceedings at Baltimore which the Supreme Court had refused to accept as a test case.[14] The constituent companies of the Institute had also tried to deluge the Department of Justice with lawsuits which the Supreme Court had permitted to be stayed until the trial of the test case.[15]

Shortly before the Public Utility Holding Company

---

13 Roger Babson, business adviser and director in public utility holding companies, sent a letter to utilities officials shortly before the registration deadline, saying:

" In this crisis a lapse by us into lawlessness would do more to degrade and damage the utilities than any attack made by hostile critics. It would be hailed as proof that some of the severest charges made against this industry are perhaps true.

" Irrespective of the moral questions involved in registration, we public utility directors would be playing directly into the hands of Communists, Socialists and Fascists by flouting the law at this critical time. How can we expect radical groups to abide by democratic principles if we ourselves are to defy the law whenever it suits our convenience! . . .

" Naturally we all cannot approve every feature of this act or some other features of the so-called New Deal legislation. We do not relish heavy income taxes, the new estate taxes and various other Administration policies. Nevertheless our plain duty as citizens of a democracy is to obey its laws.

" All of us are better off than if we lived in any other country on the face of the globe."

See *The Washington Daily News,* December 4, 1935.

14 See discussion of this case *supra,* pp. 119–121.
15 See discussion of this case *supra,* pp. 197–8.

Act was to become effective, the much-sued Securities and
Exchange Commission boldly took the offensive and
brought a suit in the Southern District of New York to
compel the Electric Bond and Share Company and a number of its holding subsidiaries to register as required by
the Act. This company was one of the largest and oldest
and most respectable of the holding company systems.
The Government won the case in the district court and
in the Circuit Court of Appeals for the Second Circuit.
The issue was pending in the Supreme Court.

The Public Utility Holding Company Act was based on
extensive investigations by Congressional committees and
upon an exhaustive study of the electric power industry by
the Federal Trade Commission, running into some seventy
volumes. The Act was one of the most carefully drafted
regulatory acts ever passed, and the utility holding company exploiters knew their lush days were over if it could
not be thrown out by the courts.

Broadly speaking, the Act provided for regulation by
the Securities and Exchange Commission of those public
utility holding companies whose activities transcended
state lines. The Act did not attempt any regulation whatever of local or operating utility companies, but only of
holding companies which actually controlled electric or gas
utility companies. The Act required utility holding companies either to register or to cease from doing business
in interstate commerce. Upon registration the Commis-

sion had extensive regulatory powers over the issuance of securities, the acquisition of securities and utility assets, the making and performance of service contracts, and other inter-company transactions. It required detailed reports and authorized the requirement of uniform accounting. The Act also authorized the Commission to formulate and ultimately to enforce plans for the reorganization and corporate simplification of holding companies to bring them within the policy of the Act. This provision, similar to the dissolution decrees long used by courts against violators of the Sherman Anti-Trust Act, was labeled by the utility propagandists " The Death Sentence," and they pleaded for its unconstitutionality like condemned prisoners for a pardon.

The suit was based upon the provisions of the Act which required registration. Unregistered holding companies were prohibited from using the mails or instrumentalities of interstate commerce to negotiate or perform service, sales, or construction contracts for any public utility company or for making any offering of securities or for negotiating for any assets. They were also prohibited from operating utility assets for the distribution of gas or electric energy in interstate commerce and were denied the right to own or control any security of any subsidiary company which did any of those things. Registration was, therefore, compelled, and upon registration the other regulatory provisions of the Act became effective.

The Bond and Share Company system, which the Government selected for its test case, had acquired control of gas and electric properties in thirty-two states, from Pennsylvania to Oregon and from Minnesota to Florida. The system served approximately two and a half million electric customers and derived therefrom in a year $214,-600,000. This exceeds the annual revenues of any state in the United States with the exception of New York. More than twenty-five per cent of all the electric energy transmitted across state lines in the United States was handled by Bond and Share subsidiaries, and the system handled approximately fifteen per cent of all the electric energy generated in the United States. It also handled more than twenty per cent of the gas transmitted across state lines. Its gas system operated in fifteen states of the United States and Mexico, with a million and a half acres of producing gas lands under lease and more than six thousand miles of main gas line. It served 450,000 gas customers, and its annual operating revenues from gas sales in 1935 amounted to approximately $45,000,000.

The Bond and Share Company was organized in 1905 by the General Electric Company with a modest capitalization of $4,000,000. Beginning in 1927, Bond and Share began to expand its capitalization. It rose from $50,-000,000 in 1926 to $300,000,000 in 1929, and its surplus was carried up to a figure in excess of $670,000,000. At the time of the trial its stock was capitalized on its books at a stated value of $171,901,233, and its surplus at $371,-108,201, while the combined market value of its outstanding securities was only about $237,000,000.

The Federal Trade Commission had found write-ups in the capital accounts of Bond and Share's domestic subsidiaries which it computed at $458,902,664. Subsequent write-downs totaled $196,839,000. The total utility assets controlled by Bond and Share exceeded a billion dollars in 1927.

Bond and Share's control over a major part of the great utility industry had been financed through sale of non-voting securities to the public while it maintained control by investing only a relatively small amount of its own funds in stocks with the voting power. More than eight hundred thousand persons held securities in the system.

The Bond and Share system for many years maintained a servicing system for nearly all of its subsidiaries. For a service fee it did all of the work — executive, managerial, and financial — of the underlying holding companies, with one exception. These service contracts with its subsidiaries were entered into with no semblance of arms-length bargaining. It also supervised construction work and purchased supplies for the various companies. By these devices the top holding company extended its control down to the finest detail of operation of the local companies. Its service fees for these services from 1926 to 1931 had ranged from over $6,000,000 to about $10,000,000 per year, and from 1932 to 1935 had ranged from about $2,700,000 to over $3,900,000. The Federal Trade Commission had concluded in 1931 that the net profits realized from services during 1931 were one hundred thirteen per cent in excess of the expenses attributable to such services.

The suit to test the Holding Company Act was brought against Bond and Share because it touched the Act at more points than any other system, and not because of any claim that Bond and Share had been guilty of more abuses than other systems. In fact, Bond and Share would have to be ranked as one of the best of the utility holding company empires.

As a whole, the holding companies had been guilty of grave abuses. They had purchased electric properties at extravagant prices and had then written them up to scandalous valuations and unloaded inflated securities on the public on the basis of the write-up. They had been under pressure to squeeze the maximum possible revenue out of operating companies. They resisted reasonable rate reductions which would have increased the consumption of gas and electricity. Unfair insiders' profits were realized through a great variety of inter-company transactions. They obstructed state regulation and concentrated the actual control in the hands of a few powerful groups which had a relatively insignificant stake in the ownership of the properties they manipulated for their own ends. They had concentrated control of these great industries and destroyed local ownership and local initiative. They were utterly beyond the reach of any state to regulate, and now their ablest lawyers announced that neither had the United States any power to control their operations.

On March 28, 1938, the Supreme Court brought the public utility holding company rebellion to an end in an opinion by Mr. Chief Justice Hughes in which he sustained the constitutionality of the Act in all respects in which the Government then sought to enforce it.[16] The Court declined the invitation of the utilities to pass upon, and strike down, the whole structure of the law, including the host of provisions, such as the " death sentence," which could affect the utilities only after administrative proceedings were had. The Court declined to let itself, instead of the Commission, be made the battleground, or to anticipate the outcome of the proceedings there. Mr. Justice McReynolds was the sole dissenter.

Still another phase of the attack by the utilities came to an end on January 30, 1939, when the Court decided *Tennessee Electric Power Co.* v. *Tennessee Valley Authority.*[17] After the Government had succeeded in sustaining the constitutional validity of the Wilson Dam,[18] nineteen electric power companies brought an action to enjoin the Tennessee Valley Authority from generating, distributing, and selling electric power and from other acts alleged to be

---

16 *Electric Bond Co.* v. *Comm'n,* 303 U. S. 419.
17 306 U. S. 118.
18 *Ashwander* v. *Valley Authority,* 297 U. S. 288; see pp. 142–6.

harmful and destructive competition with privately owned
utilities. This presented a real test of the constitutionality
of the Government's experiment in the Tennessee Valley,
which rested upon a coordinated engineering project to
create and maintain a continuous 9-foot waterway
throughout the 650-mile length of the Tennessee River
through a series of dams as aids both to navigation and to
flood control. It was intended to convert the water power
created by these projects into electric energy and sell it to
municipalities, rural cooperatives, and industrial consumers. The Government proposed to sell the power at wholesale. The power companies contended that if the river
was to be improved for navigation the works constructed
should be a series of low dams, which would be incapable
of creating a head for water power. Faced with the fact
that such structures would also be incapable of controlling
floods, the companies minimized the need of flood control
and finally suggested a novel type of reservoir, whose
chief virtue seemed to be that it would produce no power
and would destroy the potentialities of the river system
for power.

All this despite the fact that for a generation the leaders of the conservation movement, from the first Roosevelt
on down, had been preaching the sensible gospel of making
a river system " pay its way," by conserving its power
resources at the same time that it is developed for navigation and flood control. " It is poor business," Theodore

Roosevelt pointed out in 1908, " to develop a river for navigation in such a way as to prevent its use for power, when by a little foresight it could be made to serve both purposes." [19] If the Government could lawfully adopt this policy of conservation, the utilities contended, then at least the power created by the multiple-purpose dams must be turned over to the private companies for resale by them to consumers. That the Government should dispose of this power at wholesale to municipalities and rural cooperatives, the utilities argued, was a threat of illegal and destructive competition.

This case thus brought from Congress to the courts conflicting social philosophies which produced conflicting engineering projects. It was conceded that giant flood control and navigation projects could, as a practical matter, be undertaken and financed only by the Government. But it was the philosophy of many business, banking, and utility interests that the power created thereby must pass to the public only through the intervention of private interests who would be in a position to profit by their position as intermediaries. The thought of this publicly created power flowing to the consumers without a profit to some private interest en route was terrifying to them. The argument was an old one in new dress. Andrew Jackson led a struggle to grant western lands directly from the

___
[19] Message transmitting preliminary report of Inland Waterways Commission, Sen. Doc. 325, 60th Cong., 1st sess.

government to homesteaders who would live upon them,[20] thus eliminating land companies which had taken up great tracts to resell to the settlers at a profit.[21] James Buchanan, on the other hand, vetoed a proposal to grant public lands to homesteaders at a low price upon the ground that such a cheap land policy, obviously a detriment to speculators, would introduce among us " pernicious social theories." [22] The great reclamation program which brought life to the arid West was bitterly assailed because it was not left to private hands. " The United States is not a dealer in real estate," said the minority report on the Reclamation Act of 1902, " and has not the constitutional power to become such; it is not a real estate improvement society and has not the constitutional power to become such." [23] The same philosophy now demanded that publicly created power on the road to public consumption must pass through a private bottle neck at which a profit could be taken, and anyone who opposed this taking was an enemy of private business.

The course of this case in the lower courts was most unusual. The utility companies brought their suit in a state court in the State of Tennessee, and the Government removed the case to the United States District Court for

[20] Colyar, A. S.: *The Life and Times of Andrew Jackson.* Marshall & Bruce Co.; 1904. Vol. 2, p. 672.

[21] Richardson, James D.: *Messages and Papers of the Presidents.* Government Printing Office; 1896. Vol. 2, p. 601; Vol. 3, p. 68.

[22] Id. Vol. 5, p. 614.

[23] H. Rep. 794, Part 2, 57th Cong., 1st sess., p. 10.

Eastern Tennessee, although it reached a hardly more favorably disposed tribunal than the one from which it had fled. The utilities asked and promptly obtained a temporary injunction, but on appeal it was reversed. During the delay occasioned by the application for a temporary injunction, the Act of August 24, 1937 was passed [24] which required a court of three judges. This took the control of the case away from the hostile district judge, and the court of three judges after an extensive trial dismissed the bill. Had the private utilities proceeded at once to try the merits of the case instead of warring over a temporary injunction, the case might have been decided by Judge Gore, sitting alone, and it is reasonably certain that the findings of the district court would then have been less favorable to the Government. It was a case where the tactics of the day proved bad strategy for the campaign.

During the course of this proceeding in the lower courts there were fantastic injunctions and counter-injunctions by which courts enjoined courts, and the weaknesses of legal procedure were exploited by astute counsel.[25]

The Supreme Court, however, held that the franchises of the private power companies do not grant them a freedom from competition and that the companies could not maintain their action to enjoin the Federal Government from its program of wholesale power distribution. There

[24] 28 U. S. C. A., Sec. 380(a).
[25] See pp. 121–2.

was a strong dissent by Mr. Justice McReynolds and Mr. Justice Butler, but the utilities had then lost their last stand. The practical upshot of the case was that the private utility interests sold many existing facilities and retired from Tennessee Valley territory.

The legal upshot of the case was that the Court found that objections to public competition were not a matter for judicial settlement, but for legislative and administrative adjustment.

The utilities and their holding companies thus waged a long contest with the Government on many fronts to prevent federal regulation, to prevent utilization of public dams for generation of electric energy, and to prevent federal aid to municipalities and farm cooperatives which desired to finance distribution of such power. But, except in local courts, they uniformly lost in their appeal that judicial power take the electric power companies under its protecting wing to shield them from such regulation and competition as the popularly chosen branches of government thought proper.

## CHILD LABOR AMENDMENT

The Court was asked by opponents of the Child Labor Amendment, which had been pending for some thirteen years without getting the requisite number of state ratifications, to hold that it was no longer capable of ratification. In refusing so to declare, the Court characterized the issue as a " political question," that is, one to be settled exclusively by the political branches of the government.

This amendment had been proposed to overcome the effect of the Court's child labor decisions which had prevented the Federal Government from taking any effective steps to discourage child labor by taxation or even to exclude its products from interstate commerce. The difficulty of amending the Constitution to make sure that it says what it already was intended to say was illustrated by the fate of the proposed amendment. In the effort to use language broad enough so that judicial construction could not again mutilate it, a sweeping authority to the Federal Government was proposed. Its breadth aroused the apprehensions of many people, some of whom had no sympathy with the Court's disposition of the *Child Labor* cases. But because of these apprehensions it made slow progress towards ratification.

Meanwhile, those who were opposed sought to kill the amendment judicially. Had they succeeded, the precedent thus created would have placed serious restrictions upon the amending process for all time to come. Members of the state legislatures of Kansas and Kentucky endeavored to nullify the ratifying votes of those bodies through litigation. They contended that, since the amendment had been pending a long time, the Court could judicially declare it to be dead merely by holding that a reasonable time for ratification had already elapsed. They further sought a declaration that a state having once rejected the amendment lost all power to ratify it thereafter. The latter contention would have cast doubt on the adoption of the Fourteenth Amendment. The Court, however, declined the invitation to assume control of the amending process and left the function of amendment where the Constitution placed it, with the legislative branch of the government.[26] The Court wrote four opinions, which leaves the case somewhat unsatisfactory as a precedent, but it left the amending process free. The Court however had rendered decisions which virtually overruled *Hammer* v. *Dagenhart*, and thereby removed the need for the Child Labor Amendment and demonstrated that the fault to be corrected was not in the Constitution itself but in its interpretation.

## ADMINISTRATIVE AGENCIES — INTERLOPERS OR PARTNERS?

In the litigation entitled *United States* v. *Morgan*, the Supreme Court has come to grips with a new phase of an old controversy as to the relation between the judiciary and the administrative agencies of the government.

The first decision of the Supreme Court in this litigation was regarded as a significant admonition to and disci-

---

[26] *Coleman* v. *Miller*, 307 U. S. 433.

pline of administrative agencies, but the later course of
the litigation has become an admonition to the judiciary.
The case has been pending in the federal courts for up-
wards of six years; it has been tried four times in the
District Court, each time before a court of three judges;
it has three times been appealed to the Supreme Court;
and it is now on its way to the Supreme Court again. And
the Supreme Court has never yet passed on the ultimate
merits, but only on questions of procedure.

After hearings and rehearings before an examiner, the
Secretary of Agriculture, on June 14, 1933, held the rates
charged to farmers by the commission brokers at the Kansas City Stock Yards were excessive, and he fixed maximum charges pursuant to the Packers and Stockyards Act.
The brokers at once sought from the District Court an
order to set aside the Secretary's decision. They complained, among other things, that they did not have a full
and fair hearing as required by the Act, because the Secretary had not personally weighed all of the evidence presented before the examiner and also because they had not
been served with a tentative report informing them what
the Secretary proposed to decide. The District Court
itself reviewed the evidence and upheld the rates as fixed
by the Secretary and overruled, without hearing evidence,
the complaint that they had been denied a fair trial.

At the 1935 term, the Supreme Court reversed without
passing on the rates. It held that the brokers were en-

titled to a chance to prove that the Secretary had not personally weighed the evidence and thereby had failed to give a fair trial. But at the same time the Supreme Court rejected their complaint that they had not been served with a tentative report showing what the Secretary proposed to decide. The Court pointed out that while service of such a report was desirable practice, its absence did " not go to the root of the matter " and its service was not " essential to the validity of the hearing." [27]

The second trial took place in the District Court. The Supreme Court had sent the case back for retrial, with the statement that the only one of the objections which, if proved, would invalidate the Secretary's order was the claim that the Secretary had not personally considered the evidence or argument. The District Court therefore confined new evidence to that issue, which it regarded as the only one open, and it found that the Secretary had personally considered the evidence and argument. The District Court also reiterated that it found evidence to sustain the Secretary's order and so again overruled the broker's complaint.

On a second appeal the Supreme Court apparently reached the same conclusion as to the consideration of the evidence and argument by the Secretary, but it then revived the question as to a tentative report which it had previously declared not " essential to the validity of the

---

[27] *Morgan* v. *United States,* 298 U. S. 468, 478.

hearing." Now it held the proceeding " fatally defective " because no such report was served.[28] Again it reversed without considering whether the evidence justified the rates as fixed.

The two opinions seemed inconsistent, and the Solicitor General filed a petition for reargument which bluntly said so. The Court resorted to the unusual practice of writing a sharp *per curiam* opinion defending its consistency against what it considered the unwarranted statements of the Solicitor General.[29] The heated reply by the Court would probably have ended the matter, except that several hundred thousand dollars had been paid into the District Court to await final decision. That came about because the District Court had allowed the brokers during the litigation to collect the higher rates from the farmers, but had ordered the amounts in excess of the rates as reduced by the Secretary to be paid into court for distribution in accordance with the final decision. So the Solicitor General asked the Supreme Court to hear reargument as to what disposition should be made of the money. The Court was in no mood to do that either and shipped the whole case back to the District Court, saying that the issue of ownership of the impounded fund was for that court to decide. But the District Court, which had twice tried to decide the merits of the question as to the rates, was unable to find

---

28 *Morgan* v. *United States,* 304 U. S. 1.
29 *Morgan* v. *United States,* 304 U. S. 23.

any issue to try — it considered that the Supreme Court's decision left it no discretion, and it ordered the money paid to the brokers. The Government appealed and so, after another year's delay, the case bounced back to the Supreme Court to decide who owned the excess payments or at least to decide whether its previous decisions foreclosed disposition of the moneys in accordance with what the lower courts had held to be just charges to the farmers. After one argument the Court requested another. By this time it was apparent that the Court was on the spot even more than the Secretary had been. Its dilemma was this:

The lower court which had now ordered the money paid to the brokers had twice held that it represented collections in excess of a fair and lawful rate. It had said of the Secretary's decision:

" This court has found that those findings not only are supported by some evidence, but also that they are supported by the weight of the evidence. Upon its own independent consideration of the evidence this court arrived at the same findings as those which were reached by subordinates of and by the Secretary."

But the lower court, as the consequence of a decision by the Supreme Court which had not even decided that point, but reversed only on a question of procedure, felt compelled to pay the impounded money over to those who it had twice held were not fairly entitled to it. In giving the brokers a full hearing with a tentative report, the Supreme Court had taken the money away from the farmers with no hearing on the rates at all in Supreme Court. This was claimed to be the inexorable legal logic of the Supreme Court's action.

The Government appealed to the Supreme Court, however, and contended that no right to the moneys could accrue to the brokers as a result of a procedural error of the Secretary and that the impounded fund should be distributed according to equity and good conscience and after a decision upon the evidence as to fairness of the rates.

The Supreme Court heard argument as to whether it was legally necessary that the five or six years' litigation should result in the payment of the money to the parties who were found by the only court that passed on the merits not to be entitled to it, or whether the Court would grant the farmers a hearing on the merits, either before the Secretary or the lower court, before disbursing the funds. The result was that the Court extricated itself from the consequences of its decision by holding that the procedural error could be corrected by the Secretary himself; and the Court, as if scolding itself, said:[30]

". . . in construing a statute setting up an administrative agency and providing for judicial review of its action, court and agency are not to be regarded as wholly

---

30 *United States* v. *Morgan,* 307 U. S. 183, 191.

independent and unrelated instrumentalities of justice, each acting in the performance of its prescribed statutory duty without regard to the appropriate function of the other in securing the plainly indicated objects of the statute. Court and agency are the means adopted to attain the prescribed end, and so far as their duties are defined by the words of the statute, those words should be construed so as to attain that end through coordinated action. Neither body should repeat in this day the mistake made by the courts of law when equity was struggling for recognition as an ameliorating system of justice; neither can rightly be regarded by the other as an alien intruder, to be tolerated if must be, but never to be encouraged or aided by the other in the attainment of the common aim."

It fell back on the inherent power of a court of equity to control its processes to prevent any injustice. Mr. Justice Butler, Mr. Justice McReynolds, and Mr. Justice Roberts took the view, in a dissent, that the strictly logical results of the previous decision bound the Court to deliver the impounded funds to the commission brokers, regardless of the equities.

Had such a view prevailed, interests litigating before administrative tribunals might gain or lose substantive rights because the tribunal made errors in its procedure. This would have defeated the very purpose for which such tribunals had been introduced — elimination of technicalities of procedure, cheapening the cost of litigation, and speeding up of decision.

The creation of these fact-finding tribunals had been one of the significant legal movements of the twentieth century. Administrative fact-finding is especially important to the Federal Government because, if judicial bodies must be used for such purposes, the Constitution compels the appointment of the members for life. The administrative fact-finding tribunal has been the heart of nearly every social or economic reform of this century. Workmen's compensation systems, regulation of railroad and utility rates, the Securities Act, the Labor Relations Act, and many other regulatory plans would fail if the administrative body charged with enforcement could be smothered in litigation similar to that in the *Morgan* case.

The problems which grow out of the use of the administrative tribunal are not peculiar to the New Deal. Some agencies have been guilty at times of injudicious conduct, and at times extreme assertions of power have been made in their behalf. It was once — in the administration of William Howard Taft — contended that an administrative tribunal's decision of fact bound the courts, even though there was no evidence in the record to sustain it, and the party affected had no chance to meet or refute evidence. It was then argued that the Court must presume that the commission had evidence to sustain its decision, even if it was not put into the record.[31]

But no claim to such arbitrary authority has ever been asserted by any administrative tribunal in recent years, and the controversy as to the constitutionality of fact-finding by such bodies was settled by the Supreme Court in *Crowell* v. *Benson* [32] more than a year before President Roosevelt took office.

But the controversy will not down. The lawyers have never liked the informal procedures of these commissions and administrative bodies, which often have laymen as members. These bodies are given the enforcement of new laws which excite the bitterest animosities and affect the largest interests. On the other hand, friends of effective government point out that it is impossible effectively to establish such policies as the Truth-in-Securities Act or the Labor Relations Act without the administrative agency, and they battle to establish them and to maintain their powers. The Supreme Court's work is increasingly that of reviewing the determinations of such bodies and its declaration in the latest decision of the *Morgan* case leaves no doubt that its spirit will be one of cooperation with, not one of hostility to, such agencies as Congress creates.

A similarly cooperative attitude toward administrative agencies as partners in the administration of law was taken

---

[31] *Interstate Com. Comm.* v. *Louisville & Nash. R. R.*, 227 U. S. 88.
[32] 285 U. S. 22.

in a case in which the Supreme Court was obliged to discipline the Circuit Court of Appeals for the Third Circuit — a court long notorious for its antipathy to labor and to the Government, as well as for an unenviable record of being reversed.[33] Happily this important court has now been reconstituted; in fact, at the time of this decision it had one new judge who stoutly dissented from its excesses of power.

The National Labor Relations Board had entered an order against Republic Steel Corporation, and Republic claimed that the Board had made an error in procedure somewhat similar to that in the *Morgan* case which denied it the full hearing which the law allowed. Thereupon the Board attempted to correct the error by giving Republic another hearing, but Republic did not want the error corrected. It wanted to use the error as the basis for declaring void the whole order which required it to reinstate many men with pay. In other words, it valued the error more than it valued its right to a full hearing.

The judges of the Third Circuit Court of Appeals at this point issued an order, the effect of which was to restrain the Board from correcting its error and to force a final hearing on the merits of the Board's order without allowing the correction of what Republic had complained of as an error. There was utterly no authority for such inter-

---

[33] Cf. Report of Solicitor General in *1938 Report of the Attorney General* for statistical record of this court, p. 31.

ference by that court with the proceedings still pending in the administrative agency.

On May 31, the Supreme Court, Mr. Justice Butler and Mr. Justice McReynolds dissenting, issued its extraordinary writ of prohibition and mandamus to require the judges of the Third Circuit to cease this unlawful inter-ference with the procedure of the Labor Relations Board.[34]

## A VOLUNTEERED CONFESSION OF A CENTURY OF ERROR

Perhaps the most remarkable decision of this period and in some respects one of the most remarkable in the Court's history was that of *Erie Railroad Co. v. Tompkins.*[35] This decision reversed the ninety-six-year-old-doctrine of *Swift v. Tyson* [36] under which the federal courts had been making their own law in the fields of commercial law, negligence, and the like, in disregard of the state courts' decisions, where the state legislature had not passed a statute covering the point.

The significance of the overruling of this doctrine has probably not been fully appreciated.[37] It was a change of a legal doctrine, the very existence of which was but lit-

---

[34] In re *Labor Board,* 304 U. S. 486.
[35] 304 U. S. 64.
[36] 16 Pet. 1.
[37] For full discussion of the history of this case, see my address " The Rise and Fall of Swift v. Tyson: A Dramatic Episode." Amer. Bar Assn. Journal, Vol. XXIV, p. 609 (Aug. 1938).

tle known outside of the legal profession. The change was not impelled by " supervening economic events," nor was it a part of the program of any political party. The change was made on the initiative of a majority of the Court itself, without even a demand by a litigant or argument of the point at the bar. It involved a volunteered confession that the federal judiciary almost from the foundation of our government has pursued a course clearly unconstitutional, has all these years been exercising a power not conferred by the Constitution, and in so doing has invaded rights reserved by the Constitution to the several states.

When the federal courts first began to hear cases which involved no issue of federal statutory or constitutional law, but over which they had jurisdiction solely because they arose from controversies between citizens of different states, they were confronted with the question, " Where will the Court get the law it applies in such cases? " Congress attempted to answer the question by enacting Section 34 of the Judiciary Act of 1789 which provided that : " The laws of the several States . . . shall be regarded as rules of decision in trials of common law, in the courts of the United States, in cases where they apply." This made it clear that the federal court must follow " the laws of the several States " but in that day few rules of law had been codified or reduced to statute, and the law of contracts, negotiable instruments, negligence, and many other subjects was to be found only in decisions of the courts. Lawyers promptly questioned whether the Judiciary Act bound the federal courts to follow the state court decisions, for in a technical sense it was said decisions were not " laws."

This placed before the federal courts a dilemma, and they have since shifted from horn to horn finding either position very uncomfortable. If they followed state court decisions, which often conflict, the Supreme Court might one day declare one rule of law, and the next day a contrary one, depending on the state whose laws were applicable. On the other hand, if the federal courts made up and declared their own rules, they might be uniform for federal courts, but they would be applied only in the few cases where one could get into federal courts, which would often be because of purely accidental factors. So the federal courts found, and they still find, that if they are to be uniform among themselves they must be at variance with some of the states; if they try to be uniform with the state in which they sit, they are then at variance among themselves.

Prior to 1842 the Court had been more anxious to avoid a conflict of decisions between state and federal courts sitting within a state and deciding similar questions. In 1814, Justice Bushrod Washington, sitting at circuit, pointed out the danger of this conflict and said: [38]

---

[38] 3 Wash. 313.

" The injustice as well as the absurdity of the former [federal courts] deciding by one rule, and the latter [state courts] by another, would be too monstrous to find a place in any system of government."

But in 1842 the Court reversed its first position on the question and shifted to the other horn of the dilemma. What was pronounced absurd and monstrous in 1814 became the law in 1842. In making this change the Court was undoubtedly influenced by a desire to promote uniformity of federal decision, which would not be possible if state decisions controlled them, and also through the persuasive example of uniform federal court decisions to promote uniformity of state decisions. And so in reaching the decision of *Swift* v. *Tyson*, Justice Story proceeded to lay down the rule that on questions of general commercial law the decisions of the courts of the state were not binding on the federal courts sitting there, and that the federal courts were free to apply the rules of the common law in accordance with their judgment of what those rules were. Quoting Cicero, that the law is not one thing at Rome and another at Athens, Justice Story in effect concluded that the same must be true of New York and Boston. As for Section 34 of the Judiciary Act of 1789, which provided that " The laws of the several States, . . . shall be regarded as rules of decision in trials of common law, in the

courts of the United States, in cases where they apply,"
he ruled that the concept of laws as there used was limited to statute laws and perhaps also to well-settled local
usages in matters of purely local concern, such as title to
real estate. Accordingly, Justice Story announced independence of the federal courts in matters of " general
law," such as ordinary commercial law, and that the federal courts could apply rules of their own different from
those which would be applied if the case were tried in a
state court.

The Court's shift from one kind of confusion and conflict to another was followed by an aftermath that could
not have been anticipated. The newly announced power
of the federal courts to disregard the decisions of a state
grew by what it fed on.

*Gelpcke* v. *Dubuque*,[39] together with its sequels, deserves
special attention. Certain Iowa cities and counties had
issued bonds for the purchase of stock in railroad companies which were extending their lines westward. The
validity of the bonds under the Constitution of Iowa was
challenged, and the Iowa court, in a series of divided
decisions, had sustained the power of municipalities to
issue the bonds and take the railroads' stock. The question, however, appeared not to be regarded as settled, and
finally the Supreme Court of Iowa in a unanimous decision overruled its former decisions and held the bonds to

[39] 1 Wall. 175.

be invalid and the municipalities not liable to the bond-holders. But when non-resident bondholders brought suit in the federal court and carried the case to the Supreme Court of the United States, a contrary judgment was rendered holding the bondholders entitled to recover against the municipalities.

This was the beginning of a most unseemly conflict between the Iowa courts and the federal courts on the question of municipal bonds. The result was that whether a bondholder could recover against a municipality depended upon whether he could get into a federal court by reason of citizenship outside of Iowa. The Supreme Court compelled the levy of a local tax to pay federal court judgments on the bonds even though a statute of Iowa limited the amount of taxes to be levied annually, and even though that limitation had already been reached.[40] It was in the latter case that Justice Miller gave vent to the personal suffering which these decisions occasioned him, particularly when he was called upon, sitting at circuit, to enforce the federal decrees in his own State of Iowa. He said:

" These frequent dissents in this class of subjects are as distasteful to me as they can be to any one else. But when I am compelled, as I was last spring, by the decisions of this court, to enter an order to commit to jail at one

---

[40] *Butz* v. *City of Muscatine,* 8 Wall. 575.

time over a hundred of the best citizens of Iowa, for obeying as they thought their oath of office required them to do, an injunction issued by a competent court of their own State, founded, as these gentlemen conscientiously believed, on the true interpretation of their own statute, an injunction which, in my own private judgment, they were legally bound to obey, I must be excused if, when sitting here, I give expression to convictions which my duty compels me to disregard in the Circuit Court."

It is evident, of course, that in these matters of commercial law, involving the validity of bonds and the liability of stockholders, the independence of the federal courts created conflict in the name of uniformity. The same was true in the field of tort liability. The doctrine of *Swift* v. *Tyson* assumed dominion here, too. The result depended in any case on whether the action could be brought in a federal court, if the rule there was more favorable to the plaintiff, or could be removed to a federal court if the rule there was more favorable to the defendant. Characterizing this state of affairs, George Wharton Pepper observed, writing in 1889: [41]

" Of two persons sitting in the same seat in a train, and injured in the same accident, one can recover in damages and the other cannot. Surely this state of things

---

[41] Pepper, George Wharton: *The Border Land of Federal and State Decisions.*

approaches very nearly to that which has excited much comment among eminent jurists, who tell us that so great was the mingling of nations and national laws after the downfall of the Roman Empire, that of four men sitting on the same bench each was presumably governed by a different law."

Perhaps the chief beneficiaries of the doctrine of *Swift* v. *Tyson* were corporations doing business in a number of states. Such a corporation could claim that it was a citizen only of the state of its incorporation, and so when sued elsewhere, where they did business, they could remove cases freely to the federal courts on the ground of diversity of citizenship.[42] Where the corporation was the plaintiff, it likewise had an advantage. A Delaware corporation suing a New York citizen with respect to a transaction in New York could bring suit there in either the federal or state court; but the defendant could not remove the case from a state to a federal court, being a citizen and resident of the state where suit was brought.

In considering the extent to which uniformity may have been promoted, account must be taken of other factors than the rule of *Swift* v. *Tyson*. State courts may be brought into harmony with one another by recourse to exposition of the law in semi-authoritative treatises or by

---

42 Cf. Frankfurter: "Distribution of Judicial Power between United States and State Courts," 13 Cornell L. Q. 499, 524.

common training of lawyers and judges in modern law schools, or by the work of organizations like the American Law Institute and the Commissioners on Uniform State Laws.[43]

But even if uniformity in rules of law was promoted by the practice of the federal courts, that conclusion would not establish that *Swift* v. *Tyson* was a sound or wise doctrine. There remains the further and fundamental question whether the making of uniform rules of law should be entrusted to the federal judiciary in the fields where the national legislature is powerless to act.[44] It is not merely that the legislature is entitled to share at least equally in the law-making process. The most serious objection is that the national legislature was powerless to alter rules of law after they were declared by the federal courts in such matters as ordinary commercial law and torts.

The anomaly was particularly striking in the case of the law of insurance. At the very time when the federal courts were announcing or making rules of law with respect to the construction and enforcement of insurance contracts, the Supreme Court refused to reconsider its long-standing decision that insurance is not commerce.[45] Thus the making of insurance law was held to be within

---

[43] Cf. Shulman: "The Demise of Swift v. Tyson," 47 Yale L. J., 1336, 1349 (June 1938).

[44] Cf. Dobie: "Seven Implications of Swift v. Tyson." 16 Va. L. Rev., 225, 234; Hornblower: "Conflict Between Federal and State Decisions," 14 Am. L. Rev. 211, 226.

[45] *New York Life Insurance Co.* v. *Deer Lodge County,* 231 U. S. 495.

federal judicial power, but not within federal Congressional power.

With American jurisprudence in this tangle, one Harry Tompkins took a walk on the Erie Railroad Company's right of way in Pennsylvania. He was injured by a swinging door of a freight car in a passing train. Tompkins then took a trip to the law, and there he got hit by a swinging Supreme Court, and his experience illuminates both the operation of the rule of *Swift* v. *Tyson* and the effect of the judicial process of law-making by the case system.

Tompkins did not sue in the courts of the State of Pennsylvania where the accident occurred. The Erie Railroad happened to be incorporated in the State of New York. And so a federal court would have jurisdiction because Tompkins, a citizen of Pennsylvania, was suing a corporation for jurisdictional purposes treated as a citizen of New York. This was luck for Tompkins, for the Pennsylvania court decisions were highly unfavorable to a trespasser on a railroad right of way. Tompkins sued in the Southern District of New York, which was clearly justified by *Swift* v. *Tyson* in applying the rule of so-called " federal common law " developed by the federal courts in the exercise of their independent judgment, rather than being bound by state law. The federal rule was more tolerant of the trespasser, and Tompkins was awarded a verdict of $30,000 by the jury. The Circuit

Court of Appeals for the Second Circuit affirmed, and Tompkins must have felt pretty sure of his money.

His confidence might well have been shaken, however, when the Supreme Court granted the railroad's application to review. The railroad asked to be relieved of the judgment but not on any argument that involved a repudiation of *Swift* v. *Tyson*. " We do not question the finality of the holding of this Court in *Swift* v. *Tyson*," the company stated. In view of the rule followed in the first minimum-wage case from New York, the *Tipaldo* case,[46] that the Court would not reconsider a precedent unless asked to do so by the petitioner, Tompkins seemed to run little risk of losing his judgment. He reckoned, however, without the Court, for its opinion opened with the statement: " The question for decision is whether the oft-challenged doctrine of *Swift* v. *Tyson* shall now be disapproved." The Court disapproved by a vote of six to two.

The Court reconsidered the meaning of Section 34 of the Judiciary Act of 1789, and also reconsidered the constitutional power of the courts to set up doctrines of their own in place of the law of the states as fixed by their own highest courts. It chose to confer the role of executioner of *Swift* v. *Tyson* and its offspring on the Constitution, holding that the fundamental charter itself had been misconstrued by the Court of 1842. The Court, as Justice Reed preferred, might well have avoided resort to con-

---

[46] 298 U. S. 587; see pp. 171; 186.

stitutional grounds and placed its decision on sound rules of practice for federal courts. It apparently sought, however, to place the most formidable obstacles possible in the way of another shift of the Court.

In doing so, the Court in effect has declared that thousands of decisions of federal courts, which are no longer subject to correction, were wrongly decided. It adjudges federal courts for almost a century guilty of taking the property of one and giving it to another without warrant of law, and federal judges of doing daily what, in the case of administrative officers, would be denounced as exercising an unlawful discretion, having no regard to the standards which must confine their judgment. But these implications were passed over in silence and were not proclaimed with "denunciatory fervor" as had been done with brief and minor errors of the Securities and Exchange Commission. And Harry Tompkins probably thinks courts as unpredictable as car doors.

## THE COURT ON GUARD

The Court thus withdrew along a wide front. But it would be misleading to suggest that the withdrawal was indiscriminate. Of equal importance is the fact that in certain sectors the Court strengthened the barricades — in sectors where it is the Court's special task to stand on guard.

On February 27, 1939, Mr. Justice Frankfurter delivered his first opinion for the Court in *Hale* v. *Bimco Trading Co.*[47] It held that a Florida statute which had plainly attempted to impose a Florida tariff on foreign cement for the protection of Florida cement manufacturers was in collision with the Constitution of the United States and indicated that the Court was in no mood to tolerate efforts of the states to disintegrate national commerce by raising local barriers to foreign or interstate trade. It may seem odd, at first blush, that Mr. Justice Frankfurter's first pronouncement should have been to declare a statute unconstitutional. But he spoke in the great tradition of the Court, one of whose most vital functions has been to prevent local parasitic endeavors from profiting at the expense of the nation's trade.

Moreover, the Court has been particularly vigilant in stamping out attempts by local authorities to suppress the free dissemination of ideas, upon which the system of responsible democratic government rests.[48] Whether in the form of handbill ordinances, anti-picketing laws, or bans on public meetings, these attempts have suffered the same end in the Court.

There is nothing covert or conflicting in the recent judgments of the Court on social legislation and on legis-

---

[47] 306 U. S. 375.

[48] *Lovell* v. *Griffin*, 303 U. S. 444; *Hague* v. *C.I.O.*, 307 U. S. 496; *Schneider* v. *State*, 308 U. S. 147; *Thornhill* v. *Alabama*, No. 514, October Term, 1939, decided April 22, 1940; compare, however, *Minersville School District* v. *Gobitis*, No. 690, October Term, 1939, decided June 3, 1940.

lative repressions of civil rights. The presumption of validity which attaches in general to legislative acts is frankly reversed in the case of interferences with free speech and free assembly, and for a perfectly cogent reason. Ordinarily, legislation whose basis in economic wisdom is uncertain can be redressed by the processes of the ballot box or the pressures of opinion. But when the channels of opinion and of peaceful persuasion are corrupted or clogged, these political correctives can no longer be relied on, and the democratic system is threatened at its most vital point. In that event the Court, by intervening, restores the processes of democratic government; it does not disrupt them.

I am far from suggesting that our civil liberties can be adequately assured by the courts. Some of the most subtle and pervasive forms of intolerance are not technically violations of the Constitution or laws, and cannot be dealt with in the courts. And at best the courts can intervene only sporadically, as isolated cases are brought by persons with sufficient resources and fortitude to gird for litigation. But to the extent that the courts can serve to vindicate civil liberties, the recent decisions of the Supreme Court show how the job can be done. It is of more than passing interest to observe that a court which is governed by a sense of self-restraint does not thereby become paralyzed. It simply conserves its strength to strike more telling blows in the cause of a working democracy.

# Chapter IX

# GOVERNMENT BY LAWSUIT

The long struggle between the Supreme Court and the Roosevelt administration is over. I have not recited the legal battles of that conflict for their own sakes. Each of the great cases of this period would merit a volume of its own. But from the aggregate experience there seem to me to emerge large questions that relate to the extent to which we are governed by judgments in lawsuit, the fitness of the judicial process for such a function, the restraint shown by the Court toward problems within its scope, and the very urgent necessity for improving the procedures of constitutional litigation.

We have seen a harassed government take a series of legislative actions to relieve economic depression and prevent social demoralization. For the questions I now raise it makes no difference whether one regards these measures separately or collectively as wise or unwise, and it makes no difference whether one regards any one or more of the decisions as correct.

A judgment in a lawsuit ended the **N.R.A.** experiment, and another ended the Agricultural Adjustment Act. One lawsuit killed railway pensions, another ended minimum wages, and another struck down municipal bankruptcy relief. Another lawsuit restored the right to minimum wages, railway pensions or municipal bankruptcy. Whether we might organize the soft coal industry, regulate labor relations, pay old-age benefits, regulate utility holding companies or have a system of unemployment insurance has depended in each instance on the outcome of a litigation. *This is government by lawsuit.*

These constitutional lawsuits are the stuff of power politics in America. Such proceedings may for a generation or more deprive an elected Congress of power, or may restore a lost power, or confirm a questioned one. Such proceedings may enlarge or restrict the authority of an elected President. They settle what power belongs to the Court itself and what it concedes to its " coordinate " departments. Decrees in litigation write the final word as to distribution of powers as between the Federal Government and the state governments and mark out and apply the limitations and denials of power constitutionally applicable to each. To recognize or to deny the power of governmental agencies in a changing world is to sit as a continuous allocator of power in our governmental system. The Court may be, and usually is, above party politics and personal politics, but the politics of power is a most important and delicate function, and adjudication of litigation is its technique.

Those who understand the characteristics and limitations of the conventional lawsuit technique recognize it as a very dubious instrument for the control of governmental policies. Not only are the effects and consequences of any given decision obscure to the masses of the people, but few lawyers follow the Court closely enough to sense its underlying trends and pressures. This alone makes it a somewhat irresponsible force in public affairs.

Judicial justice is well adapted to ensure that established legislative rules are fairly and equitably applied to individual cases. But it is inherently ill suited, and never can be suited, to devising or enacting rules of general social policy. Litigation procedures are clumsy and narrow, at best; technical and tricky, at their worst.

The Constitution-makers well understood the peculiarities of the lawsuit. With such knowledge they authorized the Supreme Court to do nothing except dispose of " Cases " and " Controversies." It was deliberately precluded from using any political technique, such as a veto. Since it could act or speak only through deciding lawsuits, it was certainly never expected to play much part in deciding the policy of government.

The Court itself took the position early in the life of the nation that it would not aid public officers in answering legal questions, but would only express its opinion in rendering judgment in justiciable controversies between litigating parties. George Washington, sorely puzzled, addressed a letter to Chief Justice Jay reciting his legal difficulties and suggesting: " The President would, therefore, be much relieved if he found himself free to refer questions of this description to the opinions of the Judges of the Supreme Court of the United States." The Justices, however, felt that the fact that the three departments of government were " in certain respects checks upon each other," and that they were " Judges of a Court in the last resort " were " considerations which afford strong arguments against the propriety of our extra-judicially deciding the questions alluded to," and declined to advise the President.[1] This precedent has been adhered to and extended to refuse any advisory opinions.[2]

The Supreme Court has found no way of expanding its procedure, but it has expanded the substance of the constitutional issues it will subject to that procedure. The early Court restrained itself first of all by an earnest deference to the legislative branch on all policy questions and even in the matter of constitutionality itself. But a more important restraint was that the guarantee of due process was then a guarantee of regularity of procedure and had

---

[1] Warren, Charles: *The Supreme Court in United States History,* Boston: Little, Brown & Company; 1937. Vol. 1, pp. 108–111.

[2] *Hayburn's Case,* 2 Dall. 408 (decided 1792); *Muskrat* v. *United States,* 219 U. S. 346 (1910).

not been expanded to a test of reasonableness of legislative policy. It was this latter development which carried the Court into realms of fact and of policy for which it has no adequate procedure. The difficulties into which the Court has lately run are attributable in no small part to its own abandonment of its earlier formulas for keeping its decrees within the practical scope of the lawsuit process.

Recognition by Justices of the limitations of the litigation method is not wanting, but it may be of significance that the most explicit recognition is in *dissenting* opinions. Justices Black, Frankfurter, and Douglas joined in a recent dissent saying:[3]

" Judicial control of national commerce — unlike legislative regulations — must from inherent limitations of the judicial process treat the subject by the hit and miss method of deciding single local controversies upon evidence and information limited by the narrow rules of litigation. Spasmodic and unrelated instances of litigation cannot afford an adequate basis for the creation of integrated national rules which alone can afford that full protection for interstate commerce intended by the Constitution. We would, therefore, leave the questions raised by the Arkansas tax for consideration of Congress in a nationwide survey of the constantly increasing barriers to trade among the States."

----
[3] *McCarroll* v. *Dixie Lines*, 309 U. S. 176, 188.

And they cited only the sharp comment on " the narrow scope of judicial proceedings " by Chief Justice Taney.[4] But he, too, had spoken in dissent, and the majority there had also insisted on deciding as justiciable questions matters as to which he thought adjudicative machinery inadequate.

Let us examine the practical weakness in operation of the litigation technique when it is used to review far-flung economic and social conditions which vex modern government.

## GOVERNMENT POLICY CANNOT BE TESTED BY LEGAL DOCTRINE ALONE

Custom decrees that the Supreme Court shall be composed only of lawyers, though the Constitution does not say so. Those lawyers on the bench will hear only from lawyers at the bar. If the views of the scientist, the laborer, the business man, the social worker, the economist, the legislator, or the government executive reach the Court, it is only through the lawyer, in spite of the fact that the effect of the decision may be far greater in other fields than in jurisprudence. Thus government by lawsuit leads to a final decision guided by the learning and limited by the understanding of a single profession — the law.

It is no condemnation of that profession to doubt its capacity to furnish single-handed the rounded and com-

---

[4] *Pennsylvania* v. *Wheeling & Belmont Bridge Co.*, 13 How. 518, 592.

prehensive wisdom to govern all society. No more, indeed not nearly so much, would I entrust only doctors, or economists, or engineers, or educators, or theologians, to make a final review of our democratically adopted legislation. But we must not blink the fact that legal philosophy is but one branch of learning with peculiarities of its own and that judicial review of the reasonableness of legislation means the testing of the whole social process by the single standard — of men of the law.

The legal profession, like many another, tends to become over-professionalized. We forget that law is the rule for simple and untaught people to live by. We complicate and over-refine it as a weapon in legal combat until we take it off the ground where people live and into the thin atmosphere of sheer fiction. If you doubt this statement, listen to the Supreme Court session of May 29, 1939. Speaking of intangible rights, Mr. Justice Stone, in one case, declared: [5]

" These are not in any sense *fictions*. They are indisputable realities," * and added, " While *fictions* are sometimes invented in order to realize the judicial conception of justice, we cannot define the constitutional guaranty in terms of a *fiction* so unrelated to reality. . . ." *

On the same day, in a second case, Mr. Chief Justice Hughes said: [6]

---

[5] *Curry* v. *McCanless,* 307 U. S. 357, 366, 374.
* Italics supplied.
[6] *Graves* v. *Elliott,* 307 U. S. 383, 387.

" I think that the decision in this case pushes the *fiction* . . . to an unwarranted extreme. . . ." *

In presenting his views in a third case, Mr. Justice Reed said: [7]

" It is not the substitution of a new *fiction* as to the mass of choses in action for the established *fiction* of a tax situs at the place of incorporation." *

Of course *fictions* played a more prominent part than usual in the pronouncements of that day, but lawyers and judges do think in terms of fictions quite as readily as in terms of realities.

These fictions tend to mischief whenever they are accepted as having a validity of their own apart from any purpose they serve. Of course the flexibility of the process and its capacity to do justice has often been achieved only by setting up a fiction as a bridge with the past in order to reach new ground. Thus, there may be preserved a measure of continuity while the law advances. John Doe and Richard Roe, those fictional gentlemen of the law, are men of straw where once they were flesh and blood, but they enable lawyers to use old forms and procedures to gain new ends. Fictions are often the hostages that the forces of movement give to the forces of position. But frequently

---

\* Italics supplied.
[7] *Newark Fire Ins. Co.* v. *State Board,* 307 U. S. 313, 321.

lawyers' fictions serve no such useful purpose; too often they are employed as a screen to cover up a retreat. To regard a giant corporation, with its stockholders, directors and employees, as a single person is a useful and convenient fiction to enable the corporation to sue and be sued as simply as any individual; but to maintain that a worker dealing with his corporation is dealing simply with another individual like himself is to pervert a fiction as only a legal mind could do with solemnity.

When this process is carried too far in common law, legislative representatives of enfranchised men can correct the profession. Legislation rooted out the fictional doctrines about assumed risk and the acts of a fellow servant as factors in employers' liability and substituted the simple realism of workmen's compensation. The capricious capers of that " reasonably prudent man " who is the fictional standard of conduct in negligence trials is now creating a demand for automobile accident compensation. The doctrine of *caveat emptor* — let the buyer beware — became so unreal in modern marketing that it was set aside by legislation like the Securities Act.

But when such fictions as " freedom of contract " are introduced into the law of the Constitution to test the validity of legislation, the remedy is not so easy — it requires a constitutional amendment or a courageous and realistic Court to correct that.

In addition to resorting to fiction to explain facts where

modern learning would resort to facts to clarify fictions, legal doctrine has another characteristic which sets it quite apart from all science and from most philosophy. Legal learning is largely built around the principle known as *stare decisis*. It means that on the same point of law yesterday's decision shall govern today's decision. Like a coral reef, the common law thus becomes a structure of fossils. Preparation for admission to the bar is largely a study of old authorities. At the bar, cases are won by finding in the maze of legal literature a controlling case or by distinguishing or discrediting the case found by an adversary. Precedents largely govern the conclusions and surround the reasoning of lawyers and judges. In the field of common law they are a force for stability and predictability, but in constitutional law they are the most powerful influence in forming and supporting reactionary opinions. The judge who can take refuge in a precedent does not need to justify his decision to the reason. He may " reluctantly feel himself bound " by a doctrine, supported by a respected historical name, that he would not be able to justify to contemporary opinion or under modern conditions.

Under this doctrine decisions made today become the guide and precedent by which future similar cases will be governed. So, when the Court announces a rule that strikes down a law, it not only binds the executive and judicial departments; it does far more than this. It binds

*itself* and its *successors* and all inferior courts and future
judges to decide similar cases by like logic. It not only
limits the judgment of other judges, but, so long as the
rule stands, it destroys the discretion even of the men who
made it.

It was this paralyzing influence of the precedent that
made the series of decisions outlawing New Deal experiments so serious. These decisions became precedents for
limitations upon the power of all future Congresses. Their
cumulative effect aroused apprehensions as to the ability
of representative democracy to meet the future problems
that beset its people in a day of change.

It was this process of whittling down by precedent that
led Chief Justice Hughes, on behalf of himself and Justices Brandeis, Stone, and Cardozo, to protest in *Railroad
Retirement Board* v. *Alton R. R. Co.*[8] He said:

". . . the majority finally raise a barrier against all legislative action of this nature by declaring that the subject
matter itself lies beyond the reach of the congressional
authority to regulate interstate commerce. . . . That is
a conclusion of such serious and far-reaching importance
that it overshadows all other questions raised by the Act.
. . . I think that the conclusion thus reached is a departure from sound principles and places an unwarranted limitation upon the commerce clause of the Constitution."

---

8 295 U. S. 330, 375.

This was a paraphrase by the Chief Justice of Portia's:

> " 'Twill be recorded for a precedent;
> And many an error, by the same example,
> Will rush into the state: it can not be."

Of course, such judicial misconstruction theoretically can be cured by constitutional amendment. But the period of gestation of a constitutional amendment, or of any law reform, is reckoned in decades usually; in years, at least. And, after all, as the Court itself asserted in overruling the minimum-wage cases, it may not be the Constitution that was at fault.

It is also true that the Court can limit its deference to precedent if it is composed of Justices who are so inclined. Mr. Justice Stone has said that the doctrine " has only a limited application in the field of constitutional law." [9]

Mr. Chief Justice Taney has said: [10]

" I . . . am quite willing that it be regarded hereafter as the law of this court, that its opinion upon the construction of the Constitution is always open to discussion when it is supposed to have been founded in error, and that its judicial authority should hereafter depend altogether on the force of the reasoning by which it is supported."

Mr. Justice Brandeis on another occasion said: [11]

9 *St. Joseph Stock Yards Co.* v. *United States,* 298 U. S. 38, 94.
10 *The Passenger Cases,* 7 How. 283, 470.
11 *Burnet* v. *Coronado Oil & Gas Co.,* 285 U. S. 393, 406.

" But in cases involving the Federal Constitution, where correction through legislative action is practically impossible, this Court has often overruled its earlier decisions. The Court bows to the lessons of experience and the force of better reasoning, recognizing that the process of trial and error, so fruitful in the physical sciences, is appropriate also in the judicial function."

But these were daring judges. Such are not always in a majority. And if, in the language of Justice Brandeis, the Court is to bow " to the lessons of experience and the force of better reasoning," may we ask whose experience? And whose reasoning? Can the lawyer qualify to speak for all society?

## THE CONVENTIONAL " CASE " OR " CONTROVERSY " PROCEDURE IS INADEQUATE TO COLLECT, SUMMARIZE, AND INTERPRET THE EXPERIENCE AND REASON OF OUR SOCIETY

Justices generally are learned in the theories of the law — but they cannot know the conditions in every industry or the experiences in every social layer of our national life. No form of lawsuit has yet been devised suitable to inform them adequately, with judicial standards of proof, of the factors in our mass problems. To follow the effects of a minimum-wage policy, for example, through our business and social structure or to establish the effects of the Social Security Act on the general welfare by legal testimony and exhibits would produce a mass that would be incomprehensible and exhausting.

The vice of the litigation process in broad constitutional questions is that since we cannot expand the lawsuit process to include an era, a people, and a continent, we simply cut down the problem to the scope of a lawsuit. The cases we have recited demonstrate how the broad and impersonal policy that moved Congress became subjected to the procedures of a very narrow, individual, and legalistic controversy.

The deficiencies of this lawsuit method appear clearly when we look to the make-up of the information that it provides for the judges.

Important constitutional decisions are sometimes rendered on a legal record consisting chiefly of two documents drawn by opposing lawyers. It may be an indictment and a demurrer, or it may be a bill of complaint and a motion to dismiss. These amount to little more than the conflicting and unsupported assertions of two attorneys. This really gives the Court little information apart from the situation of the party and the consequences to him of the act challenged. It personalizes the controversy. In some cases the Supreme Court has refused to decide constitutionality on such a basis and has returned the parties to the lower courts with an admonition to develop their facts.[12]

---

[12] See *Borden's Co.* v. *Baldwin,* 293 U. S. 194.

When it is attempted to prove broad assertions by legal evidence, the record usually becomes large and forbidding. Either it must contain a vast amount of testimony difficult to summarize and evaluate, or it must state agreed facts which each side thinks important. In the test of the Public Utility Holding Company Act this latter method condensed the factual background into two thousand printed pages. Records in bitterly contested cases run into lengths that defeat their very purpose. Justice Brandeis complained that the record and briefs in one rate case weighed sixty-seven pounds avoirdupois.[13]

Counsel appreciates the narrowness of the process when he begins to select the little part of the appropriate background that he can present in a " brief." At best, our presentation of economic and social backgrounds is elementary and amateurish — and generally apologetically relegated to an appendix. Most Justices have little time for supplemental reading. A few regard economic information as an " ostentatious parade of irrelevant statistics." [14]

Then comes the dramatic and decisive day of argument in the Supreme Court. No experience can be more challenging to the advocate. Counsel will have from one to four hours for argument, depending on the grace of the Court for anything more than an hour. His own prepara-

---

[13] *Baltimore and Ohio R. Co.* v. *United States,* 298 U. S. 349, 381.
[14] Mr. Justice McReynolds in *Steward Machine Co.* v. *Davis,* 301 U. S. 548, 599.

tions will be superficial as compared with those of the men who have specialized in the theory or the administration of the questioned Act. But only a fraction, even of his own background knowledge, can be imparted to the Court. To select the materials and arguments that will carry conviction, to omit nothing necessary to the persuasion of any judge, to answer off-hand the doubts and questions from the bench in so grave a cause is a responsibility no lawyer ought to be required or allowed to assume. Constitutionality should not depend on an advocate's judgment, or want of it, in argument. The Justices' avenues of information should not be so restricted or so formalized.

Such a process is utterly inadequate to educate an uninformed judge or to overcome old convictions or predilections, or to win a conversion to a new viewpoint. Success in such an enterprise is apt to be accidental or the result of pre-determination. The judge goes to conference with too little except his predilections to guide his vote. Argument is likely to leave each judge just where it found him. The wonder is, not that our courts have lately been obliged frequently to confess error, but that the instances are so few. The limitations on the litigation procedure emphasize the unheeded wisdom given to the Supreme Court by James C. Carter, leader of the bar of his day, in arguing the constitutionality of the income tax: [15]

---

[15] See *Pollock* v. *Farmers' Loan & Trust Co.*, 157 U. S. 429, 531.

" Nothing could be more unwise and dangerous — nothing more foreign to the spirit of the Constitution — than an attempt to baffle and defeat a popular determination by a judgment in a lawsuit."

## DELAY, DOUBT, AND CONFUSION

We have considered limitations inherent in legal procedures which make the lawsuit an unfit channel for exercise of political power, and which suggest that those who possess no other implements should scrupulously avoid judgments for which it is not adequate. But even if the precaution is faithfully observed, there remains a wide field in which our constitutional system requires interpretative adjudications.

Constitutional litigation is so important to the preservation of the equilibrium between departments of government, between state and nation, and between effective authority and individual liberty that no effort should be spared to make it modern, systematic, expeditious, and simple. That has not been done and the New Deal experience shows the points of weakness.

The district courts of the United States are not institutional in their proceedings so much as they are personal. Each such court is an individual, in fact, with a life tenure and independence of every other district court. The district judges, about one hundred seventy-five in number, include at all times a wide range of abilities, experiences, party affiliations and loyalties, local connections, and economic views and prejudices. A litigant may often exercise a good deal of choice as to the judge or judges who will first hear his challenge to an act of Congress. The lower court thus settled upon admits or excludes evidence, expedites or delays proceedings, finds the facts, makes the first decision on the law, and controls provisional and temporary remedies. But these lower court decisions have no finality as to the law. The lawyers who fight for them and the judges who write them know that they are inconclusive.

A statute involving a major policy is likely to be the subject of a number of attacks at about the same time in different courts. Then begins confusion. No district judge is required to, and few do, yield obedience or even respect to the decision of another. One local judge may sustain the legislation; another may hold the act partly good and partly bad; and another may hold it all unconstitutional. For a considerable period in 1939, the Agricultural Marketing Act, governing the sale of milk to handlers, was unconstitutional in New York State and constitutional in Massachusetts because the federal district judges came to opposite conclusions about the same question. Opinion and counter-opinion bewilder the citizen who wants to obey the law but who does not know what to do when one judicial star differeth from another.

Then come appeals; proceedings are printed; and, in

due time, the cases are argued in the United States Circuit
Court of Appeals. There are ten of these intermediate
courts, and conflicting opinions are likely to issue; but they
settle nothing. The Judiciary Act of 1937 authorizes in
some cases that this intermediate court be passed by, and
the Supreme Court has long had discretion to order it
skipped, but even in cases where both government and an
industry agree in urging that the time be saved, the Court
often majestically refuses to be hurried.

After these court of appeals decisions, briefs are re-
written and reprinted, and the case reaches the Supreme
Court. Once there it is promptly heard and soon decided.
The delay is in the interminable lower court proceedings.
This delay, doubt, and confusion has a social and economic
cost.

New Deal legislation was often held in a long period of
suspense and uncertainty. The *Gold Clause Cases* were
decided one year and eight months after the Joint Resolution struck down the Gold Clauses. Meanwhile, all forward commitments of the business world were subject to
a possible infirmity, so substantial that it was finally resolved by a majority of only one vote.

After almost two years of vigorous administration, the
N.R.A. was held at all times to have been invalid. A
myriad of transactions had been closed and thousands of
persons had altered their positions in reliance on it.

Two and a half years after its adoption, the A.A.A. was

struck down by a sharply divided Court with havoc to existing commitments.

While most of this delay is in the lower courts, the Supreme Court has itself delayed decision. It has a philosophy that while it has a duty to decide constitutional questions, it must escape the duty if possible.

An eminently qualified and not unfriendly authority writes: [16]

" But the Court has improved upon the common law tradition and evolved rules of judicial administration especially designed to postpone constitutional adjudications and therefore constitutional conflicts until they are judicially unavoidable. The Court will avoid decision on grounds of constitutionality if a case may go off on some other ground, as, for instance, statutory construction.

" The Court has thus evolved elaborate and often technical doctrines for postponing if not avoiding constitutional adjudication. In one famous controversy, involving a conflict between Congress and the president, the Supreme Court was able until recently to avoid decision of a question that arose in the First Congress. Such a system inevitably introduces accidental factors in decision making. So much depends on how a question is raised and when it is raised."

---

16 Frankfurter, Felix: *Law and Politics.* New York: Harcourt, Brace and Company; 1939, p. 25.

Nevertheless, Mr. Frankfurter thought this prolonged uncertainty less harmful than " the mischief of premature judicial intervention." By the latter he thinks the " Court's prestige within its proper sphere would be inevitably impaired."

Must we choose between " *premature judicial intervention* " on one hand and " *technical doctrines for postponing if not avoiding constitutional adjudication* " on the other? If that were our choice I would think Mr. Frankfurter had chosen wisely. But need we be gored by either horn of such a dilemma? Can we not establish a procedure for determination of substantial constitutional questions at the suit of real parties in interest which will avoid prematurity or advisory opinions on the one hand and also avoid technical doctrines for postponing inevitable decisions? Should we not at least try to lay inevitable constitutional controversies to early rest?

An important reason for doing so is that Supreme Court law is retroactive in its operation, and that is one of the perils and inconveniences of constitutional litigation. Normally, judicial decision is law-making after the event. The function of judges is to decide controversies, and their decisions must necessarily be made to relate back to govern the transaction which provoked the controversy. This led Bentham to assert that judges make the common law " just as a man makes laws for his dog. When your dog does anything you want to break him of, you wait till he does it, and then beat him for it." [17] But the judicial conscience is eased by a theory which denied personal guilt. " But even in such cases the subsequent judges do not pretend to make a new law, but to vindicate the old one from misrepresentation. For if it be found that the former decision is manifestly absurd or unjust, it is declared, not that such a sentence was *bad law*, but that it was *not law*. . . ." [18] This sort of theoretical fol-de-rol about a " transcendental body of law " was called by Justice Holmes a " fallacy and illusion." [19]

On some occasions, the Supreme Court has refused to allow state court decisions to become effective retroactively [20] and it has held that the Federal Constitution permits a state to provide against retroactive effect of state court decisions if it so desires. Justice Cardozo, for a unanimous court, wrote: [21]

" A state in defining the limits of adherence to precedent may make a choice for itself between the principle of forward operation and that of relation backward. It may say that decisions of its highest court, though later overruled, are law none the less for intermediate transactions."

17 See Kocourek, Albert: " Retrospective Decisions and Stare Decisis and a Proposal," 17 A. B. A. Journal, 180.

18 See Blackstone: *Commentaries*. Philadelphia: Rees, Welsh & Company; 1897. Vol. I, pp. 69–70.

19 See dissenting opinions, *B. & W. Taxi. Co.* v. *B. & Y. Taxi. Co.*, 276 U. S. 518, 533.

20 *Gelpcke* v. *Dubuque,* 1 Wall. 175.

21 *Great Northern Ry.* v. *Sunburst Co.,* 287 U. S. 358, 364.

It is hard to see why a similar choice should not be open to the Federal Government. The task of doing practical justice does not depend on solving a riddle as to whether an overruling decision serves to correct wrong law or simply to correct a wrong judge. As Solicitor General I urged that " this Court has, and should have, as an incident of its power to overrule prior decisions, the power in particular cases to prevent an overruling decision from being an instrument of injustice or hardship." [22] But, there must be definite limitations in applying such a rule, and the particular case was not appropriate for its application.

Later, the Court considered the effects of retroactivity created by holding enactments unconstitutional, in a vein that indicates that the Court will strive to mitigate hardships caused thereby.

Mr. Chief Justice Hughes wrote: [23]

" The courts below have proceeded on the theory that the Act of Congress, having been found to be unconstitutional, was not a law; that it was inoperative, conferring no rights and imposing no duties, and hence affording no basis for the challenged decree. . . . It is quite clear, however, that such broad statements as to the effect of a

---

[22] See Reply to Petition for Rehearing in *Helvering* v. *Gerhardt*. Rehearing denied 305 U. S. 669.

[23] *Chicot County* v. *Baxter Bank, No. 122,* October Term, 1939. Decided January 2, 1940.

determination of unconstitutionality must be taken with qualifications. The actual existence of a statute, prior to such a determination, is an operative fact and may have consequences which cannot justly be ignored. The past cannot always be erased by a new judicial declaration. The effect of the subsequent ruling as to invalidity may have to be considered in various aspects, — with respect to particular relations, individual and corporate, and particular conduct, private and official. Questions of rights claimed to have become vested, of status, of prior determinations deemed to have finality and acted upon accordingly, of public policy in the light of the nature both of the statute and of its previous application, demand examination. These questions are among the most difficult of those which have engaged the attention of courts, state and federal, and it is manifest from numerous decisions that an all-inclusive statement of a principle of absolute retroactive invalidity cannot be justified."

Since constitutional litigation is an essential part of our technique of government, even when confined to its appropriate exercise, both government and private interests have a right to expect from the Justices and lawyers development of a more expeditious, orderly, and centralized procedure. District courts and circuit courts of appeal are creatures of Congress with no powers except those Congress extends. It is not necessary to scatter the sov-

ereign power of judicial review of constitutionality of
legislation among them. Such power should be promptly
exercised by a court of finality as well as one of a high
sense of responsibility and a national outlook in those cases
where the power is properly invoked, and self-restraint
should lead to prompt and final declination to interfere
with the legislative process in those cases where the lawsuit
is inappropriate to overrule statecraft.

# Chapter X

# THE POLITICAL NATURE OF

# JUDICIAL SUPREMACY

The political nature of judicial review generally is either unrecognized or ignored. But it is that which gives significance to constitutional litigation and which makes it transcend mere legal proceedings.

The Supreme Court, to which this essential function is committed, is an institution of distinctive characteristics which were intended to give it independence and detachment, but which also tend to make it anti-democratic. To review the functions of the Court in conjunction with its peculiar qualities will explain its repeated drift into struggles with strong Executives and will reveal the dangers that beset its future.

The ultimate function of the Supreme Court is nothing less than the arbitration between fundamental and ever-present rival forces or trends in our organized society. The technical tactics of constitutional lawsuits are part of

a greater strategy of statecraft in our system. Supreme
Court decrees prick out roughly the drifts of national
policy. Every really important movement has been preceded by " leading cases " and has left others in its wake,
even as will the New Deal. Conflicts which have divided
the Justices always mirror a conflict which pervades society. In fact, it may be said that the Supreme Court conference chamber is the forum where each fundamental
cause has had its most determined and understanding
championship. The student of our times will nowhere find
the deeper conflicts of American political philosophy and
economic policy more authentically and intelligently por-
trayed than in the opinions and dissents of members of the
Supreme Court. Justices such as Holmes and Brandeis
have not only furnished the highest expression but they
have been the very source and the intellectual leaders of
recent liberalism in the United States. And nowhere can
one find the philosophy of conservatism and opposition to
the Administration's policy more intelligently or earnestly
expressed than in the opinions of Justices Sutherland and
Butler. The Constitution, in making the balance between
different parts of our government a legal rather than a
political question, casts the Court as the most philosophical
of our political departments. It keeps the most fundamental equilibriums of our society, such as that between cen-
tralization and localism, between liberty and authority,

and between stability and progress. These issues underlie nearly every movement in an organized society.

The Court has as its highest responsibility the duty to hold every such movement, in its legislative and executive phases, within all express bounds of the Constitution. Whether or not the Justices avow such an end, whether or not they are even aware of it, their acts and pronouncements often do tip the balance between these irrepressible forces, even in matters of constitutionally permissible policy. It is safer that they be conscious of the ultimate implications and the weight of their decisions and the tensions and pressures in a democratic society which they influence.

These important functions devolve upon a Supreme Court which was intended to be, and by its inherent nature always will prove to be, over the years, a relatively conservative institution. This was assured by the provisions that its Justices should receive office through appointment and should hold it for life.

Another assurance, not provided by the Constitution, but supplied by custom, is that such Justices are drawn only from the legal profession. The entire philosophy, interest, and training of the legal profession tend toward conservatism. As I have already remarked, it is much concerned with precedents, authorities, existing customs, usages, vested rights, and established relationships. Its method of thinking, accepted by no other profession, cul-

tivates a supreme respect for the past, and its order. Justice Cardozo has well said that the " power of precedent,
when analyzed, is the power of the beaten track." [1] No
lawyer sufficiently devoted to the law to know our existing
rules, the history of them, and the justification for them,
will depart from them lightly. The contribution of legal
philosophy to the balance of social forces will always be
on the conservative side.

This trend to conservatism in the profession of the law
is intensified in the case of judges by the weight of the official tradition of social and intellectual isolation. Mr. Taft
compared Court life to life in a monastery.[2]

The operation of our two-party system has also tended
to separate the judiciary from the elective branches and to
place them in opposition. The party system often serves
to bridge the constitutional division between the executive
and legislative branches. Adherence to a common party
organization and tradition and program tend to weld the
executive departments and the majority of Senators and
Congressmen into a cohesive group, and thus to supply co-
operation between otherwise detached units.

This extra-constitutional inducement to cooperation has
at all critical times operated in reverse between the judiciary and the elective branches of government. The Fed-

[1] Cardozo, Benjamin N.: *The Growth of the Law*. New Haven: Yale
University Press; 1939, p. 62.
[2] Pringle, Henry F.: *The Life and Times of William Howard Taft*.
New York, Toronto: Farrar and Rinehart; 1939. Vol. II, p. 961.

eralist Party Executives, Washington and Adams, had no differences with the judiciary. They appointed all of the judges. But at every turn in national policy where the cleavage between the old order and the new was sharp, the new President has faced a judiciary almost wholly held over from the preceding regime. Whatever of influence party background may have on judicial trends, whether great or little, it has been an estranging influence between the Court and the great Presidents, Jefferson, Jackson, Lincoln, and Franklin D. Roosevelt.

The Court, moreover, is almost never a really contemporary institution. The operation of life tenure in the judicial department, as against elections at short intervals of the Congress, usually keeps the average viewpoint of the two institutions a generation apart. The judiciary is thus the check of a preceding generation on the present one; a check of conservative legal philosophy upon a dynamic people, and nearly always the check of a rejected regime on the one in being. And the search for Justices of enduring liberalism has usually ended in disappointment.

This conservative institution is under every pressure and temptation to throw its weight against novel programs and untried policies which win popular elections. Its plain duty to enforce explicit constitutional provisions even in opposition to the majority is easily rationalized into enforcing its own views of good policy. To the extent that

it does so, it defeats government by representative democracy.

Our representative federation was not devised to arrest
change, but to provide peaceful and orderly methods for
the continuous changes which were recognized to be inevitable. The device of periodic election was chosen to
register and remedy discontents and grievances in time to
prevent them from growing into underground or violent
revolutionary movements. An election that can turn out
one regime and install another is a revolution — a peaceful
and lawful revolution. By such method we give flexibility
and a measure of popular responsibility to our federated
system and maintain a continuity of the government, even
though the governors be turned out from time to time. The
measure of success of a democratic system is found in the
degree to which its elections really reflect rising discontent
before it becomes unmanageable, by which government re-
sponds to it with timely redress, and by which losing groups
are self-disciplined to accept election results.

It must be remembered that our democratic system can
succeed in composing oppositions only if the effort is made
while the separation is not extreme. When the separation
becomes wide or deep, as that over slavery finally became,
the contest gets beyond the capacity of elective processes
to compose.

Lord Balfour, who found the British system " admira-
bly fitted to adjust political action to the ordinary oscilla-

tions of public opinion " was not sure it could " long survive the shocks of revolutionary and counter-revolutionary violence," and he went on to state what every intelligent liberal does feel and every intelligent conservative should comprehend: [3]

" Our alternating cabinets, though belonging to different parties, have never differed about the foundations of society. And it is evident that our whole political machinery presupposes a people so fundamentally at one that they can safely afford to bicker; and so sure of their own moderation that they are not dangerously disturbed by the never-ending din of political conflict. May it always be so."

This observation of an enlightened conservative thinker has corroboration from the opposite pole by Harold Laski, a clear-headed liberal thinker, who says: [4]

" In an interesting passage, Lord Balfour has drawn attention to the fact that the success of the British Constitution in the nineteenth century — it is worth adding the general success of representative government — was built upon an agreement between parties in the state upon fundamental principles. There was, that is, a kindred out-

[3] Bagehot: *The English Constitution.* Introduction by Balfour to World's Classics Ed., Oxford Press; 1927, p. xxiv.

[4] Laski, Harold: *Liberty in the Modern State.* New York and London: Harper & Brothers; 1930, p. 238.

look upon large issues; and since fighting was confined to
matters of comparative detail, men were prepared to let
reason have its sway in the realm of conflict. For it is significant that in the one realm where depth of feeling was
passionate — Irish home rule — events moved rapidly to
the test of the sword; and the settlement made was effected
by violence and not by reason."

These passages would be perfectly applicable to American politics if, as the provocation of violence, we substitute the issue of slavery for the issue of Irish home rule.
The very ability of democracies to settle issues peaceably
may depend on responding to them before they have developed the bitterness which comes of long-endured injustices.

Our American elections have been fought between parties which, roughly, have represented the forces advocat-
ing change and those preferring stability.

The difference in the task and function of the parties
that represent these opposite roles has been stated in terms
as applicable to America as to England.[5]

" It is, of course, a much easier thing to lead their party
than ours, as you and I will find if we ever have a share in
the work. The function of the Tories in these days is
neither to originate nor to resist *a outrance*, but to forestall

---

[5] Spender, J. A. and Asquith, Cyril: *Life of Lord Oxford and Asquith.*
London: Hutchinson & Co.; 1932. Vol. 1, p. 103.

inevitable changes by judicious compromises in the interest of threatened classes and institutions. They have, just as much as the old Tories had and even more, wealth, property and the *vis inertiae* on their side, and as their game is a difficult one and full of intellectual interest, they admit a vast deal more than they used to do of the higher intelligence of the country. But they need neither intuition, initiative, constructive power (except of a low kind), nor (what is rarest of all) the ability to organize and concentrate the scattered discontent and diffuse enthusiasm of a half-educated society."

But election as a device to defend against violence by registering and responding to this " scattered discontent and diffuse enthusiasm " fails, if the popularly elected regime is to be prevented judicially from putting its policies into force. It should, of course, be so restrained where its program violates clear and explicit terms of the Constitution, such as the specific prohibitions in the Bill of Rights. But to use vague clauses to import doctrines of restraint, such as " freedom of contract," is to set up the judiciary as a check on elections, a nullification of the process of government by consent of the governed. It leaves the grievances of the frustrated majority to grow, and more extreme remedies to commend themselves to those who would have been satisfied with more moderate, if more timely, ones.

I have little fear of legislative or political clashes between the forces of liberalism and those of conservatism in
the present state of our American society. Each is subject
to moderating influences from a constituency which has not
often in substantial numbers approved real radicalism or
extreme reactionism. The Senator in our National Congress has faced his constituents not over six years before,
and on average much more recently, and the conservative
Representative is not over two years from his ballot box.
They are all parts of a political party that never more than
four years previously has faced a Presidential election and
at least within that period must do so again. Hence, the
conservatism of legislators is moderated by elimination
and by expediency, just as liberalism among them is restrained by the average opinion of electors. Whatever
other defects the elective process under a two-party system may present, it does temper extremes of legislative
opinion. By it, if at all, issues may be compromised out
and a balance struck between the forces of stability and
those of progress.

But, after this political and legislative process has taken
place, to add another and more extreme and inflexible
hurdle in the form of judicial review of social policy loads
the dice in favor of the *status quo* and makes the constructive task of liberal leadership impossible. It is always the
dynamic party of change which is frustrated by the Court's
attitude, for the conservative party, resting on the policy

of letting well enough alone, presents for review little legislation that is untried or novel. Liberal leadership exhausts its power to persuade the discontented and the have-nots to accept ballot-box disappointments or compromises if their victories are to be nullified and if elections are effective in shaping policy only when conservatives win. This was the problem that confronted the New Deal leadership in 1937 — either the election was only a mirage to winning progressive forces or the Court must yield.

The Supreme Court can maintain itself and succeed in its tasks only if the counsels of self-restraint urged most earnestly by members of the Court itself are humbly and faithfully heeded. After the forces of conservatism and liberalism, of radicalism and reaction, of emotion and of self-interest are all caught up in the legislative process and averaged and come to rest in some compromise measure such as the Missouri Compromise, the N.R.A., the A.A.A., a minimum-wage law, or some other legislative policy, a decision striking it down closes an area of compromise in which conflicts have actually, if only temporarily, been composed. Each such decision takes away from our democratic federalism another of its defenses against domestic disorder and violence. The vice of judicial supremacy, as exerted for ninety years in the field of policy, has been its progressive closing of the avenues to peaceful and democratic conciliation of our social and economic conflicts.

In stressing this I do not join those who seek to deflate

the whole judicial process. It is precisely because I value
the role that the judiciary performs in the peaceful ordering of our society that I deprecate the ill-starred adven-
tures of the judiciary that have recurringly jeopardized
its essential usefulness.

Nor am I unmindful of the hard-won heritage of an independent judiciary which for over two hundred years has
maintained the " rule of law " in England, the living principle that not even the king is above the law. But again, the
rule of law is in unsafe hands when courts cease to function
as courts and become organs for control of policy. English
history itself is not without illuminating chapters on the
contest of the courts and the popular will. The antipathy
of the judges of the eighteenth century to popular criticism of the ruling powers, their high-handed treatment of
such criticism as seditious and libelous, led to the curbing
of the judges' powers in criminal libel trials. Through
Fox's Libel Act the jury was given powers theretofore
wielded by the judges. The stubborn refusal of the common-law judges to moderate the rigidities of legal rules led
to the rise of the chancellors presiding over courts of
equity, which the judges fought as usurpers, but it was a
losing battle, and eventually the more flexible principles
of equity penetrated even the walls of the common-law
courts. The archaism of judge-made law at the beginning
of the nineteenth century inspired the Philippics of Jer-

emy Bentham, whose writings make our current diatribes seem bland and amiable. The instrument of reform for which Bentham fought was legislation; and legislation there was, unprecedented in volume and importance. One of the most recent adjustments which the courts have had to make is the recognition of systems of arbitration in lieu of ordinary litigation for the settlement of commercial disputes. Business men grew restive at the cost in time and money of endeavoring to educate the judges, through lawsuits, in the customs and practices of trade. No one would contend that these movements for judicial reform, whether consummated within or without the courts, weakened the English judiciary for its essential tasks. But for these movements the courts in the historic home of our law might have sunk irretrievably in prestige and so in power.

With us, what is wanted is not innovation, but a return to the spirit with which our early judges viewed the function of judicial review of legislation — the conviction that it is an awesome thing to strike down an act of the legislature approved by the Chief Executive, and that power so uncontrolled is not to be used save where the occasion is clear beyond fair debate.

If the judiciary attempts to enforce a judicial conservatism after legislative and political conservatism has decided to yield and compromise, it will jeopardize its power to serve the Republic in high and undisputed functions which only it can perform. By impairing its own prestige through risking it in the field of policy, it may impair its ability to defend our liberties.

I yield to the lawyer's impulse to prove my point by citing a precedent. The lowest point in the history of the federal judiciary was May 1861. Roger B. Taney, the aged Chief Justice of the United States, was sitting in Masonic Hall in Baltimore to hear the return to a writ of habeas corpus, " that traditional bulwark of individual liberty," which he had issued. An aide-de-camp in full military uniform and appropriately wearing a sword,[6] appeared and declined obedience to the ancient writ of freedom, upon the ground that it had been " suspended." Let the Chief Justice state the case:[7]

" The case, then, is simply this: a military officer, residing in Pennsylvania, issues an order to arrest a citizen of Maryland, upon vague and indefinite charges, without any proof, so far as appears; under this order, his house is entered in the night, he is seized as a prisoner, and conveyed to Fort McHenry, and there kept in close confinement; and when a habeas corpus is served on the commanding officer, requiring him to produce the prisoner before a justice of the supreme court, in order that he may examine into the legality of the imprisonment, the answer of the

---

6 Swisher, Carl B.: *Roger B. Taney.* New York: The Macmillan Company; 1936, p. 551.

7 *Ex parte Merryman,* 17 Fed. Cas. 144, 147. Case No. 9,487.

officer, is that he is authorized by the president to suspend the writ of habeas corpus at his discretion, and in the exercise of that discretion, suspends it in this case, and on that ground refuses obedience to the writ.

" As the case comes before me, therefore, I understand that the president not only claims the right to suspend the writ of habeas corpus himself, at his discretion, but to delegate that discretionary power to a military officer, and to leave it to him to determine whether he will or will not obey judicial process that may be served upon him."

And he further recites:

" But the documents before me show, that the military authority in this case has gone far beyond the mere suspension of the privilege of the writ of habeas corpus. It has, by force of arms, thrust aside the judicial authorities and officers to whom the constitution has confided the power and duty of interpreting and administering the laws, and substituted a military government in its place, to be administered and executed by military officers.

" Yet, under these circumstances, a military officer, stationed in Pennsylvania, without giving any information to the district attorney, and without any application to the judicial authorities, assumes to himself the judicial power in the district of Maryland; undertakes to decide what constitutes the crime of treason or rebellion; what

evidence (if indeed he required any) is sufficient to support
the accusation and justify the commitment; and commits
the party, without a hearing, even before himself, to close
custody, in a strongly garrisoned fort, to be there held, it
would seem, during the pleasure of those who committed
him."

Shorn of power, but not of courage, Taney, " a great
Chief Justice," [8] in full expectation that he, too, would be
imprisoned, thundered forth the fundamental and eternal
principles of civilian freedom from military usurpation.
But with a confession of helplessness and despair, he closed
an opinion which must rank as one of the most admirable
and pathetic documents in American judicial annals: [9]

" In such a case, my duty was too plain to be mistaken.
I have exercised all the power which the constitution and
laws confer upon me, but that power has been resisted by
a force too strong for me to overcome."

And so he sent his opinion to President Lincoln in the
hope that " that high officer " would " determine what
measures he will take to cause the civil process of the
United States to be respected and enforced."

The answer, if any, was drowned out by the measured
tread of marching feet. Judicial power was all but extinct.

---

[8] See Tribute to Taney by Chief Justice Hughes, American Bar
Assn. Journal, Vol. XVII, pp. 785–790.

[9] *Ex parte Merryman,* 17 Fed. Cas. 144, 153; Case No. 9,487.

Nothing but the indispensable necessity for its function could bid it rise again.

Did the lonely and frustrated Chief Justice recall the tragic part that he, more than any other, had played in starting that march? Only four years before he had read the opinion in the *Dred Scott* case,[10] in which his Court had held the Missouri Compromise to be unconstitutional. The Missouri Compromise itself had ceased to be important. But there was still hope that American forbearance and statesmanship would prove equal to finding some compromise between the angry forces that were being aroused by the slave issue. That hope vanished when the Supreme Court held that the Constitution would allow no compromise about the existence of slavery in the territories. Taney had attempted to forestall the anticipated verdict of coming elections — the verdict that came with the election of 1860. Now the weary and weatherbeaten old Chief Justice was overmastered by the violence of forces that he had himself turned away from compromise in legislative halls and had hurried toward war.

One such precedent is enough!

10 *Dred Scott* v. *Sandford,* 19 How. 393.

*75th Congress, 1st Session.* HOUSE OF REPRESENTATIVES, *Document Number* 142

RECOMMENDATION TO REORGANIZE JUDICIAL BRANCH

# MESSAGE FROM THE PRESIDENT OF THE UNITED STATES

TRANSMITTING

A RECOMMENDATION TO REORGANIZE THE JUDICIAL BRANCH
OF THE FEDERAL GOVERNMENT

*February 5, 1937. — Referred to the Committee on the Judiciary
and ordered to be printed.*

THE WHITE HOUSE, *February 5, 1937*

To THE CONGRESS OF THE UNITED STATES:

I have recently called the attention of the Congress to the clear need for a comprehensive program to reorganize the administrative machinery of the executive branch of our Government. I now make a similar recommendation to the Congress in regard to the judicial branch of the Government, in order that it also may function in accord with modern necessities.

The Constitution provides that the President " shall from time to time give to the Congress information of the state of the Union, and recommend to their consideration such measures as he shall judge necessary and expedient." No one else is given a similar mandate. It is therefore the duty of the President to advise the Congress in regard to the judiciary whenever he deems such information or recommendation necessary.

I address you for the further reason that the Constitution vests in the Congress direct responsibility in the creation of courts and judicial offices and in the formulation of rules of practice and procedure. It is, therefore, one of the definite duties of the Congress constantly to maintain the effective functioning of the Federal judiciary.

The judiciary has often found itself handicapped by insufficient personnel with which to meet a growing and more complex business. It is true that the physical facilities of conducting the business of the courts have been greatly improved, in recent years, through the erection of suitable quarters, the provision of adequate libraries, and the addition of subordinate court officers. But in many ways these are merely the trappings of judicial office. They play a minor part in the processes of justice.

Since the earliest days of the Republic, the problem of the personnel of the courts has needed the attention of the Congress. For example, from the beginning, over repeated protests to President Washington, the Justices of the Supreme Court were required to " ride circuit " and, as circuit justices, to hold trials throughout the length and breadth of the land — a practice which endured over a century.

In almost every decade since 1789 changes have been made by the Congress whereby the numbers of judges and the duties of judges in Federal courts have been altered in one way or another. The Supreme Court was established with 6 members in 1789; it was reduced to 5 in 1801; it was increased to 7 in 1807; it was increased to 9 in 1837; it was increased to 10 in 1863; it was reduced to 7 in 1866; it was increased to 9 in 1869.

The simple fact is that today a new need for legislative action arises because the personnel of the Federal judiciary is insufficient to meet the business before them. A growing body of our citizens complain of the complexities, the delays, and the expense of litigation in United States courts.

A letter from the Attorney General, which I submit herewith, justifies by reasoning and statistics the common impression created by our overcrowded Federal dockets — and it proves the need for additional judges.

Delay in any court results in injustice.

It makes lawsuits a luxury available only to the few who can afford them or who have property interests to protect which are sufficiently large to repay the cost. Poorer litigants are compelled to abandon valuable rights or to accept inadequate or unjust settlements because of sheer inability to finance or to await the end of a long litigation. Only by speeding up the processes of the law and thereby reducing their cost, can we eradicate the growing impression that the courts are chiefly a haven for the well-to-do.

Delays in the determination of appeals have the same effect. Moreover, if trials of original actions are expedited and existing accumulations of cases are reduced, the volume of work imposed on the circuit courts of appeals will further increase.

The attainment of speedier justice in the courts below will enlarge the task of the Supreme Court itself. And still more work would be added by the recommendation which I make later in this message for the quicker determination of constitutional questions by the highest court.

Even at the present time the Supreme Court is laboring under a heavy burden. Its difficulties in this respect were superficially lightened some years ago by authorizing the Court, in its discretion, to refuse to hear appeals in many classes of cases. This discretion was so freely exercised that in the last fiscal year, although 867 petitions for review were presented to the Supreme Court, it declined to hear 717 cases. If petitions in behalf of the Government are excluded, it appears that the Court permitted private litigants to prosecute appeals in only 108 cases out of 803 applications. Many of the refusals were doubtless warranted. But can it be said that full justice is achieved when a court is forced by the sheer necessity of keeping up with its business to decline, without even an explanation, to hear 87 percent of the cases presented to it by private litigants?

It seems clear, therefore, that the necessity of relieving present congestion extends to the enlargement of the capacity of all the Federal courts.

A part of the problem of obtaining a sufficient number of judges to dispose of cases is the capacity of the judges themselves. This brings forward the question of aged or infirm judges — a subject of delicacy and yet one which requires frank discussion.

In the Federal courts there are in all 237 life tenure permanent judgeships. Twenty-five of them are now held by judges over 70 years of age and eligible to leave the bench on full pay. Originally no pension or retirement allowance was provided by the Congress. When after 80 years of our national history the Congress made provision for pensions, it found a well-entrenched tradition among judges to cling to their posts, in many instances far beyond their years of physical or mental capacity. Their salaries were small. As with other men, responsibilities and obligations accumulated. No alternative had been open to them except to attempt to perform the duties of their offices to the very edge of the grave.

In exceptional cases, of course, judges, like other men, retain to an advanced age full mental and physical vigor. Those not so fortunate are often unable to perceive their own infirmities. " They seem to be tenacious of the appearance of adequacy." The voluntary retirement law of 1869 provided, therefore, only a partial solution. That law, still in force, has not proved effective in inducing aged judges to retire on a pension.

This result had been foreseen in the debates when the measure was being considered. It was then proposed that when a judge refused to retire upon reaching the age of 70, an additional judge should be appointed to assist in the work of the court. The proposal passed the House but was eliminated in the Senate.

With the opening of the twentieth century, and the great increase of population and commerce, and the growth of a more complex type of litigation, similar proposals were introduced in the Congress. To meet the situation, in 1913, 1914, 1915, and 1916, the Attorneys General then in office recommended to the Congress that when a district or a circuit judge failed to retire at the age of 70, an additional judge be appointed in order that the affairs of the court might be promptly and adequately discharged.

In 1919 a law was finally passed providing that the President " may " appoint additional district and circuit judges, but only upon a finding that the incumbent judge over 70 " is unable to discharge efficiently all the duties of his office by reason of mental or physical disability of permanent character." The discretionary and indefinite nature of this legislation has rendered it ineffective. No President should be asked to determine the ability or disability of any particular judge.

The duty of a judge involves more than presiding or listening to testimony or arguments. It is well to remember that the mass of details involved in the average of law cases today is vastly greater and more complicated than even 20 years ago. Records and briefs must be read; statutes, decisions, and extensive material of a technical, scientific, statistical, and economic nature must be searched and studied; opinions must be formulated and written. The modern tasks of judges call for the use of full energies.

Modern complexities call also for a constant infusion of new blood in the courts, just as it is needed in executive functions of the Government and in private business. A lowered mental or physical vigor leads men to avoid an examination of complicated and changed conditions. Little by little, new facts become blurred through old glasses fitted, as it were, for the needs of another generation; older men, assuming that the scene is the same as it was in the past, cease to explore or inquire into the present or the future.

We have recognized this truth in the civil service of the Nation and of many States by compelling retirement on pay at the age of 70. We have recognized it in the Army and Navy by retiring officers at the age of 64. A number of States have recognized it by providing in their constitutions for compulsory retirement of aged judges.

Life tenure of judges, assured by the Constitution, was designed to place the courts beyond temptations or influences which might impair their judgments; it was not intended to create a static judiciary. A constant and systematic addition of younger blood will vitalize the courts and better equip them to recognize and apply the essential concepts of justice in the light of the needs and the facts of an ever changing world.

It is obvious, therefore, from both reason and experience, that

some provision must be adopted which will operate automatically
to supplement the work of older judges and accelerate the work
of the court.

I, therefore, earnestly recommend that the necessity of an increase in the number of judges be supplied by legislation providing for the appointment of additional judges in all Federal courts,
without exception, where there are incumbent judges of retirement age who do not choose to retire or to resign. If an elder
judge is not in fact incapacitated, only good can come from the
presence of an additional judge in the crowded state of the dockets; if the capacity of an elder judge is in fact impaired, the appointment of an additional judge is indispensable. This seems
to be a truth which cannot be contradicted.

I also recommend that the Congress provide machinery for
taking care of sudden or long-standing congestion in the lower
courts. The Supreme Court should be given power to appoint an
administrative assistant who may be called a proctor. He would
be charged with the duty of watching the calendars and the business of all the courts in the Federal system. The Chief Justice
thereupon should be authorized to make a temporary assignment
of any circuit or district judge hereafter appointed in order that
he may serve as long as needed in any circuit or district where
the courts are in arrears.

I attach a carefully considered draft of a proposed bill, which,
if enacted, would, I am confident, afford substantial relief. The
proposed measure also contains a limit on the total number of
judges who might thus be appointed and also a limit on the poten-
tial size of any one of our Federal courts.

These proposals do not raise any issue of constitutional law.
They do not suggest any form of compulsory retirement for incumbent judges. Indeed, those who have reached the retirement
age, but desire to continue their judicial work, would be able to
do so under less physical and mental strain and would be able to
play a useful part in relieving the growing congestion in the
business of our courts. Among them are men of eminence and
great ability whose services the Government would be loath to

lose. If, on the other hand, any judge eligible for retirement
should feel that his court would suffer because of an increase in its
membership, he may retire or resign under already existing provisions of law if he wishes so to do. In this connection let me say
that the pending proposal to extend to the Justices of the Supreme
Court the same retirement privileges now available to other Federal judges, has my entire approval.

One further matter requires immediate attention. We have
witnessed the spectacle of conflicting decisions in both trial and
appellate courts on the constitutionality of every form of important legislation. Such a welter of uncomposed differences of judicial opinion has brought the law, the courts, and, indeed, the
entire administration of justice dangerously near to disrepute.

A Federal statute is held legal by one judge in one district; it
is simultaneously held illegal by another judge in another district.
An act valid in one judicial circuit is invalid in another judicial
circuit. Thus rights fully accorded to one group of citizens may
be denied to others. As a practical matter this means that for
periods running as long as 1 year or 2 years or 3 years — until
final determination can be made by the Supreme Court — the law
loses its most indispensable element — equality.

Moreover, during the long processes of preliminary motions,
original trials, petitions for rehearings, appeals, reversals on
technical grounds requiring retrials, motions before the Supreme
Court, and the final hearing by the highest tribunal — during all
this time labor, industry, agriculture, commerce, and the Government itself go through an unconscionable period of uncertainty
and embarrassment. And it is well to remember that during these
long processes the normal operations of society and government
are handicapped in many cases by differing and divided opinions
in the lower courts and by the lack of any clear guide for the
dispatch of business. Thereby our legal system is fast losing
another essential of justice — certainty.

Finally, we find the processes of government itself brought to
a complete stop from time to time by injunctions issued almost
automatically, sometimes even without notice to the Government,

and not infrequently in clear violation of the principle of equity that injunctions should be granted only in those rare cases of manifest illegality and irreparable damage against which the ordinary course of the law offers no protection. Statutes which the Congress enacts are set aside or suspended for long periods of time, even in cases to which the Government is not a party.

In the uncertain state of the law, it is not difficult for the ingenious to devise novel reasons for attacking the validity of new legislation or its application. While these questions are laboriously brought to issue and debated through a series of courts, the Government must stand aside. It matters not that the Congress has enacted the law, that the Executive has signed it, and that the administrative machinery is waiting to function. Government by injunction lays a heavy hand upon normal processes; and no important statute can take effect — against any individual or organization with the means to employ lawyers and engaged in wide-flung litigation — until it has passed through the whole hierarchy of the courts. Thus the judiciary, by postponing the effective date of acts of the Congress, is assuming an additional function and is coming more and more to constitute a scattered, loosely organized, and slowly operating third house of the National Legislature.

This state of affairs has come upon the Nation gradually over a period of decades. In my annual message to this Congress I expressed some views and some hopes.

Now, as an immediate step, I recommend that the Congress provide that no decision, injunction, judgment, or decree on any constitutional question be promulgated by any Federal court without previous and ample notice to the Attorney General and an opportunity for the United States to present evidence and be heard. This is to prevent court action on the constitutionality of acts of the Congress in suits between private individuals, where the Government is not a party to the suit, without giving opportunity to the Government of the United States to defend the law of the land.

I also earnestly recommend that, in cases in which any court of first instance determines a question of constitutionality, the Congress provide that there shall be a direct and immediate appeal to the Supreme Court and that such cases take precedence over all other matters pending in that court. Such legislation will, I am convinced, go far to alleviate the inequality, uncertainty, and delay in the disposition of vital questions of constitutionality arising under our fundamental law.

My desire is to strengthen the administration of justice and to make it a more effective servant of public need. In the American ideal of government the courts find an essential and constitutional place. In striving to fulfill that ideal, not only the judges but the Congress and the Executive as well, must do all in their power to bring the judicial organization and personnel to the high standards of usefulness which sound and efficient government and modern conditions require.

This message has dealt with four present needs:

First, to eliminate congestion of calendars and to make the judiciary as a whole less static by the constant and systematic addition of new blood to its personnel; second, to make the judiciary more elastic by providing for temporary transfers of circuit and district judges to those places where Federal courts are most in arrears; third, to furnish the Supreme Court practical assistance in supervising the conduct of business in the lower courts; fourth, to eliminate inequality, uncertainty, and delay now existing in the determination of constitutional questions involving Federal statutes.

If we increase the personnel of the Federal courts so that cases may be promptly decided in the first instance, and may be given adequate and prompt hearing on all appeals; if we invigorate all the courts by the persistent infusion of new blood; if we grant to the Supreme Court further power and responsibility in maintaining the efficiency of the entire Federal judiciary; and if we assure Government participation in the speedier consideration and final determination of all constitutional questions, we shall go a long way toward our high objectives. If these measures achieve their aim, we may be relieved of the necessity of considering any fundamental changes in the powers of the courts or the Constitution of our Government — changes which involve consequences so far reaching as to cause uncertainty as to the wisdom of such course.

FRANKLIN D. ROOSEVELT

*February 2, 1937*

The PRESIDENT,
   *The White House.*

MY DEAR MR. PRESIDENT: Delay in the administration of justice is the outstanding defect of our Federal judicial system. It has been a cause of concern to practically every one of my predecessors in office. It has exasperated the bench, the bar, the business community, and the public.

The litigant conceives the judge as one promoting justice through the mechanism of the courts. He assumes that the directing power of the judge is exercised over its officers from the time a case is filed with the clerk of the court. He is entitled to assume that the judge is pressing forward litigation in the full recognition of the principle that " justice delayed is justice denied." It is a mockery of justice to say to a person when he files suit that he may receive a decision years later. Under a properly ordered system rights should be determined promptly. The course of litigation should be measured in months and not in years.

Yet in some jurisdictions the delays in the administration of justice are so interminable that to institute suit is to embark on a life-long adventure. Many persons submit to acts of injustice rather than resort to the courts. Inability to secure a prompt judicial adjudication leads to improvident and unjust settlements. Moreover, the time factor is an open invitation to those who are disposed to institute unwarranted litigation or interpose unfounded defenses in the hope of forcing an adjustment which could not be secured upon the merits. This situation frequently results in extreme hardships. The small business man or the litigant of limited means labors under a grave and constantly increasing disadvantage because of his inability to pay the price of justice.

Statistical data indicate that in many districts a disheartening and unavoidable interval must elapse between the date that issue is joined in a pending case and the time when it can be reached for trial in due course. These computations do not take into account the delays that occur in the preliminary stages of litigation or the postponements after a case might normally be expected to be heard.

The evil is a growing one. The business of the courts is continually increasing in volume, importance, and complexity. The average case load borne by each judge has grown nearly 50 percent since 1913, when the District courts were first organized on their present basis. When the courts are working under such pressure it is inevitable that the character of their work must suffer.

The number of new cases offset those that are disposed of, so that the courts are unable to decrease the enormous backlog of undigested matters. More than 50,000 pending cases (exclusive of bankruptcy proceedings) overhang the Federal dockets — a constant menace to the orderly processes of justice. Whenever a single case requires a protracted trial, the routine business of the court is further neglected. It is an intolerable situation and we should make shift to amend it.

Efforts have been made from time to time to alleviate some of the conditions that contribute to the slow rate of speed with which causes move through the courts. The Congress has recently conferred on the Supreme Court the authority to prescribe rules of procedure after verdict in criminal cases and the power to adopt and promulgate uniform rules of practice for civil actions at law in the district courts. It has provided terms of court in certain places at which Federal courts had not previously convened. A small number of judges have been added from time to time.

Despite these commendable accomplishments sufficient progress has not been made. Much remains to be done in developing procedure and administration, but this alone will not meet modern needs. The problem must be approached in a more comprehensive fashion, if the United States is to have a judicial system worthy of the Nation. Reason and necessity require the appointment of a sufficient number of judges to handle the business of the Federal courts. These additional judges should be of a type and age which would warrant us in believing that they would vigorously attack their dockets, rather than permit their dockets to overwhelm them.

The cost of additional personnel should not deter us. It must be borne in mind that the expense of maintaining the judicial system constitutes hardly three-tenths of 1 percent of the cost of maintaining the Federal establishment. While the estimates for the current fiscal year aggregate over $23,000,000 for the maintenance of the legislative branch of the Government, and over $2,100,000,000 for the permanent agencies of the executive branch, the estimated cost of maintaining the judiciary is only about $6,500,000. An increase in the judicial personnel, which I earnestly recommend, would result in a hardly perceptible percentage of increase in the total annual Budget.

This result should not be achieved, however, merely by creating new judicial positions in specific circuits or districts. The reform should be effectuated on the basis of a consistent system which would revitalize our whole judicial structure and assure the activity of judges at places where the accumulation of business is greatest. As congestion is a varying factor and cannot be foreseen, the system should be flexible and should permit the temporary assignment of judges to points where they appear to be most needed. The newly created personnel should constitute a mobile force, available for service in any part of the country at the assignment and direction of the Chief Justice. A functionary might well be created to be known as proctor, or by some other suitable title, to be appointed by the Supreme Court and to act under its direction, charged with the duty of continuously keep-

ing informed as to the state of Federal judicial business throughout the United States and of assisting the Chief Justice in assign-
ing judges to pressure areas.

I append hereto certain statistical information, which will give
point to the suggestions I have made.

These suggestions are designed to carry forward the program
for improving the processes of justice which we have discussed
and worked upon since the beginning of your first administration.

The time has come when further legislation is essential.

To speed justice, to bring it within the reach of every citizen,
to free it of unnecessary entanglements and delays are primary
obligations of our Government.

Respectfully submitted.

HOMER CUMMINGS,
*Attorney General.*

*March 9, 1937*

*Address of the President, broadcast from the White House.*

Last Thursday I described in detail certain economic problems which everyone admits now face the Nation. For the many
messages which have come to me after that speech, and which it
is physically impossible to answer individually, I take this means
of saying " thank you."

Tonight, sitting at my desk in the White House, I make my
first radio report to the people in my second term of office.

I am reminded of that evening in March, four years ago, when
I made my first radio report to you. We were then in the midst
of the great banking crisis.

Soon after, with the authority of the Congress, we asked the
Nation to turn over all of its privately held gold, dollar for dollar, to the Government of the United States.

Today's recovery proves how right that policy was.

But when, almost two years later, it came before the Supreme

Court its constitutionality was upheld only by a five-to-four vote. The change of one vote would have thrown all the affairs of this great Nation back into hopeless chaos. In effect, four Justices ruled that the right under a private contract to exact a pound of flesh was more sacred than the main objectives of the Constitution to establish an enduring Nation.

In 1933 you and I knew that we must never let our economic system get completely out of joint again — that we could not afford to take the risk of another great depression.

We also became convinced that the only way to avoid a repetition of those dark days was to have a government with power to prevent and to cure the abuses and the inequalities which had thrown that system out of joint.

We then began a program of remedying those abuses and inequalities — to give balance and stability to our economic system — to make it bomb-proof against the causes of 1929.

Today we are only part-way through that program — and recovery is speeding up to a point where the dangers of 1929 are again becoming possible, not this week or month perhaps, but within a year or two.

National laws are needed to complete that program. Individual or local or state effort alone cannot protect us in 1937 any better than ten years ago.

It will take time — and plenty of time — to work out our remedies administratively even after legislation is passed. To complete our program of protection in time, therefore, we cannot delay one moment in making certain that our National Government has power to carry through.

Four years ago action did not come until the eleventh hour. It was almost too late.

If we learned anything from the depression we will not allow ourselves to run around in new circles of futile discussion and debate, always postponing the day of decision.

The American people have learned from the depression. For in the last three national elections an overwhelming majority of them voted a mandate that the Congress and the President begin the task of providing that protection — not after long years of debate, but now.

The Courts, however, have cast doubts on the ability of the elected Congress to protect us against catastrophe by meeting squarely our modern social and economic conditions.

We are at a crisis in our ability to proceed with that protection. It is a quiet crisis. There are no lines of depositors outside closed banks. But to the far-sighted it is far-reaching in its possibilities of injury to America.

I want to talk with you very simply about the need for present action in this crisis — the need to meet the unanswered challenge of one-third of a Nation ill-nourished, ill-clad, ill-housed.

Last Thursday I described the American form of Government as a three horse team provided by the Constitution to the American people so that their field might be plowed. The three horses are, of course, the three branches of government — the Congress, the Executive and the Courts. Two of the horses are pulling in unison today; the third is not. Those who have intimated that the President of the United States is trying to drive that team, overlook the simple fact that the President, as Chief Executive, is himself one of the three horses.

It is the American people themselves who are in the driver's seat.

It is the American people themselves who want the furrow plowed.

It is the American people themselves who expect the third horse to pull in unison with the other two.

I hope that you have re-read the Constitution of the United States. Like the Bible, it ought to be read again and again.

It is an easy document to understand when you remember that it was called into being because the Articles of Confederation under which the original thirteen States tried to operate after the Revolution showed the need of a National Government with power enough to handle national problems. In its Preamble, the Constitution states that it was intended to form a more perfect Union and promote the general welfare; and the powers given to

the Congress to carry out those purposes can be best described
by saying that they were all the powers needed to meet each and
every problem which then had a national character and which
could not be met by merely local action.

But the framers went further. Having in mind that in succeeding generations many other problems then undreamed of
would become national problems, they gave to the Congress the
ample broad powers " to levy taxes * * * and provide for the
common defense and general welfare of the United States."

That, my friends, is what I honestly believe to have been the
clear and underlying purpose of the patriots who wrote a Federal
Constitution to create a National Government with national power,
intended as they said, " to form a more perfect union * * * for
ourselves and our posterity."

For nearly twenty years there was no conflict between the
Congress and the Court. Then, in 1803, Congress passed a statute
which the Court said violated an express provision of the Constitution. The Court claimed the power to declare it unconstitutional and did so declare it. But a little later the Court itself admitted that it was an extraordinary power to exercise and through
Mr. Justice Washington laid down this limitation upon it: " It
is but a decent respect due to the wisdom, the integrity and the
patriotism of the Legislative body, by which any law is passed,
to presume in favor of its validity until its violation of the Constitution is proved beyond all reasonable doubt."

But since the rise of the modern movement for social and economic progress through legislation, the Court has more and more
often and more and more boldly asserted a power to veto laws
passed by the Congress and State Legislatures in complete disregard of this original limitation.

In the last four years the sound rule of giving statutes the
benefit of all reasonable doubt has been cast aside. The Court
has been acting not as a judicial body, but as a policy-making
body.

When the Congress has sought to stabilize national agriculture,
to improve the conditions of labor, to safeguard business against

unfair competition, to protect our national resources, and in many other ways, to serve our clearly national needs, the majority of the Court has been assuming the power to pass on the wisdom of these Acts of the Congress — and to approve or disapprove the public policy written into these laws.

That is not only my accusation. It is the accusation of most distinguished Justices of the present Supreme Court. I have not the time to quote to you all the language used by dissenting Justices in many of these cases. But in the case holding the Railroad Retirement Act unconstitutional, for instance, Chief Justice Hughes said in a dissenting opinion that the majority opinion was " a departure from sound principles," and placed " an unwarranted limitation upon the commerce clause." And three other Justices agreed with him.

In the case holding the A.A.A. unconstitutional, Justice Stone said of the majority opinion that it was a " tortured construction of the Constitution." And two other Justices agreed with him.

In the case holding the New York Minimum Wage Law unconstitutional, Justice Stone said that the majority were actually reading into the Constitution their own " personal economic predilections," and that if the legislative power is not left free to choose the methods of solving the problems of poverty, subsistence and health of large numbers in the community, then " government is to be rendered impotent." And two other Justices agreed with him.

In the face of these dissenting opinions, there is no basis for the claim made by some members of the Court that something in the Constitution has compelled them regretfully to thwart the will of the people.

In the face of such dissenting opinions, it is perfectly clear, that as Chief Justice Hughes has said: " We are under a Constitution but the Constitution is what the Judges say it is."

The Court in addition to the proper use of its judicial functions has improperly set itself up as a third House of the Congress — a super-legislature, as one of the Justices has called it

— reading into the Constitution words and implications which are not there, and which were never intended to be there.

We have, therefore, reached the point as a Nation where we must take action to save the Constitution from the Court and the Court from itself. We must find a way to take an appeal from the Supreme Court to the Constitution itself. We want a Supreme Court which will do justice under the Constitution — not over it. In our Courts we want a government of laws and not of men.

I want — as all Americans want — an independent judiciary as proposed by the framers of the Constitution. That means a Supreme Court that will enforce the Constitution as written — that will refuse to amend the Constitution by the arbitrary exercise of judicial power — amendment by judicial say-so. It does not mean a judiciary so independent that it can deny the existence of facts universally recognized.

How then could we proceed to perform the mandate given us? It was said in last year's Democratic platform " If these problems cannot be effectively solved within the Constitution, we shall seek such clarifying amendment as will assure the power to enact those laws, adequately to regulate commerce, protect public health and safety, and safeguard economic security." In other words, we said we would seek an amendment only if every other possible means by legislation were to fail.

When I commenced to review the situation with the problem squarely before me, I came by a process of elimination to the conclusion that short of amendments the only method which was clearly constitutional, and would at the same time carry out other much needed reforms, was to infuse new blood into all our Courts. We must have men worthy and equipped to carry out impartial justice. But, at the same time, we must have Judges who will bring to the Courts a present-day sense of the Constitution — Judges who will retain in the Courts the judicial functions of a court, and reject the legislative powers which the Courts have today assumed.

In forty-five out of the forty-eight States of the Union, Judges are chosen not for life but for a period of years. In many States Judges must retire at the age of seventy. Congress has provided financial security by offering life pensions at full pay for Federal Judges on all Courts who are willing to retire at seventy. In the case of Supreme Court Justices, that pension is $20,000 a year. But all Federal Judges, once appointed, can, if they choose, hold office for life, no matter how old they may get to be.

What is my proposal? It is simply this: whenever a Judge or Justice of any Federal Court has reached the age of seventy and does not avail himself of the opportunity to retire on a pension, a new member shall be appointed by the President then in office, with the approval, as required by the Constitution, of the Senate of the United States.

That plan has two chief purposes. By bringing into the Judicial system a steady and continuing stream of new and younger blood, I hope, first, to make the administration of all Federal justice speedier and, therefore, less costly; secondly, to bring to the decision of social and economic problems younger men who have had personal experience and contact with modern facts and circumstances under which average men have to live and work. This plan will save our national Constitution from hardening of the judicial arteries.

The number of Judges to be appointed would depend wholly on the decision of present Judges now over seventy, or those who would subsequently reach the age of seventy.

If, for instance, any one of the six Justices of the Supreme Court now over the age of seventy should retire as provided under the plan, no additional place would be created. Consequently, although there never can be more than fifteen, there may be only fourteen, or thirteen, or twelve. And there may be only nine.

There is nothing novel or radical about this idea. It seeks to maintain the Federal bench in full vigor. It has been discussed and approved by many persons of high authority ever since a similar proposal passed the House of Representatives in 1869.

Why was the age fixed at seventy? Because the laws of many States, the practice of the Civil Service, the regulations of the

Army and Navy, and the rules of many of our Universities and of almost every great private business enterprise, commonly fix the retirement age at seventy years or less.

The statute would apply to all the Courts in the Federal system. There is general approval so far as the lower Federal courts are concerned. The plan has met opposition only so far as the Supreme Court of the United States itself is concerned. If such a plan is good for the lower courts it certainly ought to be equally good for the highest Court from which there is no appeal.

Those opposing this plan have sought to arouse prejudice and fear by crying that I am seeking to " pack " the Supreme Court and that a baneful precedent will be established.

What do they mean by the words " packing the Court "?

Let me answer this question with a bluntness that will end all *honest* misunderstanding of my purposes.

If by that phrase " packing the Court " it is charged that I wish to place on the bench spineless puppets who would disregard the law and would decide specific cases as I wished them to be decided, I make this answer — that no President fit for his office would appoint, and no Senate of honorable men fit for their office would confirm, that kind of appointees to the Supreme Court.

But if by that phrase the charge is made that I would appoint and the Senate would confirm Justices worthy to sit beside present members of the Court who understand those modern conditions — that I will appoint Justices who will not undertake to override the judgment of the Congress on legislative policy — that I will appoint Justices who will act as Justices and not as legislators — if the appointment of such Justices can be called " packing the Courts," then I say that I and with me the vast majority of the American people favor doing just that thing — now.

Is it a dangerous precedent for the Congress to change the number of the Justices? The Congress has always had, and will have, that power. The number of Justices has been changed several times before — in the Administrations of John Adams and Thomas Jefferson, — both signers of the Declaration of Independence — Andrew Jackson, Abraham Lincoln and Ulysses S. Grant.

I suggest only the addition of Justices to the bench in accordance with a clearly defined principle relating to a clearly defined age limit. Fundamentally, if in the future, America cannot trust the Congress it elects to refrain from abuse of our Constitutional usages, democracy will have failed far beyond the importance to it of any kind of precedent concerning the Judiciary.

We think it so much in the public interest to maintain a vigorous judiciary that we encourage the retirement of elderly Judges by offering them a life pension at full salary. Why then should we leave the fulfillment of this public policy to chance or make it dependent upon the desire or prejudice of any individual Justice?

It is the clear intention of our public policy to provide for a constant flow of new and younger blood into the Judiciary. Normally every President appoints a large number of District and Circuit Judges and a few members of the Supreme Court. Until my first term practically every President of the United States had appointed at least one member of the Supreme Court. President Taft appointed five members and named a Chief Justice — President Wilson three — President Harding four including a Chief Justice — President Coolidge one — President Hoover three including a Chief Justice.

Such a succession of appointments should have provided a Court well-balanced as to age. But chance and the disinclination of individuals to leave the Supreme bench have now given us a Court in which five Justices will be over seventy-five years of age before next June and one over seventy. Thus a sound public policy has been defeated.

I now propose that we establish by law an assurance against any such ill-balanced Court in the future. I propose that hereafter, when a Judge reaches the age of seventy, a new and younger Judge shall be added to the Court automatically. In this way I propose to enforce a sound public policy by law instead of leaving the composition of our Federal Courts, including the highest, to be determined by chance or the personal decision of individuals.

If such a law as I propose is regarded as establishing a new precedent — is it not a most desirable precedent?

Like all lawyers, like all Americans, I regret the necessity of this controversy. But the welfare of the United States, and indeed of the Constitution itself, is what we all must think about first. Our difficulty with the Court today rises not from the Court as an institution but from human beings within it. But we cannot yield our constitutional destiny to the personal judgment of a few men who, being fearful of the future, would deny us the necessary means of dealing with the present.

This plan of mine is no attack on the Court; it seeks to restore the Court to its rightful and historic place in our system of Constitutional Government and to have it resume its high task of building anew on the Constitution " a system of living law."

I have thus explained to you the reasons that lie behind our efforts to secure results by legislation within the Constitution. I hope that thereby the difficult process of constitutional amendment may be rendered unnecessary. But let us examine that process.

There are many types of amendment proposed. Each one is radically different from the other. There is no substantial group within the Congress or outside it who are agreed on any single amendment.

It would take months or years to get substantial agreement upon the type and language of an amendment. It would take months and years thereafter to get a two-thirds majority in favor of that amendment in *both* Houses of the Congress.

Then would come the long course of ratification by three-fourths of the States. No amendment which any powerful economic interests or the leaders of any powerful political party have had reason to oppose has ever been ratified within anything like a reasonable time. And thirteen States which contain only five per cent of the voting population can block ratification even though the thirty-five States with ninety-five per cent of the population are in favor of it.

A very large percentage of newspaper publishers, Chambers of

Commerce, Bar Associations, Manufacturers' Associations, who are trying to give the impression that they really do want a constitutional amendment would be the first to exclaim as soon as an amendment was proposed " Oh! I was for an amendment all right, but this amendment that you have proposed is not the kind of an amendment that I was thinking about. I am, therefore, going to spend my time, my efforts and my money to block that amendment, although I would be awfully glad to help get some other kind of amendment ratified."

Two groups oppose my plan on the ground that they favor a constitutional amendment. The first includes those who fundamentally object to social and economic legislation along modern lines. This is the same group who during the campaign last Fall tried to block the mandate of the people.

Now they are making a last stand. And the strategy of that last stand is to suggest the time-consuming process of amendment in order to kill off by delay the legislation demanded by the mandate.

To them I say — I do not think you will be able long to fool the American people as to your purposes.

The other group is composed of those who honestly believe the amendment process is the best and who would be willing to support a reasonable amendment if they could agree on one.

To them I say — we cannot rely on an amendment as the immediate or only answer to our present difficulties. When the time comes for action, you will find that many of those who pretend to support you will sabotage any constructive amendment which is proposed. Look at these strange bed-fellows of yours. When before have you found them really at your side in your fights for progress?

And remember one thing more. Even if an amendment were passed, and even if in the years to come it were to be ratified, its meaning would depend upon the kind of Justices who would be sitting on the Supreme Court bench. An amendment like the rest of the Constitution is what the Justices say it is rather than what its framers or you might hope it is.

This proposal of mine will not infringe in the slightest upon the civil or religious liberties so dear to every American.

My record as Governor and as President proves my devotion to those liberties. You who know me can have no fear that I would tolerate the destruction by any branch of government of any part of our heritage of freedom.

The present attempt by those opposed to progress to play upon the fears of danger to personal liberty brings again to mind that crude and cruel strategy tried by the same opposition to frighten the workers of America in a pay-envelope propaganda against the Social Security Law. The workers were not fooled by that propaganda then. The people of America will not be fooled by such propaganda now.

I am in favor of action through legislation:

First, because I believe that it can be passed at this session of the Congress.

Second, because it will provide a reinvigorated, liberal-minded Judiciary necessary to furnish quicker and cheaper justice from bottom to top.

Third, because it will provide a series of Federal Courts willing to enforce the Constitution as written, and unwilling to assert legislative powers by writing into it their own political and economic policies.

During the past half century the balance of power between the three great branches of the Federal Government, has been tipped out of balance by the Courts in direct contradiction of the high purposes of the framers of the Constitution. It is my purpose to restore that balance. You who know me will accept my solemn assurance that in a world in which democracy is under attack, I seek to make American democracy succeed.

*75th Congress, 1st Session.* S. J. Resolution 80

IN THE SENATE OF THE UNITED STATES. February 15 (calendar day, February 17), 1937. Mr. Wheeler (for himself and Mr. Bone) introduced the following joint resolution; which was read twice and referred to the Committee on the Judiciary.

*JOINT RESOLUTION proposing an amendment to the Constitution of the United States providing that any law held unconstitutional by the Supreme Court shall be valid if reenacted by Congress.*

*RESOLVED* by the Senate and House of Representatives of the United States of America in Congress assembled (two-thirds of each House concurring therein), That the following article is proposed as an amendment to the Constitution of the United States, which shall be valid to all intents and purposes as part of the Constitution when ratified by the legislatures of three-fourths of the several States:

" Article —, Section 1. In case the Supreme Court renders any judgment holding any Act of Congress or any provision of any such Act unconstitutional, the question with respect to the constitutionality of such Act or provision shall be promptly submitted to the Congress for its action at the earliest practicable date that the Congress is in session following the date upon which such judgment is rendered; but no action shall be taken by the Congress upon such question until an election shall have been held at which Members of the House of Representatives are regularly by law to be chosen. If such Act or provision is reenacted by two-thirds of each House of the Congress to which such Members are elected at such election, such Act or provision shall be deemed to be constitutional and effective from the date of such reenactment.

" Section 2. This article shall be inoperative unless it shall have been ratified as an amendment to the Constitution by the legislatures of three-fourths of the several States within seven years from the date of its submission."

## 75th Congress, 1st Session. S. J. RESOLUTION 98

IN THE SENATE OF THE UNITED STATES. March 11, 1937. Mr. O'MAHONEY introduced the following joint resolution; which was read twice and referred to the Committee on the Judiciary.

*JOINT RESOLUTION proposing an amendment to the Constitution of the United States relating to the power of the courts to hold laws unconstitutional.*

RESOLVED by the Senate and House of Representatives of the United States of America in Congress assembled (two-thirds of each House concurring therein), That the following article is hereby proposed as an amendment to the Constitution of the United States, which shall be valid to all intents and purposes as part of the Constitution when ratified by conventions in three-fourths of the several States:

"ARTICLE —, SECTION 1. No law of the United States or of any State shall be held to be unconstitutional by any inferior court, and not by the Supreme Court unless two-thirds of the members thereof shall specifically and by separate opinion find it so beyond a reasonable doubt.

"SECTION 2. This article shall be inoperative unless it shall have been ratified as an amendment to the Constitution by conventions in the several States, as provided in the Constitution, within seven years from the date of the submission hereof to the States by the Congress."

# TABLE OF CASES

## A

Ableman v. Booth, 18 How. 476; 21 How. 506 . . . . 17, 18
Adair v. United States, 208 U. S. 161 . . . . 65
Adkins v. Children's Hospital, 261 U. S. 525 . 53, 54, 171, 186
Alabama Power Co. v. Ickes, 302 U. S. 464 . . . 247
Amazon Petroleum Corp. v. Ryan, 293 U. S. 389 . . 87, 94
American States Public Service Co., *In re,* 12 F. Supp. 667    121
Anniston Manufacturing Co. v. Davis, 301 U. S. 337 . 139
Appalachian Coals, Inc. v. United States, 288 U. S. 344    158
Ashton v. Cameron County District, 298 U. S. 513 . 165, 240
Ashwander v. Tennessee Valley Authority, 297 U. S.
  288 . . . . . . . . . . . 145, 255
Associated Industries v. Department of Labor, 299 U. S.
  515 . . . . . . . . . . . 182
Associated Press v. National Labor Relations Board, 301
  U. S. 103 . . . . . . . . . . 216

## B

Bailey v. George, 259 U. S. 16 . . . . . . 140
Baldwin v. Missouri, 281 U. S. 586 . . . . . 68
Baltimore and Ohio Railroad Co. v. United States, 298
  U. S. 349 . . . . . . . . . . 300
Bedford Cut Stone Co. v. Journeymen Stone Cutters'
  Assn., 274 U. S. 37 . . . . . . . 63
Black & White Taxicab Co. v. Brown & Yellow Taxicab
  Co., 276 U. S. 518 . . . . . . . . 307
Borden's Farm Products Co. v. Baldwin, 293 U. S. 194    299
Bunting v. Oregon, 243 U. S. 426 . . . . . 66
Burco, Inc. v. Whitworth, 297 U. S. 724 . . . . 121
Burnet v. Coronado Oil & Gas Co., 285 U. S. 393 . 48, 297
Butz v. City of Muscatine, 8 Wall. 575 . . . . 277

## C

Carmichael v. Southern Coal & Coke Co., 301 U. S. 495    226
Carter v. Carter Coal Co., 298 U. S. 238    21, 153, 161, 163
Central West Public Service Co., *In re,* 13 F. Supp. 239    121
Champion v. Ames, 188 U. S. 321 . . . . . 67

Chicago & Grand Trunk Railway Co. v. Wellman, 143
U. S. 339 . . . . . . . . . .        41
Chicago, Milwaukee and St. Paul Railway Company v.
Minnesota, 134 U. S. 418 . . . . . . .        51
Chicot County Drainage District v. Baxter Bank (Jan. 2,
1940) . . . . . . . . . . .        308
Children's Hospital v. Adkins, 284 Fed. 613 . . .        73
Chisholm v. Georgia, 2 Dall. 419 . . . . .        13
Cincinnati Soap Co. v. United States, 301 U. S. 308 . .        220
Coleman v. Miller, 307 U. S. 433 . . . . . .        262
Colgate v. Harvey, 296 U. S. 404 . . . .        168, 169
Collector v. Day, 11 Wall. 113 . . . . . .        241
Coppage v. Kansas, 236 U. S. 1 . . . . . .        65
Crowell v. Benson, 285 U. S. 22 . . . . . .        270
Currin v. Wallace, 306 U. S. 1 . . . . .        95, 237
Curry v. McCanless, 307 U. S. 357 . . . . .        292

## D

Davidson v. New Orleans, 96 U. S. 97 . . . . .        49
De Jonge v. Oregon, 299 U. S. 353 . . . . .        203
Dred Scott v. Sandford, 19 How. 393 . . . .        24, 327
Duke Power Co. v. Greenwood County, 10 F. Supp. 854;
299 U. S. 259 . . . . . . . .        116, 200, 247

## E

Eisner v. Macomber, 252 U. S. 189 . . . . .        48
Electric Bond & Share Co. v. Securities and Exchange
Comm'n, 303 U. S. 419 . . . . . . .        255
Erie Railroad Co. v. Tompkins, 304 U. S. 64        12, 194, 208, 272
Evans v. Gore, 253 U. S. 245 . . . . . .        48, 244
*Ex parte* Merryman, 17 Fed. Cas. 144 . . . .        324, 326
*Ex parte* Milligan, 4 Wall. 2 . . . . . .        71

## F

Fairfax v. Hunter, 7 Cranch 602 . . . . .        17
Federal Trade Comm. v. Curtis Publishing Co., 260 U. S.
568 . . . . . . . . . . .        61
Federal Trade Comm. v. Gratz, 253 U. S. 421 . . .        60
Federal Trade Comm. v. R. F. Keppel & Bro., 291 U. S.
305 . . . . . . . . . . .        163

Fiske v. Kansas, 274 U. S. 380 . . . . . . 71
Florida v. Mellon, 273 U. S. 12 . . . . . . 20

# G

Gelpcke v. Dubuque, 1 Wall. 175 . . . . 41, 276, 307
Georgia Power Co. v. Tennessee Valley Authority, 17
  F. Supp. 769 . . . . . . . . . 122
Graves v. Elliott, 307 U. S. 383 . . . . . 292
Graves v. O'Keefe, 306 U. S. 466 . . . . 194, 243
Great Northern Railway Co. v. Sunburst Oil & Refining
  Co., 287 U. S. 358 . . . . . . . . 307

# H

Hague v. Committee for Industrial Organization, 307
  U. S. 496 . . . . . . . . . . 284
Hale v. Bimco Trading, Inc., 306 U. S. 375 . . . 284
Hammer v. Dagenhart, 247 U. S. 251 . . . . 67
Hans v. Louisiana, 134 U. S. 1 . . . . . 14
Hart Coal Corporation v. Sparks, 7 F. Supp. 16 . . 116
Hayburn's case, 2 Dall. 408 . . . . . . 289
Helvering v. Davis, 301 U. S. 619 . . . . . 233
Helvering v. Gerhardt, 305 U. S. 669 . . . . . 308
Hepburn v. Griswold, 8 Wall. 603 . . . . . 41
Herndon v. Lowry, 301 U. S. 242 . . . . . . 219
Hillsboro Packing Co. v. Wallace (U. S. Dist. Ct. for
  Southern Dist. of Fla. — Jan. 30, 1934) . . . . 118
Hitchman Coal & Coke Company v. Mitchell, 245 U. S.
  229 . . . . . . . . . . 65, 186
Holden v. Hardy, 169 U. S. 366 . . . . . . 53, 66
Holyoke Water Power Co. v. American Writing Paper
  Co., 300 U. S. 324 . . . . . . . . 205
Home Building & Loan Association v. Blaisdell, 290 U. S.
  398 . . . . . . . . . . . 78, 79
H. P. Hood & Sons, Inc. v. United States, 307 U. S. 588 239
Hopkins Federal Savings & Loan Assn. v. Cleary, 296
  U. S. 315 . . . . . . . . . . 21
Humphrey's Executor v. United States, 295 U. S. 602 107

# I

*In re* American States Public Service Co., 12 F. Supp. 667 121
*In re* Central West Public Service Co., 13 F. Supp. 239 121

*In re* National Labor Relations Board, 304 U. S. 486        272
International Stone Company v. Federal Trade Commission, 280 U. S. 291 . . . . . . . .        61
Interstate Commerce Commission v. Louisville and Nashville Railroad Company, 227 U. S. 88 . . .        270

## J

Jones v. Securities & Exchange Commission, 298 U. S. 1 . . . . . . . . . . .        147, 148

## K

Kentucky Whip & Collar Co. v. Illinois Central Railroad Co., 299 U. S. 334 . . . . . . . .        202
Knox v. Lee, 12 Wall. 457 . . . . . . .        43

## L

Labor Board (See National Labor Relations Board)
Landis v. North American Co., 299 U. S. 248 . . .        198
Lochner v. New York, 198 U. S. 45 . . . . 53, 55, 66
Loewe v. Lawlor, 208 U. S. 274 . . . . . .        63
Louisville Joint Stock Land Bank v. Radford, 295 U. S. 555 . . . . . . . . . . .        106
Lovell v. City of Griffin, 303 U. S. 444 . . . .        284
Luther v. Borden, 7 How. 1 . . . . . . .        30

## M

McCarroll v. Dixie Greyhound Lines, Inc. (Feb. 12, 1940)        290
McCray v. United States, 195 U. S. 27 . . . .        67
McCulloch v. Maryland, 4 Wheat. 316 . . . . 29, 92
Marbury v. Madison, 1 Cranch 137 . . . . .        24
Massachusetts v. Mellon, 262 U. S. 447 . . . .        20
Massachusetts v. Missouri, 308 U. S. 1 . . . .        13
Merryman, *Ex parte,* 17 Fed. Cas. 144 . . . 324, 326
Miles v. Graham, 268 U. S. 501 . . . . . 48, 246
Milligan, *Ex parte,* 4 Wall. 2 . . . . . .        71
Milliken v. United States, 283 U. S. 15 . . . .        205
Minersville School District v. Gobitis (June 3, 1940) .        284
Moore v. Dempsey, 261 U. S. 86 . . . . . .        71
Morehead v. New York *ex rel.* Tipaldo, 298 U. S. 587 . . . . . . . . . 171, 186, 282

Morgan v. United States, 298 U. S. 468; 304 U. S. 1;
304 U. S. 23 . . . . . . . 264, 265
Mulford v. Smith, 307 U. S. 38 . . . . . 114, 237
Muller v. Oregon, 208 U. S. 412 . . . . . 53, 66
Munn v. Illinois, 94 U. S. 113 . . . . . 50
Muskrat v. United States, 219 U. S. 346 . . . . 289
Myers v. United States, 272 U. S. 52 . . . . 108

# N

National Labor Relations Board, *In re,* 304 U. S. 486 272
National Labor Relations Board v. Fainblatt, 306 U. S.
601 . . . . . . . . . 114
National Labor Relations Board v. Friedman-Harry
Marks Clothing Co., 301 U. S. 58 . . . . 216
National Labor Relations Board v. Fruehauf Trailer
Co., 301 U. S. 49 . . . . . . . 216
National Labor Relations Board v. Jones & Laughlin, 301
U. S. 1 . . . . . . . . 114, 216
Near v. Minnesota *ex rel.* Olson, 283 U. S. 697 . . . 71
Nebbia v. New York, 291 U. S. 502 . . . . 73, 80
Newark Fire Insurance Co. v. State Board of Tax Ap-
peals, 307 U. S. 313 . . . . . . . 293
New York Life Insurance Co. v. Deer Lodge County, 231
U. S. 495 . . . . . . . . 280
Nixon v. Herndon, 273 U. S. 536 . . . . . 71
Norman v. Baltimore & Ohio Railroad Co., 294 U. S.
240 . . . . . . . . . 100, 103
Nortz v. United States, 294 U. S. 317 . . . 101, 103

# O

Old Dearborn Distributing Co. v. Seagram Distillers
Corp., 299 U. S. 183 . . . . . . 164
O'Malley v. Woodrough, 307 U. S. 277 . . . 194, 246

# P

Palmer v. Massachusetts, 308 U. S. 79 . . . . 19
Panama Refining Co. v. Ryan, 293 U. S. 389 . . . 87, 94
Passenger Cases, 7 How. 283 . . . . . 297
Penn v. Glenn, 10 F. Supp. 483 . . . . . 116

Pennsylvania v. Wheeling & Belmont Bridge Company,
    13 How. 518 . . . . . . . . . 291
Perry v. United States, 294 U. S. 330 . . . . 101, 103
Pollock v. Farmers' Loan & Trust Co., 157 U. S. 429; 158
    U. S. 601 . . . . . . . . . 44, 47, 301
Powell v. Alabama, 287 U. S. 45 . . . . . . 71

## R

Railroad Retirement Board v. Alton Railroad Co., 295
    U. S. 330 . . . . . . . . . 105, 296
Ribnik v. McBride, 277 U. S. 350 . . . . . 56
Rickert Rice Mills, Inc. v. Fontenot, 297 U. S. 110 . . 141

## S

St. Joseph Stock Yards Co. v. United States, 298 U. S.
    38 . . . . . . . . . . 52, 297
St. Louis & O'Fallon Railway Company v. United States,
    279 U. S. 461 . . . . . . . . . 52
Schneider v. State, 308 U. S. 147 . . . . . 284
Senn v. Tile Layers Protective Union, 301 U. S. 468 . . 221
Smythe v. Ames, 169 U. S. 466 . . . . . . 51
Socony-Vacuum Oil Co., Inc. v. United States (May 6,
    1940) . . . . . . . . . . 92
Sonzinsky v. United States, 300 U. S. 506 . . . . 212
Standard Oil Company of New Jersey v. United States,
    221 U. S. 1 . . . . . . . . . 58, 59, 88
Steward Machine Co. v. Davis, 301 U. S. 548 . . 227, 300
Stout v. Pratt, 12 F. Supp. 864 . . . . . . 117
Sunshine Anthracite Coal Co. v. Coal Commission (May
    20, 1940) . . . . . . . . . 165
Swift v. Tyson, 16 Pet. 1 . . . . . . . 272
Swift and Company v. Federal Trade Commission, 272
    U. S. 554 . . . . . . . . . 61
Swift and Company v. United States, 196 U. S. 375 . . 58

## T

Tennessee Electric Power Co. v. Tennessee Valley Au-
    thority, 306 U. S. 118 . . . . . . . 255
Texas v. Florida, 306 U. S. 398 . . . . . . 13
Thornhill v. Alabama (April 22, 1940) . . . . 284

Truax v. Corrigan, 257 U. S. 312 . . . . . . 65
Tyson & Brother v. Banton, 273 U. S. 418 . . . . 56

# U

United States v. American Tobacco Company, 221 U. S.
106 . . . . . . . . . . . 59
United States v. Bankers Trust Co., 294 U. S. 240 . . 103
United States v. Bekins, 304 U. S. 27 . . . . 194, 240
United States v. Booth, 18 How. 476, 21 How. 506 . . 17, 18
United States v. Brims, 272 U. S. 549 . . . . . 64
United States v. Butler, 297 U. S. 1 . . 21, 125, 131, 232
United States v. Curtiss-Wright Export Corp., 299 U. S.
304 . . . . . . . . . . . 201
United States v. E. C. Knight Company, 156 U. S. 1 . . 57
United States v. Gearhart, 7 F. Supp. 712 . . . . 117
United States v. Grimaud, 220 U. S. 506 . . . . 92
United States v. Hudson, 299 U. S. 498 . . . . 203
United States v. Morgan, 307 U. S. 183 . . . . 267
United States v. Rock Royal Co-operative, Inc., 307 U. S.
533 . . . . . . . . . . . 239
United States v. Socony-Vacuum Oil Co., Inc. (May 6,
1940) . . . . . . . . . . . 92
United States v. Sutherland, 9 F. Supp. 204 . . . 117
United States v. Trans-Missouri Freight Association, 166
U. S. 290 . . . . . . . . . . 58
United States v. United States Steel Corporation, 251
U. S. 417 . . . . . . . . . . 63
Untermyer v. Anderson, 276 U. S. 440 . . . . 205

# V

Virginian Railway Co. v. System Federation No. 40, 300
U. S. 515 . . . . . . . . . . 212

# W

West v. Chesapeake & Potomac Telephone Company,
295 U. S. 662 . . . . . . . . . 52
West Coast Hotel Co. v. Parrish, 300 U. S. 379 38, 194, 206, 208
Williams v. Standard Oil Co., 278 U. S. 235 . . . 56
Worcester v. Georgia, 6 Pet. 515 . . . . . . 17
Wright v. Vinton Branch, 300 U. S. 440 . . . . 213

# INDEX

Acts of Congress held unconstitutional by Supreme Court, statistics of, 40.
Adams, John, 315.
Administrative agencies, relation of courts to, 262 f.
Agricultural legislation, 125 f., 175, 220, 236 f., 304.
   See also Farm debtors' relief.
Akerman, Alexander, 118.
Amendment of Constitution, 179, 261, 297.
   See also Child Labor Amendment.
Anti-trust laws, 57 f.
Arbitration, commercial, 323.

Baldwin, Simeon, 72.
Balfour, Lord, 316.
Bank of the United States, 29, 34.
Beck, James M., 140, 144.
Bentham, Jeremy, 323.
Bituminous Coal Act, 21, 153 f.
Black, Hugo L., 290.
Brandeis, Louis Dembitz, 134, 146, 161, 165, 169, 172, 182, 190, 221, 229, 245, 296, 297, 300, 312.
Buchanan, James, 258.
Butler, Pierce, 187, 206, 210, 218, 221, 226, 229, 238, 247, 260, 268, 272, 312.

Cardozo, Benjamin Nathan, 94, 134, 146, 149, 161, 165, 169, 172, 187, 227, 229, 233, 296, 307, 314.
Carter, James C., 301.
Chase, Salmon P., 32.
Chase, Samuel, 28.
Child labor, 67, 203.
Child Labor Amendment, 180, 260.
Choate, Joseph, 45.

Civil liberties, 22 f., 71, 203, 219, 284.
Clarke, John H., 186.
Coal industry, see Bituminous Coal Act.
Coleman, William C., 119.
Collective bargaining, see Labor unions; National Labor Relations Act.
Conservation of resources, 257.
Constitution, Judiciary Article of, 10.
Constitutional convention, 4, 5.
Cooley, Thomas, 35.
Corwin, Edward S., 141.
Court bill of 1937, 187 f., 234, 328 f.
Cummings, Homer S., 188.

Daugherty, Harry, 184.
Davis, John W., 119.
Dawson, Charles I., 116.
Decisions in constitutional cases, 1933–1937, 181.
Delay in constitutional cases, 302 f.
Delegation of power, 92 f., 163.
District courts, 115 f., 302.
Dorr's rebellion, 30.
Douglas, William O., 147, 290.
Dred Scott decision, 30, 36, 327.
Due process clause, 48, 54.
Duke Power Company, 200.

Election of 1936, 176.
Electric Bond and Share Company, 198, 252 f.
Electric power companies, see Public Utility Holding Company Act; Public works, loans and grants for.
Eleventh Amendment, 14.
England, judicial reform in, 322.

Farm Board, 127.
Farm debtors' relief, 106, 213.
Federal common law, 272 f.
Federal Register, 91.
Federal Trade Commission, 60 f.,
  250.
Federalism, 69.
*Federalist, The,* 7.
Federalists, 25.
Fictions, legal, 292 f.
Foreign relations, power of President over, 201.
Fourteenth Amendment, 23, 66,
  173.
  See also Civil liberties; Due process clause; Freedom of contract.
Frankfurter, Felix, 115, 290, 305,
  306.
Frazier-Lemke Act, see Farm debtors' relief.
Freedom of contract, 53, 173, 209,
  294, 319.
Freedom of the press, 219.
Fugitive Slave Law, 17.

General-welfare clause of Constitution, see Spending power of Congress.
Gold cases, 96 f., 205, 304.
Gore, John J., 122, 259.
Grant, Ulysses S., 42.
Grier, Robert C., 41–42.

Habeas corpus, 324.
Haines, Charles G., 72.
Hamilton, Alexander, 8, 245.
Harding, Warren G., 184.
Holding companies, see Public Utility Holding Company Act.
Holmes, Oliver Wendell, 16, 24, 54,
  65, 68, 174, 245, 307, 312.
Homestead Act, 258.
Hoover, Herbert, 185.
Hopkins, Harry L., 223.
Hough, Charles M., 50–51.

Hours-of-labor legislation, 66.
Hughes, Charles Evans, 3, 43, 71,
  75, 79, 83, 105, 161, 172, 190,
  208, 216, 255, 296, 308.
Humphrey, William E., 107.

Income tax, 39, 41 f.
Injunctions against collection of taxes, 139.
Injunctions against enforcement of Federal laws, 115, 139, 198, 216.
Interstate commerce, power of Congress to regulate, 18, 89,
  105, 114, 202, 215, 218, 236 f.,
  284.

Jackson, Andrew, 28, 257, 315.
Jay, John, 289.
Jefferson, Thomas, 315.
Jurisdiction of Federal courts, 11.

Kennedy, Joseph P., 147.

Labor unions, 63 f., 163, 212, 216 f.,
  221.
Landis, James M., 147.
Landon, Alfred M., 87, 176.
Laski, Harold, 317.
Legal Tender Acts, 32, 33, 41 f.
Lincoln, Abraham, 31, 315, 326.
Litigation, government by, 286 f.

McReynolds, James C., 73, 81, 139,
  146, 206, 210, 218, 221, 226, 227,
  255, 260, 268, 272.
Madison, James, 7.
*Marbury v. Madison,* 24 f.
Marshall, John, 25 f., 174.
Milk control law of New York, 80.
Milk marketing orders, 238 f., 303.
Miller, Samuel F., 41, 49, 277.
Minimum-wage legislation, 66, 160,
  162, 170 f., 191, 206 f.
Minnesota mortgage moratorium law, 78.

Monetary legislation, see Gold cases.
Monopoly, see Anti-trust laws.
Municipal bankruptcy legislation, 165 f., 240.

National City Bank, 130.
National Firearms Act, 212.
National Industrial Recovery Act, 88 f., 109 f., 158, 175, 304.
National Labor Relations Act, 178, 191, 214 f., 271.
Nields, John P., 121.
Norris, George W., 189.

Old age benefit payments, 228, 230 f. See also Social security legislation.
Otis, Merrill E., 117.
Overruling decisions, 297, 308.

Packers and Stockyards Act, 263.
Pecora, Ferdinand, 147.
Pepper, George Wharton, 130, 278.
Petroleum industry, regulation of, 87 f.
Pierce, Franklin, 227.
Powell, Thomas Reed, 82.
Power to declare acts of Congress unconstitutional, 4, 24 f., 34, 37, 40, 288 f., 299.
Power to declare acts of states unconstitutional, 15, 34, 288 f., 299.
Price-fixing legislation, 159, 161, 240.
Privileges and immunities clause of Fourteenth Amendment, 169.
Processing taxes, 136, 140, 220. See also Agricultural legislation.
Public Utility Holding Company Act, 119 f., 178, 198, 248 f.
Public works, loans and grants for, 116, 199, 247.

Railroad Retirement Act, 104.
Railway Labor Act, 212.
Rate regulation, 51, 300.
Reclamation program, 258.
Reed, Stanley, 282.
Removal power of President, 107.
Republican National Convention of 1936, 173.
Resale price-maintenance laws, 164.
Retroactive effect of decisions, 306 f.
Roberts, Owen J., 83, 84, 146, 191, 208, 229, 237, 238, 268.
Robinson, Joseph, 193.
Roosevelt, Franklin D., 75, 176 f., 315. See also Court bill of 1937.
Roosevelt, Theodore, 190, 257.

Salaries of judges, tax on, 244 f.
Securities and Exchange Commission, 146 f., 250. See also Public Utility Holding Company Act.
Shays' insurrection, 7.
Sherman Anti-Trust Act, see Anti-trust laws.
Sibley, Samuel H., 121.
Silver Purchase Act, 203.
Sixteenth Amendment, 47.
Smith, Adam, 6.
Smith, Young B., 193.
Social security legislation, 178, 182, 221 f.
Spending power of Congress, 131 f., 224, 227, 232.
*Stare decisis*, rule of, 295, 313.
States' rights, 20, 168.
Statutes of Congress held unconstitutional by Supreme Court, statistics of, 40.
Statutes passed on by Supreme Court, 1933–1937, 181.
Stockholders' suits, 118, 143, 153.
Stone, Harlan F., 134, 136, 146, 161,

166, 169, 172, 173, 212, 226, 229, 296, 297.
Story, Joseph, 275.
Strikes, 154, 178, 214, 249.
Sutherland, George, 148, 160, 164, 184, 187, 206, 210, 218, 221, 226, 228, 312.

Taft, William Howard, 58, 108, 182 f., 314.
Taney, Roger B., 29, 291, 297, 324 f.
Tax immunity, 241 f., 244 f.
Taxes, see Income tax; Injunctions against collection of taxes; National Firearms Act; Processing taxes; Silver Purchase Act; Social security legislation.
Tennessee Valley Authority, 121, 142 f., 255 f.

Tobacco, inspection and marketing quotas, 237.

Unemployment, 222. See also Social security legislation.

Van Devanter, Willis, 187, 192, 206, 210, 218, 221, 226, 228, 244.
Van Orsdel, Josiah A., 73.

Waite, Morrison Remick, 50, 65.
Washington, Bushrod, 274.
Washington, George, 289, 315.
Watkins, Henry H., 116.
Wheeler, Burton K., 179.
White, Edward Douglass, 184.
Wilson, Woodrow, 60, 182, 186.

This book was set on the Linotype in *Scotch Modern*, a type-face that has been in continuous service for more than one hundred years. It is usually considered that the style of " modern face " followed in our present-day cuttings of Scotch was developed in the foundry of Alexander Wilson and Sons of Glasgow early in the nineteenth century. The new Wilson patterns were made to meet the requirements of the new fashion in printing that had been set going at the beginning of the century by the " modern " types of Didot in France and of Bodoni in Italy. It is to be observed that the *modern* in these matters is a modernity of A.D. 1800, not of today. The " modernist " type-faces of today are quite another story.

The book was designed by W. A. Dwiggins and manufactured by The Plimpton Press, Norwood, Massachusetts.